Dreamweaver MX 2004 Solutions

Dreamweaver® MX 2004 Solutions

Ethan Watrall

SYBEX® San Francisco • London

Associate Publisher: DAN BRODNITZ
Acquisitions Editor: MARIANN BARSOLO
Developmental Editor: PETE GAUGHAN
Production Editor: ERICA YEE
Technical Editor: DENISE TYLER
Copyeditor: JUDY FLYNN
Composer: MAUREEN FORYS, HAPPENSTANCE TYPE-O-RAMA
Proofreaders: LAURIE O'CONNELL, AMY RASSMUSSEN, NANCY RIDDIOUGH
Indexer: TED LAUX
Book Designer: FRANZ BAUMHACKL
Cover Designer: JOHN NEDWIDEK, EMDESIGN
Cover Illustration: JOHN NEDWIDEK, EMDESIGN

Library of Congress Card Number: 2003115544

ISBN: 0-7821-4299-0

Software License Agreement: Terms and Conditions

For my son, Sam, with all the love in the world that a father can give

 # Acknowledgments

Any book (large or small) is the product of not only the author, but also a host of other people working behind the scenes whose presence (either directly or indirectly) helps bring the project to fruition. This book is hardly any different.

At Sybex, special thanks to Erica Yee and Pete Gaughan. This book was delayed slightly as I finished the other Sybex book I was writing at the time, and both Erica and Pete were incredibly tolerant and understanding during the process. Kudos to my technical editor, Denise Tyler, for all her help and great suggestions. As always, I must express my profound thanks and gratitude to Mariann Barsolo, my acquisitions editor, who was phenomenally helpful throughout this project—as she has always been. Also, many thanks to Dan Brodnitz, associate publisher at Sybex, who championed this book and who, with the help of Mariann Barsolo, made sure that I was given the time to write the best book possible without sacrificing my other literary obligations.

Many thanks to my agent, David Fugate of Waterside Productions. I am forever in his debt for all the work, help, and wonderful advice he gave during this project. I certainly hope I'll have his wise counsel for years to come.

I must offer my gratitude to all the people who kindly let me use screen shots from their own digital creations for the book's color insert.

I thank my friend (and co-conspirator) Norb Herber. Besides offering the usual helpful suggestions, he also selflessly took on many of the little "end of project" responsibilities for our book *Flash MX 2004 Savvy* so that I could focus on this book. Thanks to my dad, who, besides lots of encouragement and thoughtful advice, still never asks what an archaeologist was doing writing a book about web design. Thanks also to my mom for her support during the project. My love and thanks to my daughter, Taylor. All of my love to my wife, Jenn, without whose unwavering support I wouldn't be able to manage sitting in front of a computer, day after day, pounding away at the keyboard.

Finally, my sincere apologies to anyone whom I managed to forget. Thanks, everybody!

Dear Reader

Thank you for choosing *Dreamweaver MX 2004 Solutions*. This book is part of a new wave of Sybex graphics books, all written by outstanding authors—artists and teachers who really know their stuff and have a clear vision of the audience they're writing for.

Founded in 1976, Sybex is the oldest independent computer book publisher. More than twenty-five years later, we're committed to producing a full line of consistently exceptional graphics books. With each title, we're working hard to set a new standard for the industry. From the paper we print on, to the writers and photographers we work with, our goal is to bring you the best graphics books available.

I hope you see all that reflected in these pages. I'd be very interested to hear your comments and get your feedback on how we're doing. To let us know what you think about this or any other Sybex book, please visit us at www.sybex.com. Once there, go to the product page, click on Submit a Review, and fill out the questionnaire. Your input is greatly appreciated.

Please also visit www.sybex.com to learn more about the rest of our growing graphics line.

Best regards,

DAN BRODNITZ
Associate Publisher
Sybex Inc.

Contents

Chapter 5   Creation and Care of Hyperlinks   101

Chapter 6   Laying Out Tables and Frames   123

Introduction

Back in 1989, Tim Berners-Lee of the Centre Européenne pour la Recherche Nucléaire (which, in English, translates as the European Center for Nuclear Research, or CERN for short) wrote an innocent little document titled *Information Management: A Proposal* that, among other things, outlined the development of Hypertext Markup Language (HTML). Little did he realize that the modest 18-page document would forever change the way in which we access, acquire, and share information.

HTML caught on like wildfire. By July 1993, there were hundreds of computers worldwide that could deliver HTML documents. The world had just gotten a whole lot bigger.

Fast-forward to 1997 when, much to the joy of the web design community (and the average web user, for that matter), Macromedia Dreamweaver 1.0 was released. No more writing HTML by hand, no more puzzling over cryptic lines of code, and certainly no more head scratching for those who weren't trained programmers. Macromedia had unveiled the future, and the future looked good.

While Dreamweaver certainly wasn't the first WYSIWYG (what you see is what you get) web design tool, it was easily one of the best and brightest. Including such revolutionary features as an intuitive and flexible visual authoring environment, Roundtrip HTML, and support for Dynamic HTML, Dreamweaver was easily one of the most powerful web tools to come down the pipe.

Several years and several versions later, Dreamweaver is arguably the most popular visual web authoring tool available. With over 700,000 users and a market share of more than 75 percent, Dreamweaver has made high-level web authoring accessible to both professional and amateur designers. In the fall of 2003, Macromedia announced the release of Dreamweaver MX 2004, a phenomenal upgrade that pushes the boundaries of visual web design.

About This Book

The sheer popularity of the Web has created a large group of people clambering to get their digital creations out there. It's only natural that many of these people would turn to Dreamweaver as their visual web design application of choice. It's at this point that this book comes in.

I've found that the vast majority of computer books are one of two types. Either they are the bare-bones introduction to an application and intended for those who have little or no experience, or they are the huge-tome-with-which-you-can-kill-a-rat variety of book that often leaves many readers scratching their head in confusion as to where exactly to start. I've written *Dreamweaver MX 2004 Solutions* to fit somewhere in between these two extremes. While it is designed to provide a fundamental introduction to creating websites with Dreamweaver MX 2004, it also covers more mature intermediate topics. The tone of the book, which is in line with the other books in Sybex's Solutions series, is geared toward those readers who are experienced in the digital realm but might not be particularly at ease with Dreamweaver.

Beyond the technical, "how-to" purpose of the book, I've attempted to weave in a strong web design theme—a topic that I firmly believe is neglected in many tool-based web design books. Not only will you find an entire chapter (Chapter 1) dedicated to an introduction to the art and science of web design, but you'll also find many design-oriented tidbits scattered throughout the book. While these reminders refer back to many of the topics raised in Chapter 1, they are designed to also call attention to many of the unspoken laws of web design that are usually gained through applied design experience.

As an instructor of new media, interactive design, and digital storytelling, I am proudest of the fact that this book is written for *students*. I'm not just taking about people involved in classroom-based studies, but anyone who finds instructor-led education fruitful. This doesn't mean that *Dreamweaver MX 2004 Solutions* is geared toward only one learning style—quite the contrary! The point is that when I was writing this book, I not only thought about the content itself, but also who the audience was and the way they'd approach and absorb the content.

Mac or Windows: The Eternal Dilemma

One of the great joys of most Macromedia products (and Dreamweaver MX 2004 is hardly any different) is that they function almost identically from platform to platform. There are some superficial visual differences (which are a result of the different operating systems and not the programs themselves) and different hotkeys, but generally speaking, you find very little difference whether you are using Dreamweaver on a Mac or a Windows PC. On top of this, I teach on both Macs and PCs, have both a Mac and a PC in my office at the university, and am a PC user at home.

However, I've had to put a little more thought into the "eternal dilemma" as I wrote this book. To begin with, Dreamweaver MX 2004 for Windows features the MDI (multiple document interface) workspace. Not only does it feature the same streamlined integrated panel-based interface that is the hallmark of all Macromedia's next-generation MX 2004 applications, it also features a tabbed Document window that allows you to easily switch back and forth between multiple documents during the design and development process.

But the MDI workspace is only available on the Windows version of the program. This will come as a pretty heavy blow to those working on a Mac, who must make due with a Dreamweaver 4 version interface.

The second reason I had to put a little more thought into the Mac/Windows dilemma while writing this book had to do with Dreamweaver MX 2004's dynamic database-driven application development tools. Generally speaking, this type of development has traditionally taken place on Windows PCs instead of Macs. This doesn't mean that Mac users can't create cool dynamic web applications with Dreamweaver MX 2004—quite the contrary. However, Windows users wanting to take advantage of 2004's dynamic database-driven application development features will generally find themselves with more tools at their disposal.

So I made the decision to focus primarily on the Windows workspace, look, and tools. I apologize to Mac users; my decision was motivated by the desire to look forward instead of back. This doesn't mean that Mac users are totally alienated. Where necessary, I've gone to great lengths to point out important differences between Dreamweaver MX on Mac OS and Dreamweaver MX on Windows (especially in the later chapters).

> **Note:** Hotkeys are always given for both Macintosh and Windows users, in that order. For example, Alt/Option +F7 indicates that the Mac shortcut is Option+F7 and the Windows shortcut is Alt+F7.

Who Needs This Book

It's impossible to write a book that is all things to all people. This being said, I did my best to write a book that is many things to a lot of different people. I carefully selected the topics discussed and crafted the way I discussed them so that many different people, with varying levels of expertise and different goals, could pick the book up and find it useful. Granted, if worse comes to worst, the book is large enough to prop up the wobbly leg on your bed or serve as a pretty decent doorstop.

If you were to corner me in a dark alley, I would feel comfortable (*relatively* comfortable, that is, since I'm not used to being cornered in dark alleys by my readers) in saying that the people who will get the most out of this book will range from the savvy computer user who feels comfortable in the digital realm (but hasn't necessarily worked with Dreamweaver) to someone who is experienced in the foundation of Dreamweaver and wants to tackle more mature intermediate topics.

I strongly feel that this book is not that appropriate for people who already have advanced Dreamweaver skills. I certainly don't want to discourage any interested individual from using the book—it does cover a lot of stuff that even the more experienced user might not be familiar with. If everyone who looked at this volume in their local bookstore ended up buying it, I would definitely be a happy camper. However, I feel that those advanced Dreamweaver users might not find exactly what they are looking for in *Dreamweaver MX 2004 Solutions* and would therefore be disappointed—something I definitely don't want.

How This Book Is Organized

I firmly believe that there is a natural progression of skills involved in working with Dreamweaver MX 2004. The chapter-by-chapter structure of this book is designed to emulate this progression. Although each chapter builds on the previous ones, the book is also written in such a way that you can zero in on specific topics when you're searching for a solution to a particular problem.

Here is a quick look at what you can expect in each chapter:

Chapter 1, "The Path to Harmonious Web Usability and Design" You'll start off by getting a nice (and very important) introduction to some of the fundamental principles of interactive design.

Chapter 2, "Laying the Groundwork" You'll explore how to work with the Dreamweaver MX 2004 workspace and delve deeply into the earliest steps that need to be taken when creating your first web page/website. Topics such as opening and saving a document, setting page properties, and previewing your work in a browser are all covered.

Chapter 3, "Communicating Effectively with Text" You'll learn how to create and manipulate text using Dreamweaver MX 2004.

Chapter 4, "Working with Images" This chapter covers the addition and manipulation of images in your digital creation.

Chapter 5, "Creation and Care of Hyperlinks" You'll look at the lifeblood of the Web: hyperlinks. You'll learn, among other things, how to attach links to text and images, change link color, and create named anchors.

Chapter 6, "Laying Out Tables and Frames" This chapter covers the fine art of page layout using both tables and frames.

Chapter 7, "Using Templates, Library Items, and Digital Assets" You'll explore a host of tools (including Templates and Library Items) geared toward streamlining the production process.

Chapter 8, "Adding Multimedia" You'll learn how to add some serious "oomph" to your website with all manner of different types of multimedia.

Chapter 9, "Adding Interactivity to Your Site with JavaScript Behaviors" This chapter explores how to add JavaScript-based interactivity using Dreamweaver MX 2004's behaviors.

Chapter 10, "Formatting with CSS and Layers" You'll learn how to use the next-generation layout tool, Cascading Style Sheets (CSS), to create inspiring layout and design.

Chapter 11, "Managing and Publishing Your Site" Here you explore the tools that empower you to manage and manipulate an entire website (as opposed to just a web page).

Chapter 12, "Handcrafting Code in Dreamweaver" You'll leave Dreamweaver's visual authoring environment behind and learn how to use the program to directly edit and create HTML.

Chapter 13, "Extending Dreamweaver" Here you'll explore how to extend Dreamweaver MX 2004 beyond its original, "out of the box" configuration by integrating new behaviors, creating custom program menus, and adding custom commands to the Insert bar.

Chapter 14, "Collecting Information with Forms" You'll look at how to get information from the user by employing forms.

Appendix, "Web Resources" The appendix features a bevy of online resources that will help you further your design skills.

Bonus Chapter 1, "Working with Dynamic Databases" Located on the book's accompanying CD, this chapter explores how to set the groundwork for your very own dynamic database-driven application.

Bonus Chapter 2, "Displaying Dynamic Data and Applications" Located on the book's accompanying CD, this chapter will explore the basics of displaying information from a database in your web page. The chapter will also take a tutorial-based approach to teach you how to develop some of the more common database-driven applications, such as a registration/login page combination or a simple search engine.

About the CD

As with many computer books out nowadays, *Dreamweaver MX 2004 Solutions* comes with a handy-dandy companion CD, which is compatible with both Macintosh and Windows platforms. I've included some pretty useful stuff on it. You'll find a whole bevy of demo and trial software from Macromedia (including Dreamweaver MX 2004). Also, the CD contains all the necessary support and example files that are used in some of the chapters.

Getting in Touch

As an author, I love hearing from readers. I always get a serious jolt out of getting an e-mail from anyone who has bought any of my books and goes to the trouble of actually sending me e-mail. While I love getting praise, I also value constructive criticism. Think the tone of the book was inappropriate? Confused by the way in which I covered a particular topic? Wish I would have covered some additional topics? Send me an e-mail! I not only respond to all the e-mail sent from readers, but I also take suggestions into account when writing the next edition (seriously). So, drop me a digital line at ethan@captainprimate.com.

About the Author

Given the fact that Ethan Watrall is an archaeologist by training, people often ask, "What the heck is an archaeologist doing writing books about interactive design?" Well, to understand this, you need to understand that he has two great loves in his academic life. The first, which represents a culmination of years of archaeological experience, is household craft production in Predynastic Egypt. He has worked at both Nabta Playa (an extremely large Neolithic habitation site in the Egyptian Western Desert) and Hierakonpolis, where he has excavated such cool things as prehistoric wells, clay mines, households, animal enclosures, pottery kilns, and cemeteries.

The second—and here comes the answer to the big question—is the place of interactive media in archaeology. Whether from the standpoint of an educational tool, a method for scholarly publication, or simply an issue deserving academic discussion, Watrall has dedicated himself to expanding the dialog surrounding the use of interactive media in archaeology. He is particularly interested in the role that interactive entertainment plays in the public perception of archaeology—a topic on which he has published and delivered papers targeted to both professional archaeologists and professional game designers. Not content to simply comment on the situation, Watrall practices what he preaches: active involvement on the part of academics in the interactive entertainment industry.

He is currently a visiting faculty member in the Department of Telecommunications at Indiana University, where he teaches classes in interactive new-media design, the social dimension of new information and communication technologies, and interactive entertainment. He has written several books, including *Dreamweaver 4/Fireworks 4 Visual Jump-Start*, *Dreamweaver MX: Design and Technique*, *Flash MX Savvy*, and *Flash MX 2004 Savvy* (the last two co-authored with Norbert Herber).

Ethan Watrall's digital alter ego can be found hanging out at www.captainprimate.com.

The Path to Harmonious Web Usability and Design

1

The fundamental issues you need to address when you're designing your website are relatively universal (at least when it comes to interactive design): you need to create something that fulfills the needs of your audience. Even the most insignificant of interactive creations is usually intended for a wider audience than just the designer. As such, there are some extremely *important issues you should consider during the creative process.*

Chapter Contents
Preparing Your Site
Designing Effective Web Pages
Getting from Here to There: Developing
  Intuitive Navigation

Preparing Your Site

When creating a website, you should spend as much time and effort in the predigital production process as you spend in the actual production process. The *predigital* process includes everything that must be done before you create a single line of HTML—from choosing your look and style to developing textual content. When you're creating a website of any complexity, there are a lot of things to keep track of. The best sites out there are an artful mix of technology, design, and usability that haven't been slapped together over a weekend. Instead, they've been created with a great deal of thoughtful predigital planning and preparation.

In the following sections, you are going explore several topics that fit into the predigital production process: information design and architecture, developing a visual metaphor, and creating storyboards and concept art.

Note: Before diving into this chapter, it's important to remember that the information that will help you become a master of interactive design can hardly fit into one chapter. Heck, it can't even fit into a single book (or a stack of books for that matter). The whole point of this chapter is to provide you with tools, guidelines, and advice that will empower you to start thinking about the necessity of efficient and elegant interactive design. In addition, the chapter should act as the foundation upon which to further your own exploration of the topic. So, if you are already versed in the principles of interactive design and are looking right away for specific solutions in Dreamweaver, you may want to skip this chapter.

Creating Your Site's Information Design and Architecture

Information architecture is the organization of a website's content into easily accessible components that support a wide variety of user access techniques (casual browsing, direct searching, and so on). As one would expect, information architecture is intimately related to the navigational system of a site. You'd have a difficult time designing one without the other.

Note: This section of the chapter is designed to be a simple introduction to information architecture. Extra resources are a must. You might want to seek out Louis Rosenfeld and Peter Morville's *Information Architecture for the World Wide Web* (O'Reilly, 1998). If you are interested in extending your search to the Web, check out the Argus Center for Information Architecture at www.argus-acia.com.

At its most basic, the process by which you develop a site's information architecture is usually a two-step affair. The first step involves organizing your site's information into a variety of categories. You need to decide how many sections, subsections, and categories you need; how your site's content will fit into those categories; and how the units of information (individual web pages) will relate to units of information within the same category and to units in other categories. This is arguably one of the most difficult things about designing a site. The way we human beings organize information is largely determined by our cultural context. As a result, what constitutes well-organized information is subjective. One must contend with all manner of problems, such as linguistic ambiguity (a word or term may mean different things to different people) or different perspectives of how information should be organized.

As with many other issues in web design, the way you organize information will depend largely on your audience. You must put yourself in their shoes and predict the best way to develop an information architecture so that your users' needs are met. Developing a way to organize your content can often be a fairly painful process, but it is absolutely necessary in developing a functional and usable information architecture.

Once you've decided how to organize your information, the second step requires you to formalize the structure you created with something called an information architecture diagram (IA diagram). Designed to provide a visual representation of the information architecture of your site, an IA diagram can take many different forms (see Figure 1.1). Ultimately, the specific style is up to you.

An IA diagram isn't supposed to show the links between various pages within your site. Instead, it represents the hierarchical relationship between sections/subsections and individual pages.

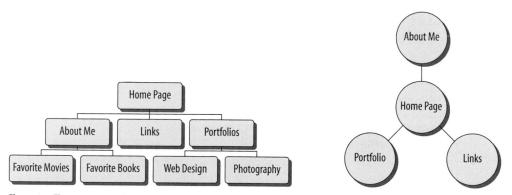

Figure 1.1 There are many different ways to create an information architecture diagram. The example on the left is a reverse branching tree model; the example on the right is the spherical model.

So, what is the big deal about creating an information architecture diagram? Well, there are a couple of things to consider. First, if you are working in a design group or making a proposal to a client or a boss, an IA diagram allows you to communicate the structure and information flow of the site to other people. Second, a well-designed IA diagram provides you with a blueprint of the site's structure that you can refer back to during the production process.

 Note: An IA diagram is also very useful for developing the structure of your site on the server (folders, subfolders, and so on).

Developing a Visual Metaphor

A visual metaphor is often a pretty slippery concept to put into words, but it can be easy to unconsciously interpret when it's used properly. A visual metaphor, which is universally applied to an entire website, leverages familiar visual elements (such as images, interface elements, icons, colors, or fonts) to unconsciously reinforce the site's subject matter. The visual metaphor for a major Hollywood movie's promotional website will be completely different from that of an interactive design firm or an online merchant.

For example, in the screen shot depicted in Figure 1.2, the goal was to create a website for the Arizona State Institute of Human Origins for an online exhibit that would explore human evolution from our earliest ancestors to the emergence of *Homo sapiens*. Because of the archaeological theme, the website used an earthy palette of colors consisting of shades of brown, gray, rust, dark green, and tan combined with archaeologically oriented design elements to visually reinforce its content.

Creating an effective visual metaphor requires some serious brainstorming and inspired free association. You need to sit down and think about what kinds of colors, fonts, images, icons, and interface/layout elements unconsciously reinforce the site's content.

 Note: Before you even begin brainstorming for your visual metaphor, be rock-solid sure of your audience. You can't effectively design a visual metaphor if you aren't exactly positive of the demographic profile of those who'll be using the site.

Say, for example, you are creating a children's online community site geared toward ages 7 to 10. You might think about using bold primary colors with cartoony interface elements and fonts. On the other hand, the website for a movie would draw its visual metaphor from the film's look and feel (check out the *Planet of the Apes* website at www.planetoftheapes.com for a great example).

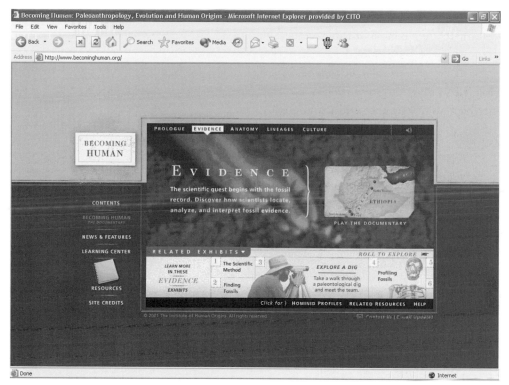

Figure 1.2 The Becoming Human website employs earth tone colors and archaeologically oriented imagery to create a solid visual metaphor.

There are no hard and fast rules for creating a visual metaphor. The only real guideline is that they should be used wisely: be subtle and don't overdo it. Always have your ideas vetted by individuals not associated with the project; they will often have suggestions or comments you never thought of. Don't get too attached to a visual metaphor because it's quite possible that, given an outside opinion (perhaps one of a prospective user), you'll decide that it doesn't work for your site.

Conceptualizing a Site's Layout and Design with Storyboards

One of the most important steps in the paper and brain predigital production process is creating storyboards or concept art, an idea swiped from the film industry. Generally one of the last steps before you go digital with your grand creation, storyboards are used to visualize your design as a complete entity. With them, you get a chance, among other things, to see how colors interact with one another, how interface elements play off one another, how your navigational system is realized, how your visual metaphor plays out, and whether content is represented in the best way possible. Storyboards provide you with a painless way of catching any potential design problems before you get to the stage where you build your design in HTML and they become major obstacles. Storyboards are also a great way to play with design ideas and visually brainstorm.

As illustrated in Figure 1.3, there is no hard-and-fast rule as to how they should look. If you are brainstorming ideas, the back of a cocktail napkin is as good a medium as any. However, if you are preparing a pitch to a potential client, it's a good idea to come up with something more polished and formal. The bottom line is that storyboards, in whatever form they appear, should efficiently communicate your design ideas without too much ambiguity.

You may even want to create your storyboards in a photocopy of an empty browser window. This is a great way to give your client the necessary context. A browser template for the purpose of storyboarding has been included in the Chapter 1 folder of this book's companion CD.

Designing Effective Web Pages

The whole point of a website is that it's composed of a series of individual pages that are linked together. While designing the website as a whole is the ultimate goal of good web design, you need to give special attention to the pages within your website, and, more specifically, how those pages fit into your site as a whole. Today's browser technology allows users to view only one page at a time, so the pages within your site are the way the user interfaces with your site. The user doesn't really browse a site; they browse pages that make up a site.

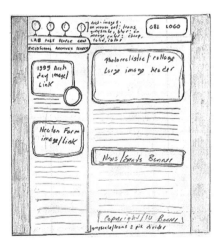
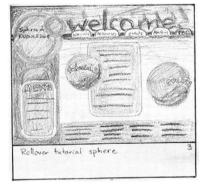

Figure 1.3 Storyboards can range from "quick and dirty" (left) to quite formal and polished (right). Whatever their level of quality, they should effectively communicate your design ideas.

The Web User and Experience-Based Expectation

An expectation (based on previous experience) is a subject that is hardly unique to response time. You are going to see the issue pop up again and again when it comes to user-centered web design. Why is experience-based expectation so important? Well, look at it this way: Every day you stop at many red lights and then go when they turn green. What would happen if, one day, you were sitting at a red light, happily waiting for it to turn green, and it turned blue? Would you be confused? Probably. Would you sit there, unsure of what you should do? Most likely. The abrupt change in the pattern (which was established based on experience) forces the formation of new behavior—which may take some time. The same applies in the world of user-centered web design. If the user has become accustomed to doing something one way (navigating, downloading, etc.) and you force them to learn how to do it another way, they may get annoyed, frustrated, or even angry and then go elsewhere.

Let's explore some of the key characteristics of creating a well-designed and usable web page—minimizing response times, writing for the Web, and creating usable links. It's very important to remember that what's covered in this section of the chapter is just the tip of the iceberg. You can use the information as a set of guidelines upon which to base your own design process.

Minimizing Response Times

One of the other fundamental issues for page design is response time, also known as download time, which is the amount of time it takes for a page to totally download after a user has clicked the link or typed in the URL.

Although you will need to balance visual design with response time, the guideline is "the faster the better." Unfortunately, even with Internet connections getting faster and more and more people getting access to high-speed connections, we won't be getting sub-second response time anytime in the near future. Even with the fastest Internet connections, it still takes time to download a web page. As a result, the current goal for response time should range from 5 to 8 seconds. Anything more than that and the user will generally become bored and leave the site.

Note: When you start working with Dreamweaver MX 2004, you'll discover that the Document window's Document Size/Download Time indicator is a great way to get an idea as to the size (in kilobytes) of your page and how long it will take to download over a specified connection. However, for reasons that will be covered shortly, knowing the size of your page is hardly a guarantee as to the length of time it will take to download.

Beyond a fast response time, you also have to strive for low variability in your response time. The satisfaction of a user is partially based on their expectations as well as the actual response time performance.

When it comes to response time, if the same action sometimes happens fast and sometime slow, the user won't know what to expect and, therefore, won't be able to adjust their behavior to optimize their use of the system. If people assume that a page will download quickly, they'll be disappointed when it doesn't. In extreme cases, the variability in response time might prompt the user to think there is something wrong with the web page, their browser, or even their computer. Say, for example, a user visits a website and for the first five or six pages they visit, the response time is a respectable 6 seconds. However, when they visit the seventh page, it doesn't download in 6 or so seconds. In fact, after 25 seconds it hasn't downloaded. Now, it's entirely possible that the page itself is very large and it needs a long time to download. However, the user doesn't know this. They are forced to sit there, twiddling their thumbs, wondering whether their browser has had a nervous breakdown. They might even get so frustrated that they point their browser elsewhere. It's for all of these reasons, and more, that you should do your absolute best to keep response time variability to a minimum.

There is, however, a factor that contributes to response time that is completely out of your control. Response time (as well as the predictability in the response time itself) is determined by the weakest link in the chain from server to browser. So, the time it takes for a page to download is determined not only by the size of the page itself, but also by the throughput to the server, the server's connection to the Internet, the Internet itself, the user's connection to the Internet, and the rendering speed of the user's browser and computer.

So, given these issues, what can you do to minimize response time (and variability in response time)? Here are some suggestions:

- When you create your web pages, always try to keep their size as small as possible (given your design needs and the page's contents). It's important that you realize that there isn't an "ideal" file size that you need to hit. Instead, the size of your page should be based on your audience. For example, if the site you are creating is targeted toward an audience that you know will have fast Internet connections, you can employ media that uses more bandwidth. However, if your audience is accessing the Web with slower connections, you need to optimize your site so that it can be easily accessed.

- If you have a page whose contents make its file size much larger than many of the other pages within your site, use strategies to provide the user with feedback about the loading process. For instance, if you are working with Flash, you can use a preloader to indicate the amount of the file left to load. In HTML, when you are working with particularly large images, you can use Low Source images (for more information on Low Source images, see Chapter 4 "Working with Images").

- It's always important to constantly test your web pages. By doing this, you can get an idea of any cross-browser or cross-platform compatibility issues, but you can also get a "realistic" idea of response time by uploading your site to a server and then testing it on different connections.

Writing for the Web

Even though the Web is getting more and more visual by the second, textual content is still easily one of the most important types of content. The thing you need to realize is that, because of the unique nature of the medium, writing for the Web is a type of writing unto itself. There are two important issues (both of which are linked to each other) that make the process of writing for the Web so unique.

First, when people read web pages, they don't read them like they would read a book—from left to right, top to bottom. Instead, they scan the page in an irregular manner, looking for something of interest. Second, studies have shown that screen-based text is more difficult to read than printed text—which results in a reading rate that's 25 percent slower than you would normally expect from printed media. Given these two facts, when you are writing for your website, you can't just slap together text or copy and paste from a printed document. Instead, you need to put a lot of thought into how your text is structured and attempt to craft what you write so that it takes these two issues into consideration.

Understanding Bandwidth

Bandwidth is a measure of the amount of data that can be sent across an Internet connection over a certain unit of time (second, minute, and so on).

An Internet connection is the method by which you connect to the Internet itself and can range from a modem to a digital subscriber line (DSL). Each method has a different level of bandwidth, which can range from very low (downloads data from the Web slowly) to very high (downloads from the Web quickly).

Bandwidth is usually measured in terms of Kbps—kilobits per second. Most standard modems range from 14.4 to 56Kbps, while high-speed connections (such as cable modems, DSL, or T1 lines) range from 64 to 1500Kbps (and even higher).

You can think of your Internet connection as a pipe through which the material you're downloading is shoved. A faster connection means a larger pipe, which means more stuff can be downloaded at a quicker rate. A slower connection, on the other hand, means a smaller pipe, which means things are downloaded at a far slower rate.

In the following sections, you are going to explore some strategies for creating text that supports scanning. In addition, you are going to look at some steps that you can take to increase the legibility of your text, thereby avoiding a situation in which you contribute to the difficulty of reading digital text.

Creating Scannable Text

Because people find it is so uncomfortable to read text on a screen (as well as the fact that the online experience can often foster impatience), users tend not to read long streams of online text. Instead, they scan text and pick out keywords, sentences, and paragraphs that interest them, while skipping over those parts of the text they care less about.

As a result, you need to craft your text so that it supports scanning. How do you do this? Well, here are some great guidelines:

- Structure articles with two, or even three, levels of headlines. As illustrated in Figure 1.4, using headlines allows people to quickly identify and focus in on areas of particular interest to them.

As a species, human beings are completely infatuated with themselves. Its nothing to be ashamed of, we're actually a really interesting bunch of primates. I'm certainly not embarrassed to admit that I've spent majority of my academic career scratching my head and trying to figure out why we act the way we do. It's no great surprise that this fixation has worked its way into the world of interactive entertainment. I'd suspect that most designers realize that computer games frequently mirror our thoughts about ourselves and the world around us. How did we get to where we are now? What is going to happen to us in the future? Both are questions that are posed time and again in processual story based strategy titles. Processual who? Story based what? Basically, its just a fancy shmancy name for God Games like Activision's *Civilization: Call to Power*, Sierra's *City Builder* Series, or Firaxis' *Alpha Centauri* . Each time the "new game" button is clicked, the player not only gets the opportunity to explore these questions, but also to play god (something all of us love but don't always admit to) and immerse themselves in a "what could have been" or "what could be" scenario.

Humans are Interesting

As a species, human beings are completely infatuated with themselves. Its nothing to be ashamed of, we're actually a really interesting bunch of primates. I'm certainly not embarrassed to admit that I've spent majority of my academic career scratching my head and trying to figure out why we act the way we do.

Computers Games Mirror Us

It's no great surprise that this fixation has worked its way into the world of interactive entertainment. I'd suspect that most designers realize that computer games frequently mirror our thoughts about ourselves and the world around us.

God Games

How did we get to where we are now? What is going to happen to us in the future? Both are questions that are posed time and again in processual story based strategy titles. Processual who? Story based what? Basically, its just a fancy shmancy name for God Games like Activision's *Civilization: Call to Power,* Sierra's *City Builder* Series, or Firaxis' *Alpha Centauri* . Each time the "new game" button is clicked, the player not only gets the opportunity to explore these questions, but also to play god (something all of us love but don't always admit to) and immerse themselves in a "what could have been" or "what could be" scenario.

Figure 1.4 The text on the top lacks headlines, while the text on the bottom has been broken up using headlines. The difference between the two can easily be seen.

- Use meaningful, rather than "cute," headlines. A heading should tell the user what the page or section is about; the reader should not be forced to read the actual text to find out what it is about.

- As illustrated in Figure 1.5, bulleted lists and similar design elements should be used to break the flow of uniform text blocks.

How did we get to where we are now? What is going to happen to us in the future?
Both are questions that are posed time and again in strategy games that attempt to emulate social evolution such as Activision's *Civilization: Call to Power* , Impressions Games' City Builder Series, or Firaxis' *Alpha Centauri or Civilization III* .
Each time the "new game" button is clicked, the player not only gets the opportunity to explore these questions, but also to play god (something all of us love but don't always admit to) and immerse themselves in a "what could have been" or "what could be" scenario.
For the most part, however, traditional game designers really don't have a firm grasp of the process of social change.
As a result, most games depend on a skewed view of human culture change that translates into an infamous system most often referred to as the Tech Tree.

- How did we get to where we are now? What is going to happen to us in the future?

- Both are questions that are posed time and again in strategy games that attempt to emulate social evolution such as Activision's *Civilization: Call to Power* , Impressions Games' City Builder Series, or Firaxis' *Alpha Centauri or Civilization III* .

- Each time the "new game" button is clicked, the player not only gets the opportunity to explore these questions, but also to play god (something all of us love but don't always admit to) and immerse themselves in a "what could have been" or "what could be" scenario.

- For the most part, however, traditional game designers really don't have a firm grasp of the process of social change.

- As a result, most games depend on a skewed view of human culture change that translates into an infamous system most often referred to as the Tech Tree.

Figure 1.5 The text on the top has been broken up using bullets, while the text on the bottom hasn't. You can see that the bulleted text is far easier to scan than the un-bulleted text.

- Use highlighting and emphasis—such as color differences, bold text (as in Figure 1.6), or italicized text—to make important words catch the user's eye.

> How did we get to where we are now? What is going to happen to us in the future? Both are questions that are posed time and again in **strategy games** that attempt to **emulate social evolution** such as Activision's *Civilization: Call to Power* , Impressions Games' City Builder Series, or Firaxis' *Alpha Centauri or Civilization III* .
>
> Each time the "new game" button is clicked, the player not only gets the opportunity to explore these questions, but also to **play god** (something all of us love but don't always admit to) and immerse themselves in a "**what could have been**" or "**what could be**" scenario.
>
> For the most part, however, traditional game designers really **don't have a firm grasp of the process of social change**. As a result, most games depend on a **skewed view of human culture change** that translates into an infamous system most often referred to as the **Tech Tree**.

Figure 1.6 Text that has been emphasized (bold text was used in this example) tends to stand out and draws the reader's eye toward it.

Creating Legible Text

Given the fact that people find it more difficult to read screen-based text than it is to read traditional printed text, you don't want to add to their burden by creating text that is any harder to read. Remember, all else—spectacular design, low response time, compelling content—fails when the user can't actually read the text. As a result, there are some general guidelines you should follow in order to craft legible text:

- Use colors with high contrast between text and background. As illustrated in Figure 1.7, optimal legibility requires black text on white background (called positive text) or white text on a black background (called negative text).

  The worst color schemes are those that result in too little contrast (thereby making them almost impossible to read)—like pink text on a red background.

> Lorem ipsum dolor sit amet, consectetuer adipiscing elit. Donec adipiscing quam sit amet orci. Morbi feugiat dolor id nunc. Donec cursus. Etiam adipiscing tempus ligula. Donec dapibus magna vitae erat. Nam nonummy metus a ante. Nullam sollicitudin luctus wisi. Donec neque lacus, commodo vitae, accumsan quis, scelerisque ut, magna. Cras consectetuer. Cras blandit. Curabitur aliquam elementum lorem. Maecenas sed nisl nec arcu lacinia tincidunt. Nullam pulvinar placerat diam.

> Lorem ipsum dolor sit amet, consectetuer adipiscing elit. Donec adipiscing quam sit amet orci. Morbi feugiat dolor id nunc. Donec cursus. Etiam adipiscing tempus ligula. Donec dapibus magna vitae erat. Nam nonummy metus a ante. Nullam sollicitudin luctus wisi. Donec neque lacus, commodo vitae, accumsan quis, scelerisque ut, magna. Cras consectetuer. Cras blandit. Curabitur aliquam elementum lorem. Maecenas sed nisl nec arcu lacinia tincidunt. Nullam pulvinar placerat diam.

Figure 1.7 Example of positive text (top) and negative text (bottom).

Note: Although the contrast ratio is almost as good for negative text, the inverted color scheme often throws people off a little and slows their reading slightly.

- Use either plain-color backgrounds or extremely subtle background patterns. As illustrated in Figure 1.8, complex background patterns interfere with the eye's ability to resolve the lines in the characters and recognize word shapes.

Figure 1.8 Text placed over a background with complex shapes or a "busy" pattern is *very* difficult to read.

- Use fonts that are big enough to make the text easy to read even if the viewer doesn't have perfect vision. Tiny font size should be relegated to footnotes or legal text.
- Make sure the text stands still. Moving, blinking, or zooming text is far harder to read than static text.
- Almost all text should be left justified. By having a steady starting point for the eye to start scanning, the user can read much faster than when faced with centered or right justified text.
- At all costs, avoid using all uppercase text. Users read uppercase text about 10% slower than lower and mixed-case text case text.

Getting from Here to There: Developing Intuitive Navigation

One could easily argue that designing an intuitive and usable system of navigation is one of—if not *the*—most important goals when it comes to creating a usable and well-designed website. User experience on the Web is all about moving in space from one location to another in search of *something*. Whether or not the user knows what they are looking for is moot. It's up to you to crawl inside the heads of the users, figure out what they want from your site, and then figure out the easiest way for them to get it. If you don't provide a system for them to get from where they are to where they need to be, they'll go elsewhere, and this is the last thing you want.

Don't be fooled into thinking that a navigation scheme is simply buttons and hyperlinks. The best-designed navigation is a highly artful mix of many different things: a pinch of interface design, a dash of information architecture, and a generous dollop of psychology.

As I've mentioned, there is no way that I could effectively condense all that you need to know about designing intuitive navigation into one section of one chapter of one book. However, there are certain general, basic concepts that are both fundamentally important and self-contained enough that they can be discussed.

Keeping Navigation Consistent

We've already talked about the fact that one of the ways human beings define the world around them, and the way they interact with it, is based on the consistency and predictability of events. When a navigational system works properly, people come to unconsciously rely upon it. For this to happen, the navigational system must be consistent. This means (as shown in Figure 1.9) that on all the site's pages, the menu must remain in the same location, it must retain the same appearance and contents, and the interface where the navigational elements reside must not change to any significant degree.

One of the obstacles to designing a consistent and predictable navigation system revolves around the interplay between navigational elements and interface design at deep levels within the website. Often, as one gets deeper and deeper into a site, a certain point is reached at which the navigation scheme breaks down due to a lack of foresight. Designers tend to put most of their effort into developing a navigation scheme that will work best in the more consistently accessed areas of a site. As they move deeper and deeper into their site and the amount of information in any given screen increases, they spend less and less time ensuring that the navigation scheme they developed will function properly.

Note: The best-designed websites have a pyramid-shaped information distribution. The top levels of the site contain information that doesn't take up a great amount of screen real estate. As you move deeper into the site and into more specialized information, a larger amount of screen real estate is consumed by the website's content.

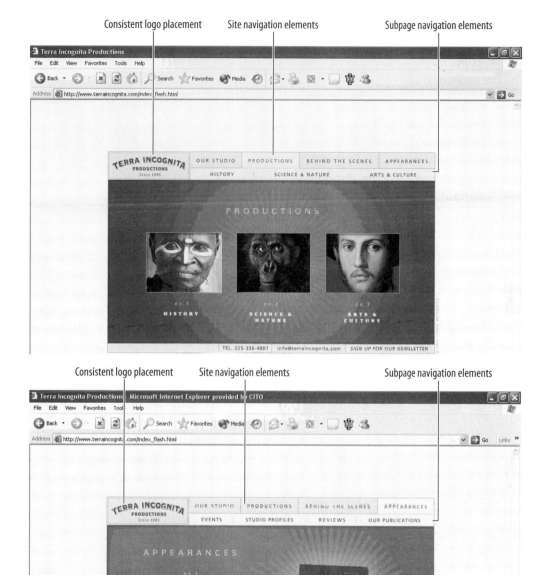

Figure 1.9 These two screen shots are of two different pages within the same site. Note that the navigational elements remain exactly the same.

It's at this point that chaos often sets in and the all important consistency and predictability goes out the window. To cope with the additional information, designers will toss in additional navigational elements (menus, buttons, and so on) or even alter the existing navigational scheme that worked just fine in the upper levels of the site.

Instead of succumbing to bedlam and anarchy, make sure that when you create the navigational scheme, you think deep into your site's structure. It may seem time consuming, but it could save you valuable time later. Because your user will probably spend more time in the deeper sections of your site, ask yourself whether what you've laboriously designed will work just as well with the content in the upper sections of your site as it will work with the content in the deeper sections of your site. If you can't answer with a resounding "yes," start again.

Note: Remember, the Web is a nonlinear medium. Users don't always enter your site through the front door: they can just as easily enter through a side or back door into a section deep within your site's hierarchy. Because of this, you should make sure that your entire site maintains a consistent scheme of navigation.

Help Users Quickly Learn Your Navigation Scheme

When you create a website of any kind, you are providing something to your user. Whether it's a mega online bookstore like Amazon.com, the site of a major educational institution like the University of Toronto, or your own personal corner of cyberspace, content is king. You don't want users to have to spend a huge amount of time learning how to locate what they desire. In other words, you don't want an overly complex navigational system to stand in the way of the user and what they want.

The key to easily learned navigational systems lies in several different issues. First, as I just mentioned, your navigational system should be consistent. If you switch the way you require your user to move about the site, they'll have to start from scratch and relearn your navigational scheme—not good. Second, as will be covered shortly, make sure your navigational elements (labels, visual imagery, and so on) are straight to the point and not overly complex or confusing. There is nothing worse than a series of buttons with labels that make no sense. Don't create navigational schemes that are counterintuitive and thereby difficult to learn.

Providing Clear and Obvious Visual Cues

Because the Web is a visual medium, effective navigational schemes should provide clear visual messages. I'm not just talking about the buttons here. Integrating clear visual cues into a navigational scheme requires some very broad (and often subtle) thinking.

Color

One of the best ways to provide your users with a quick and easy (and often unconscious) method of identifying exactly where they are located in your site is to use color. You may have noticed that many large sites use a consistent navigational system whose color changes slightly depending on the section or subsection where the user currently resides. This is a very effective technique that, when used properly, creates "signposts" for the user that are easily learned and recognized. When using color to increase the usability of your navigational system, you've definitely got some options. Changing the background color of individual pages is one way, but you can also use color for subtle emphasis—highlighting certain navigational or interface elements like buttons, banners, or header graphics.

There are, however, a couple of caveats to using color in this way:

- To avoid overwhelming the user with a new color for each subsection, pick a very limited palette and apply those colors to the top-level sections of your site. For example, say you're designing your own personal website and you use a nice light rust color for the "About Me" section. To avoid overwhelming the user, you'd also use that color for the "My Favorite Movies," "My Family," and "My Favorite Music" sections, all of which are subsections of the "About Me" page.

- Choose your colors carefully so that they fit in nicely with your visual metaphor.

Branding

Consistent and clear branding is also a good way to provide your audience with visual cues. Given the nature of the Web, people have a tendency to quickly jump from site to site with mouse clicks. When your audience is cavorting about your site, you want them to know *exactly* where they are. This is best accomplished with clearly and consistently placed logos, as shown in Figure 1.10.

Prominent logo placement

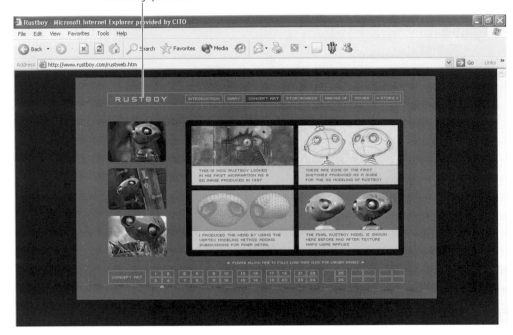

Prominent logo placement

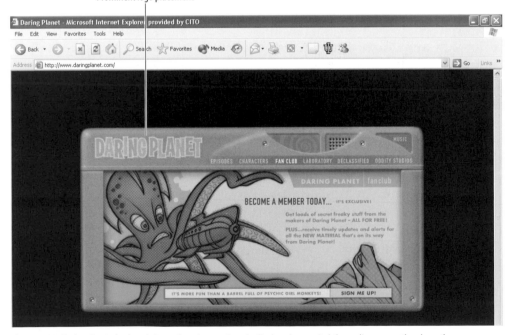

Figure 1.10 Notice that in both websites, a logo is prominently displayed to remind the audience exactly where they are.

Breadcrumb Trail

One of the biggest problems in particularly large, content-heavy websites is that people can easily get lost and end up with no clue of where they are located and no idea how to get back to where they were several clicks ago. One of the easiest and most elegant ways (and most cost effective in terms of effort and screen real estate consumed) to work around this problem is to create a simple navigational tool called a breadcrumb trail (Figure 1.11). A breadcrumb trail (sometimes referred to as a link buildout) is a horizontal line of hyperlinked words indicating the location of the current page within the site's overall information architecture. An example of a breadcrumb trail would be something like Home > About Me > Favorite Movies. Each item in the trail would be a hyperlink to that specific section or subsection.

Breadcrumb trail

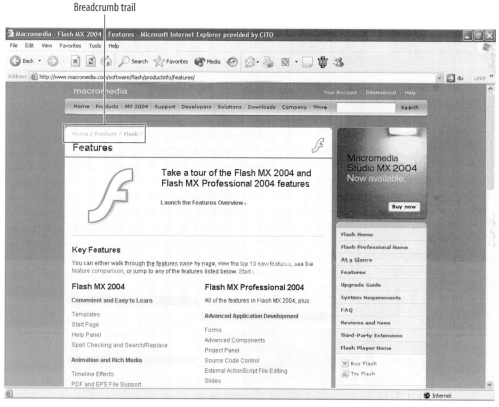

Figure 1.11 A breadcrumb trail provides a clear indication of the position of the current page within the site's overall structure; it also provides an easy way of moving back up that particular section or subsection's hierarchy.

Labels

One of the most often overlooked methods to provide clear and concise visual cues to your audience is to use effective labels. We're not just talking about ordinary labels here; we're talking about concepts that have been boiled down to their basic understandable components. For example, suppose a section of your site had images of all the photographs you've taken, all the paintings you've painted, and all the sculpture you've sculpted. Instead of having a link or a button that said "Everything I've ever created on film, with canvas, or with clay," you could simply use the word "Portfolio" or "Gallery."

Note: It's important to remember that many of the conventional web labels used are culturally based. While your average web user in North America wouldn't have any difficulty understanding your intentions if you used the word *Home* in your navigational scheme, someone from Egypt, the Czech Republic, or Malaysia may have absolutely no clue as to what you are referring.

When creating clear labels, you must avoid using what I call *geekspeak*, or terminology familiar only to those individuals within a specific field. For example, as an archaeologist, I've created websites where the term *Gray Literature* is used. If you have no experience in the field of archaeology, you probably don't have a clue what gray literature is. However, there are individuals out there who, despite the fact that they aren't familiar with the strange terms we archaeologists use, would be interested in gray literature. (*Gray literature* refers to the excavation reports generated by federally mandated salvage archaeological excavations.) To avoid geekspeak in this particular situation, I substituted *Gray Literature* with the term *Excavation Reports*, which is a lot more understandable to the general public.

Visual Vocabulary: Navigational Elements

Another good way to provide users with clear visual cues is by using consistent and universally understandable visual vocabulary. There are three general schools of thought when it comes to creating navigational elements (buttons, menus, and so on). The first one tends to emphasize the use of icons or imagery, while the second one emphasizes the use of purely textual-based navigation. The third, which I think is the most rational, encourages the appropriate and contextually suitable use of both text and images as navigational elements.

If you've decided to use a purely visually based navigation system, you are in for some serious obstacles. Using icons or images in navigation is fine, but you must realize that the Web itself has no real standardized conventions for visual vocabulary. So, for instance, if you've created a button on your main page that links to your "About Me" section, what icon do you use? The possibilities are literally endless. The problem especially pops up when you choose an icon that, while significant to you, has no significance for your audience. In this situation, your audience will be faced with a series of acontextual (at least for them) icons with which they are expected to navigate your site. The only true universal solution for this problem is to create navigational elements that incorporate both text and images. If you include text that answers the user's "what the heck is this button for" kinds of questions, you can use funky icons that fit into your visual metaphor.

Multiple Roads from Here to There

Lots of people do things in lots of different ways. People drive differently, have different tastes in movies and music, talk differently, eat differently, and most important to this discussion, use different methods to move about the Web. Some like to wander aimlessly until they stumble across something interesting, while others want to locate specific information as quickly and efficiently as possible. Some people use the newest browser on a fast machine with a fast Internet connection, while others have an older browser on a slower machine with a slow Internet connection. Some people use text browsers or screen readers. Get the point? It's up to you to try to accommodate all of these "profiles" so that you don't alienate possible visitors.

Note: A screen reader is a piece of software that "reads" the content of a website for those who are visually impaired or blind.

To ensure that your website is accessible to as wide an audience as possible, you have to create a navigational system that supports many different personal styles. For instance, provide a low-bandwidth version for those whose Internet connection and computer is on the slower side. You can also employ a series of different tools, such as a search feature, a site map, and a traditional text and icon menu, so that a user can choose how to move about your site.

Laying the Groundwork

It would be tempting to just jump right into creating a web page with Dreamweaver MX. However, as with any program of any complexity, it's best to take a moment, sit back, and familiarize yourself with the program's features. By doing so, you'll build a foundation that will make your work easier and help you produce a truly inspiring interactive creation. Throughout this chapters, you'll explore topics that will help you accomplish this:

Chapter Contents

Choosing the Workspace That's Best for You

Several years ago, Macromedia came to the realization that many different kinds of people were using Dreamweaver to do web design. It was no longer the visual web design program of choice for just the masses. Professionally trained designers and programmers were also using it for their own needs. As a result, the folks at Macromedia eventually took the idea of workspace customization a step beyond what you normally see in many programs—they introduced two separate versions of the workspace (each tailored to meet the needs of different users) that could be dynamically toggled on and off.

 Note: In all honesty, the two aren't really two different workspaces; they are just two ways of configuring the same workspace.

Designer The Designer workspace (Figure 2.1) is an integrated workspace (using the multiple document interface, or MDI) in which in which all Document windows and panels are integrated into one larger application window, with the panel groups docked on the right.

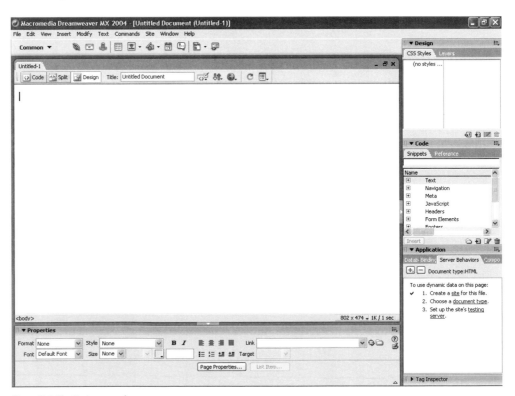

Figure 2.1 The Designer workspace

Coder The Coder workspace (Figure 2.2) is the same integrated workspace but with the panel groups docked on the left—in a layout similar to that used by Macromedia HomeSite and Macromedia ColdFusion Studio—and with the Document window showing Code View by default.

Note: Unfortunately, the Designer and the Coder workspaces are only available in the Windows version of Dreamweaver MX 2004. Mac users are restricted to the old-style Dreamweaver 4 workspace —which is just as functional, only visually diferent.

If you are starting up Dreamweaver MX 2004 for the first time, you'll be greeted by a dialog box (Figure 2.3) that allows you to make a choice right off the bat.

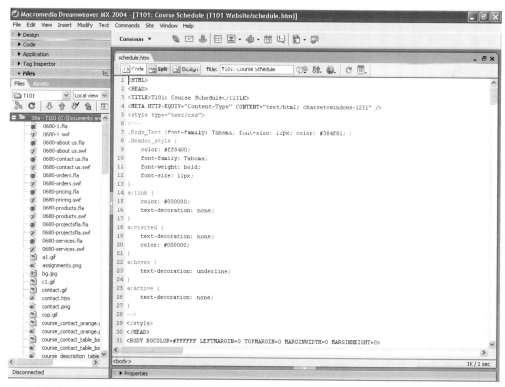

Figure 2.2 The Coder workspace

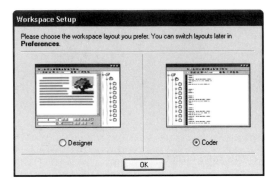

Figure 2.3 When you initially start up the program on a Windows machine running Dreamweaver MX 2004, the Workspace Setup dialog box lets you decide which workspace you want.

Not only can you choose your workspace when you first start up Dreamweaver MX 2004 on a Windows machine, you can also switch from one workspace to another later. To do so, just follow these steps:

1. Choose Edit > Preferences.

2. When the Preferences dialog box (Figure 2.4) appears, select the General category in the Category list box.

3. Click the Change Workspace button [Change Workspace...].

4. When the Workspace Setup dialog box appears, select the workspace to which you would like to change, and click OK.

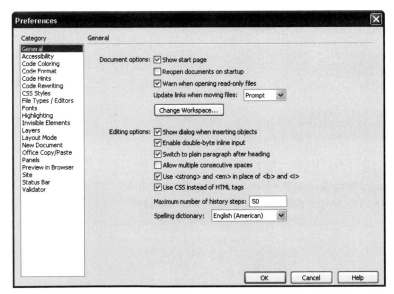

Figure 2.4 The General section of the Preferences dialog box

5. From here, you'll get a pop-up alert telling you that the change will take effect the next time you start Dreamweaver. Click OK to dismiss the alert.

Note: If you've selected the same workspace that you are currently working in, the alert will not appear.

6. Back in the Edit Preferences dialog box, click OK.

7. Restart the program, and your change will take effect.

Customizing Your Workspace

Beyond the two preset workspace styles (Designer and Coder), Dreamweaver MX 2004 also allows you a host of ways to customize the interface so that you can streamline your work and get the most out of the production process. In the following sections, you are going to explore how to customize panels, create custom keyboard shortcuts, and add custom rulers and grids to the Document window.

Customizing Panels

One of the most obviously useful features of Dreamweaver's interface is that its panels can be combined into different panel groups and then collapsed/expanded as your needs require. The panel groups can also float free or dock as you wish.

In the following sections, you'll learn how to make the most of Dreamweaver's great panel paradigm by creating, docking, and undocking panel groups, shifting panels from one panel group to another, and expanding and collapsing panels.

Panels vs. Panel Groups

What exactly is the difference between panels and panel groups? Well, panels are the individual tools that are accessible through the Window menu. Panel groups, on the other hand, are made up of a series of similar panels that are grouped together under one name (Code, Design, Files, Tags, etc.). You can also easily create new custom panel groups that contain panels that you've specified. Panel groups can be docked with one another or with the underlying interface. Strictly speaking, individual panels cannot be docked (either with each other or with the underlying interface); it's the panel group in which they reside that does the docking and undocking. Panel groups can also be collapsed and expanded, thereby hiding or displaying their panels.

Collapsing and Expanding Panel Groups

The Dreamweaver MX 2004 interface has become a little crowded. As a result, Macromedia has provided users with the ability to expand and collapse panels (see Figure 2.5), thereby economizing on space while still keeping the necessary tools at their fingertips.

To expand a collapsed panel group (or collapse an expanded panel group), click the small black arrow to the left of the panel group's name in the title bar. It's that easy.

Docking Panel Groups

To dock two panel groups to each other to create one large, floating panel group, follow these steps:

1. Open any two panels by using the Window menu.

Note: Remember that when you initially open up Dreamweaver, the panel or panels you want to use to create your mega floating panel might be docked with the interface. In order to undock them, follow the instructions later in this section.

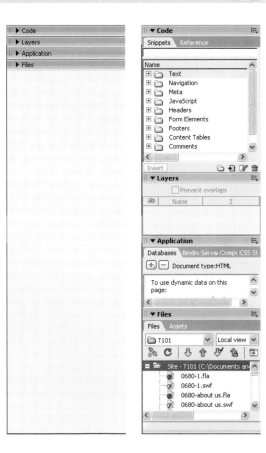

Figure 2.5 The left screen shows a series of panels that have been collapsed, and the right one shows the same panels expanded.

2. Click the gripper region of one panel group's title bar (represented by the small dots on the left side of the title bar) and drag it toward the target panel (Figure 2.6). Notice that a ghost image of the panel appears as you drag your mouse.

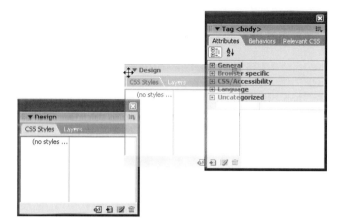

Figure 2.6 When you are combining one panel group with another, you'll notice that a ghost image of the dragged panel will appear as you are moving it toward the target panel group.

Note: You'll notice that your cursor will change when it moves over the gripper region of the panel's title bar.

3. Move your cursor over the target panel group.

4. When a black highlight appears around the target panel, release the mouse button and the two panel groups will be combined, as in Figure 2.7.

Figure 2.7 You can combine two or more panels to create a mega floating panel.

When you are working in Dreamweaver MX 2004 on a Windows machine, you have the benefit of an interface in which you can dock floating panel groups with the underlying interface—here's how:

1. Click the gripper region of one panel group's title bar (the small dots on the left side of the title bar) and drag it toward the left or the right side of the interface. Notice that a ghost image of the panel appears as you drag your mouse.

2. When a black highlight appears around the area where you dragged the panel group, release the mouse button and the group will dock with the underlying interface.

Moving Panels between Groups

You certainly aren't limited by which panels can go in which panel groups. Dreamweaver MX 2004 has a default organization, but you can easily move panels from one panel group to another.

Open the panel you would like to group with another existing panel group. Right-click/Control-click the panel's tab, and from the context menu, choose Group *Panel Name* With. Choose the panel group with which you'd like to combine the panel from the submenu of available options.

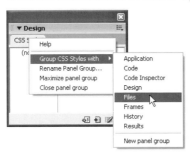

CHAPTER 2: LAYING THE GROUNDWORK ■

 Note: In Mac OS X, you press the Control key and click to get the context menu, and that's how I'll state it throughout this book. But in some earlier versions of the Mac OS, you press the Command key (⌘).

Creating a New Panel Group

While Dreamweaver has some default panel groups, you can easily create your own.

 Note: A panel group must have at least one panel in it. As a result, you create a new panel group by taking a panel that sits in an already existing group and telling Dreamweaver to create a new group around that panel.

Let's take a look at how:

1. Open the panel around which you would like to create a new panel group.

2. Right-click/Control-click the panel's tab and, from the context menu, choose Group *Panel Name* With > New Panel Group. A new panel group will automatically be created. The new group takes its name from the panel itself.

3. To rename the newly created panel group, right-click/Control-click the panel group's name and choose Rename Panel Group from the context menu.

4. When the Rename Panel Group dialog box appears, enter a new name into the Name field and click OK.

Customizing Keyboard Shortcuts

Keyboard shortcuts are a quick and easy way to access a program's various functions. Until now, most programs only offered the user an immutable set of shortcuts. However, Dreamweaver MX 2004 offers a Keyboard Shortcuts editor that allows you to create your own shortcuts, edit existing shortcuts, or choose from the fixed list of shortcut sets.

Let's take a look at how to define a custom set of shortcuts and start assigning shortcuts in that set:

1. Choose Edit > Keyboard Shortcuts to open the Keyboard Shortcuts editor (Figure 2.8).

> **Note:** If you've already defined a shortcut set and want to edit it, skip forward to step 5.

2. If it isn't already selected, choose Macromedia Standard from the Current Set drop-down menu.

3. Click the Duplicate Set button 🔁.

4. When the Duplicate Set dialog box appears (Figure 2.9), enter a name for the set and click OK. Notice that the name of the duplicate set you just created appears in the Current Set drop-down menu.

Duplicate Set

Figure 2.8 The Keyboard Shortcuts editor

Figure 2.9 The Duplicate Set dialog box

5. From the Commands drop-down menu, choose the group of commands with which you'd like to work.

6. If you choose Menu Commands or Site Panel, a list of command categories appears in the window below the Commands drop-down menu. Click the plus sign to expand the command category (File, Edit, View, Insert, and so on) with which you want to work. If you choose any of the other options in the Commands drop-down menu, go directly to step 8.

7. Select the specific command you want. Notice that the existing shortcuts attached to that command appear to the right of the command (the shortcut will also appear in the Shortcuts text box shown).

8. Select the command's existing shortcut in the Shortcuts text box.

9. Click the Remove Item button ▬ to strip the command's existing shortcut.

10. Click the Add Item button ✚; the Press Key field will automatically become accessible.

11. Press the key combination you want to add; the combination will appear in the Press Key field.

12. Click the Change button [Change] to assign the new shortcut to the command.

> **Note:** If your key combination is already assigned to another command, Flash will alert you and let you either reassign the shortcut or cancel it.

13. When you finish, click OK and the new keyboard shortcut will be assigned.

Customizing the Ruler and Grids

In Dreamweaver MX 2004, you can add both rulers and grids to the Document window in order to better lay out your page.

> **Note:** It's important to remember that when your HTML document is viewed in a browser, neither the rulers nor the grids are visible—they are a purely internal Dreamweaver thing.

To add rulers to your document, choose View > Rulers > Show, and two rulers, one along the top of the Document window and one along the left side of the Document window, will appear (Figure 2.10).

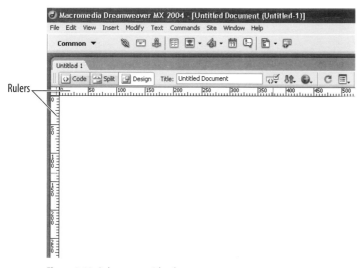

Figure 2.10 A document with rulers

By default, the rulers display pixels. It's easy to switch the rulers around so they display either inches or centimeters. To do so, choose View > Rulers > Centimeters or View > Rulers > Inches, depending on the unit of measurement you want displayed.

While rulers are displayed along the outside of the Document window, a grid is displayed inside the Document window (Figure 2.11), allowing you to line up the elements in your web page in a consistent manner. To view your document's grid, just choose View > Grid > Show Grid.

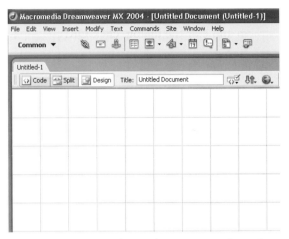

Figure 2.11 By adding a grid to your document, you can line up elements with greater consistency.

You'll notice that when you display your document's grid, it has a default appearance. You can easily change that appearance to better suit your needs. To do so, choose View > Grid > Grid Settings. When the Grid Settings dialog box (Figure 2.12) appears, set up your grid's appearance using the following options:

- Click the Color swatch ▣, and select a color for the grid from the color picker.
- To make the grid visible, click the Show Grid check box.
- If you want items to snap to the grid lines as you drag them near, click the Snap to Grid check box.
- To change the distance between the lines in the grid, select a unit of measurement (pixels, inches, or centimeters) from the Spacing drop-down menu and then enter a value into the Spacing field.
- Choose whether you would like the grid lines to be displayed as dots or as solid lines by clicking either the Dots or the Lines radio button.

To see your choices in effect, click Apply. When you've finished setting the properties of the grid and want to apply them and exit the dialog, click OK.

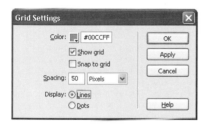

Figure 2.12 The Grid Settings dialog box

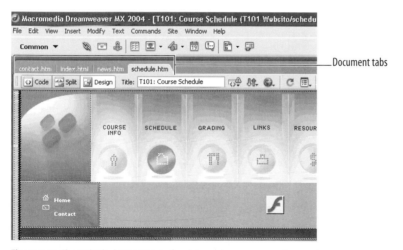

Document tabs

Figure 2.13 The multiple document interface lets you have numerous documents open at the same time and navigate fluidly between them.

Adjusting Document Window Size and Checking Page Download Time

Down along the bottom of your Document window on the right side, you'll see a pixel value (452×234, for example). This is a handy little feature called the Window Size indicator (Figure 2.14), which serves two primary functions. First, it provides an indicator of the current size (in pixels) of the Document window you're currently working in. Second, if you resize your window, the Window Size indicator changes immediately to reflect the new value. If you click the Window Size indicator and open the drop-down menu, you can easily choose from a preset list of window sizes.

By customizing the size of your Document window, you can get a rough preview of how your web page would look in a smaller browser window—which is particularly handy if you are using the Open Browser Window behavior (something that will be discussed in Chapter 9, "Adding Interactivity with JavaScript Behaviors") to open a custom-sized browser window.

One of the great things about the Window Size indicator drop-down menu is that you can create your own presets from which to choose. To do so, follow these steps:

1. Choose Edit > Preferences.

2. Select Status Bar from the Category list box (Figure 2.15).

3. When you click your mouse button with the cursor below the list of preset window sizes, a blank edit box will appear. Enter the new width in the Width column.

4. Press Tab and enter the new height in the Height column.

5. Press Tab and enter a description of your custom settings.

6. When you are finished, click OK.

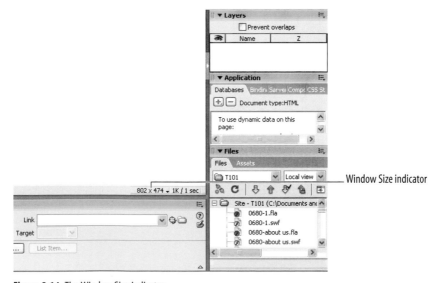

Figure 2.14 The Window Size indicator

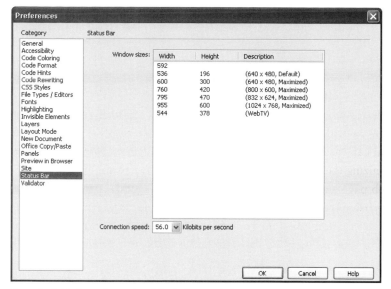

Figure 2.15 The Status Bar section of the Preferences dialog

Checking Document Size and Download Time

The Document Size/Download Time indicator (located along the bottom of the Document window right next to the Document Window Size indicator, as illustrated in Figure 2.16) is one of the unsung heroes of the Dreamweaver environment. Basically, it tells you the current size of your page (in kilobytes) and the amount of time (in seconds) it will take to download it over a 28.8Kbps modem connection.

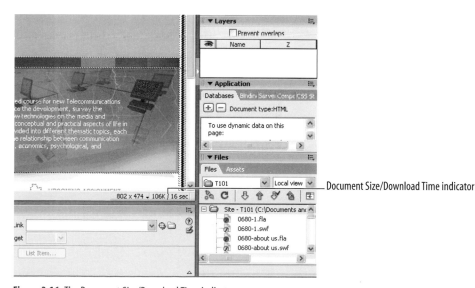

Document Size/Download Time indicator

Figure 2.16 The Document Size/Download Time indicator

As you add objects to your page, both numbers will increase. For those who spend a lot of time thinking about bandwidth (which should be most people), this is definitely a tool to keep your eye on.

Note: Although the Document Size/Download Time indicator provides a nice indication of the speed at which your page will download over a given connection, it's quite important to realize that it's just a rough indicator. As discussed in Chapter 1, there are more factors than the size of the page and the speed of the user's connection that affect the speed at which your page downloads, such as the speed of the user's computer processor or network traffic.

Now, you're probably thinking to yourself, "Hmmm…great tool, but what if I want to know how long my page will take to download over a 56Kbps modem, or even a cable modem?" Don't worry, you can easily change the speed of the modem: Open the Preferences dialog box (Edit > Preferences) and choose Status Bar from the Category list box (shown back in Figure 2.15).

Just below the Window Sizes field, you'll see a drop-down menu labeled Connection Speed (Kilobytes Per Second) from which you can choose the modem speed (Figure 2.17). Once you've set this, click OK to close the Preferences dialog box.

Using a Browser to Preview Your Work

After the first true public web browser, Mosaic, was released, the size of the World Wide Web increased exponentially. Many software companies realized that the browser was the key to the whole shebang and quickly responded. The most notable were Microsoft and Netscape. Despite the fact that both companies are now the giants of the scene, many smaller companies still offer their own take on the browser.

You can never be absolutely sure what kind of browser is being used to view your page, and every browser displays HTML a little differently.

This is where Dreamweaver's Preview in Browser function comes in. You can set it so that a simple stroke of a hotkey will load your page in a browser of your choice.

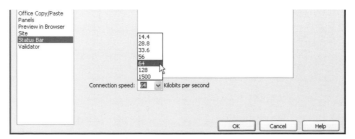

Figure 2.17 Selecting a new option from the Connection Speed drop-down menu changes what is displayed in the Document Size/Download Time indicator.

Browser Power

All browsers (especially Netscape and Internet Explorer) are hardly created equal. Not only do you have to contend with browsers of the same generation (at this point 6 for both Netscape and IE) that nonetheless do not support the same features, you also have to deal with older browsers. This is why it's extremely important to either get to know your audience and design specifically for the browser they most commonly use or design your page for the lowest common browser denominator. Want to know which browsers support which specific features? Check out CNET's Browser topic center at www.browsers.com.

Adding a Target Browser

Before you can preview your work in a browser, you need to tell Dreamweaver which browsers you've loaded on your computer and which hotkeys you want to associate with them.

Note: You can only preview work in a browser that you have installed on your computer.

To set a target browser, follow these steps:

1. Open the Preferences dialog box (Edit > Preferences).

2. Select Preview in Browser from the Category list box (Figure 2.18).

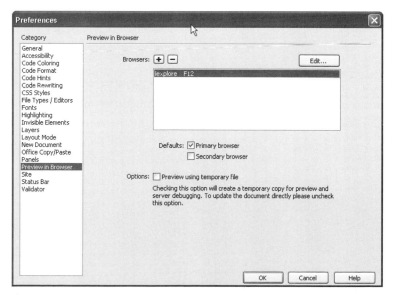

Figure 2.18 The Preview in Browser section in the Preferences dialog box

3. Click the plus symbol  to open the Add Browser dialog box (Figure 2.19).

Figure 2.19 The Add Browser dialog box

4. In the Name field, type the browser name as you want it to appear in the browser list.

5. Click Browse ⬚ Browse... ⬚ to open the file navigation screen. Navigate to the browser program file and select it.

6. If you want Dreamweaver to preview a temporary copy of your document (as opposed to the document itself), click the Preview Using Temporary File check box.

7. Click OK.

Editing Your Browser List

Because there are many different browsers on the market, and new browser versions are released regularily, you may find it necessary to edit your browser list so that new browsers can be added and old browsers removed:

1. Open the Preferences dialog box (Edit > Preferences).

2. Select Preview in Browser from the Category list box.

Note: Depending on your preference, you can designate one browser as primary and another as secondary. The primary browser will be designated the default.

3. Select the browser you wish to edit and click the Edit ⬚ Edit... ⬚ button to open the Edit Browser dialog box.

4. Make your changes and click OK.

Launching Your Target Browser

Once you've defined your target browser and its associated hotkeys, there are two ways to preview your creation:

- Press the hotkey you defined for the target browser. In most cases, the default for your primary browser is F12, while the default for your secondary browser is ⌘/Ctrl+F12.

- Click the Preview/Debug in Browser button in the Toolbar above your Document window to open a drop-down list of target browsers to choose from.

Note: If you've defined only one target browser in the Preferences dialog box, clicking the Toolbar's Preview in Browser button automatically launches that browser.

Creating and Managing New Documents

By default, Dreamweaver opens a new document when it's launched. However, at some point while working in Dreamweaver MX 2004, you'll probably need to open an additional new document. Here's how to create a new document:

1. Open the New Document dialog box (Figure 2.20) by choosing File > New.

2. Make sure the General tab is selected.

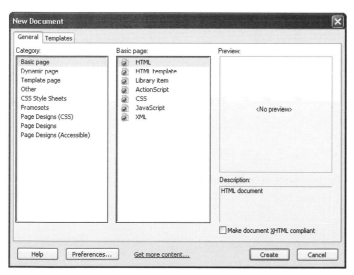

Figure 2.20 The New Document dialog box

3. In the Category list box, select the category of document you would like to create.

Note: If you want to use an existing predesigned page layout, select either Page Designs or Page Designs (Accessible).

4. Select the specific type of document from the Basic Page list box (to the right of the Category list box).

5. Click Create Create .

Changing the Default Document Type

As you've already seen, when Dreamweaver launches, it opens a default new HTML document in the Document window. However, as you well know, Dreamweaver can work with a far wider variety of document types than just HTML. So, what if, when you start up the program, you want the default new document to be a PHP file instead of an HTML file?

Well, changing the default document type is an easy process; all you need to do is open the Preferences dialog box (Edit > Preferences) and choose New Document from the Category list box (Figure 2.21).

Select the desired type from the Default Document Type drop-down menu. When you're finished, click OK.

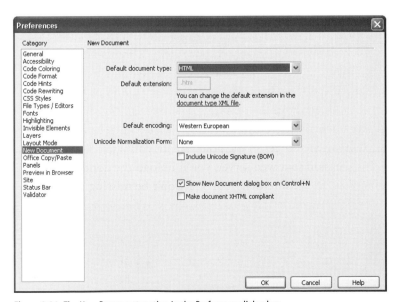

Figure 2.21 The New Document section in the Preferences dialog box

Changing the Default Document Encoding

Document encoding, which is specified in a meta tag in the head section of the document, tells the browser and Dreamweaver MX 2004 how the document should be decoded and, more specifically, what fonts should be used to display the decoded text.

For example, if you specify Western European (Latin1), the following meta tag is inserted:

```
<meta http-equiv="Content-Type" content="text/html; charset=iso-8859-1">
```

In this case, Dreamweaver displays the document using the fonts you specify in Fonts Preferences for the Western European (Latin1) encoding. On the other hand, a browser displays the document using the fonts its user specifies for the Western European (Latin1) encoding.

If you specify Japanese (Shift JIS), the following meta tag is inserted:

```
<meta http-equiv="Content-Type" content="text/html; charset=Shift_JIS">
```

In this case, Dreamweaver displays the document using the fonts you specify for the Japanese encodings, and a browser will display the document using the fonts its user specifies for the Japanese encodings.

By default, all newly created documents have a set document encoding. It's quite easy to change the default encoding. To do so, open the Preferences dialog box by choosing Edit > Preferences and select the New Document category (shown back in Figure 2.21). Choose one of the options from the Default Encoding drop-down menu and then click OK.

The Fine Art of Local Sites

Dreamweaver MX 2004 is as much a website creation and management tool as it is an individual web page creation tool. While you can certainly create a stand-alone page, Dreamweaver has a host of great tools designed to help you create, manipulate, and manage whole sites. All of these tools revolve around the initial creation of a local site.

The local site (which will include all the files in your site) should reside in a separate folder on your hard drive (or another form of portable media such as a CD-RW or a Zip disk), mainly because when you get to the point where you want to establish a remote site and upload your creation to a web server, you'll upload the contents of the entire site's folder. By doing this, you ensure that your site won't be missing any components when you upload it. When you set up your local site, you'll also be able to track and maintain your links.

It's important to note that without having set up a local site, you'll be unable to set up a *remote* site and, therefore, won't be able to take advantage of Dreamweaver MX 2004's integrated FTP client or invoke the series of tools (such as the Check In/Check Out feature and Design Notes) that allow you to work collaboratively with a team of other designers on a site residing on a remote web server. You will get ample time to explore the intricacies of creating and manipulating a remote site in Chapter 11.

Note: If you are inserting elements (images, multimedia files, and so on) that reside outside of the folder in which your local site sits, Dreamweaver will always prompt you to save them to your local site. If you want your site to be complete when you upload it to your remote server, be sure to take advantage of Dreamweaver's prompt and move external files over to your local site.

There are two ways of setting up a local site. The first, which is outlined in the following section, involves manually inputting the local site information into the Site Definition dialog box. The second involves using the Site Definition Wizard, a handy tool that walks you through the process of setting up a local site (and also walks you through setting up a remote site and a testing server, for that matter).

Creating a Local Site Manually

The first thing you must do when you set up a local site is tell Dreamweaver where on your hard drive you want your site to reside and what you want to call it. You also need to input some additional information about the structure and properties of your local site. To do this, follow these steps:

1. Choose Site > Manage Sites to open the Manage Sites dialog box (Figure 2.22).

Figure 2.22 The Manage Sites dialog box

2. Click the New button ![New...], and select Site from the subsequent drop-down menu.

3. If it isn't already selected, click the Advanced tab at the top of the Site Definition dialog box (Figure 2.23).

4. Make sure Local Info is selected in the Category list box.

5. In the Site Name field, enter the name you want to give to your site.

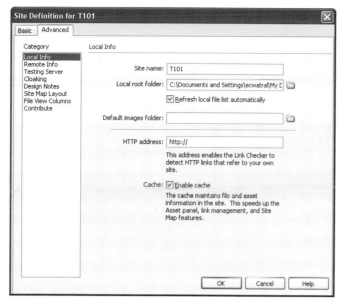

Figure 2.23 The Advanced tab of the Site Definition dialog box

Note: The site name is not your filename or your page title; it's a name that is used when you're working with the Dreamweaver MX 2004 site tools. When you upload your site to a remote web server, the name won't appear anywhere on your pages. Giving each a unique name is very handy if you are working with more than one local site—it will help you avoid getting mixed up.

6. Click the browse button to the right of the Local Root Folder field. When the file navigation screen appears, locate and select the folder on your hard drive where you want your new local site to reside.

7. If you want the structure and content of the site to refresh automatically every time you copy a file into your local site, check the Refresh Local File List Automatically option. If you leave this option unchecked, Dreamweaver will copy files to your local site more quickly.

8. If you are planning on storing all of the images in your site in single folder, click the browse button to the right of the Default Images Folder field. When the Choose Local Images Folder dialog box appears, navigate to the folder and click Select.

Note: For a default images folder to work properly, you need to make sure it's within the local root folder of your local site—otherwise, when you upload your site to a web server, the images won't go with it and you'll have nothing but broken images.

9. If you know what the URL, or *domain name*, of your site will ultimately be after you've uploaded it to a remote web server, enter it in the HTTP Address field.

Note: If you fill out the HTTP Address field, Dreamweaver can verify links within the site that use absolute URLs.

10. If you want your local site to have a cache, click the Enable Cache check box. The cache essentially saves your site's file information, thereby speeding up many of the tools that rely on a local site, like the Assets panel and the Site Map.

11. When you are finished, click OK.

12. When you are returned to the Manage Sites dialog box (where you'll see that your newly created site will be displayed), click Done.

After you finish entering all the local site information, the Files panel will automatically open, displaying the files in your local site's root folder. If the Files panel doesn't actually display any files, you need not worry: your local site doesn't have any files in it yet.

Creating a Local Site with the Site Definition Wizard

Instead of manually setting up your local site, you can take advantage of the Site Definition Wizard. If you're new to Dreamweaver, the Site Definition Wizard might be a good choice to start with. However, in the grand scheme of things, setting your site information manually gives you more control over the process. Follow these steps to use the Site Definition Wizard:

1. Choose Site > Manage Sites to open the Manage Sites dialog box.

2. Click the New button New... and select Site from the subsequent drop-down menu.

3. If it isn't already selected, click the Basic tab at the top of the Site Definition Wizard (Figure 2.24).

4. In the first screen of the Site Definition Wizard, enter the name of your site into the field and click Next.

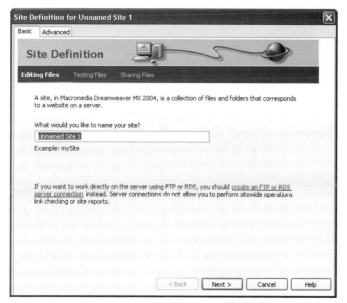

Figure 2.24 The Site Definition Wizard

5. Click the "No, I don't want to use server technology" radio button. Although you very well might be interested in creating a dynamic database-driven site (something we'll look at in Bonus Chapters 1 and 2 on the CD), you don't want to complicate things at this stage. Click Next.

6. Click the Edit Local Copies on My Machine radio button. You can set up a remote site on this screen, but we won't cover that here (for more information on this topic, see Chapter 11).

7. From here, you need to tell Dreamweaver MX 2004 where on your hard drive all of the files in your local site are going to be stored (this is called the Local Root folder). Click the browse button to the right of the "Where on your computer do you want to store your files" field. When the file navigation screen appears, locate and select the folder on your hard drive where you want your new local site to reside. Then click Next.

8. When the Sharing Files section of the Site Definition Wizard appears, select None from the "How do you want to connect to your remote server" drop-down menu. You don't have to worry about how you are connecting to a remote server until you set up your remote site—something you'll look at in Chapter 11. Then click Next.

9. From here, the Site Definition Wizard will give you a rundown of the parameters of your local site. If you see something wrong, back up to the appropriate point in the process by clicking the Back button. If you are happy with the results, click Done [Done].

Visualizing Your Local Site with a Site Map Layout

The Site Map is a handy feature that produces a visual representation (a reverse branching tree) of the structure of your website; Figure 2.25 provides an example. Located in the left side of your local Site panel (after you click the Site panel's Expand/Collapse button), the Site Map not only lets you get a comprehensive structural representation of your entire site, it also lets you add new files or add, modify, or delete links between files in your site.

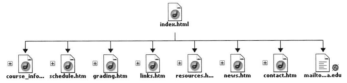

Figure 2.25 The Site Map layout displays the structure of your site as a reverse branching tree issuing forth from a single page—your home page.

In the following sections, you are going to learn how to define and view your site map, manipulate the Site Map layout, work with files in the Site Map layout, and save the Site Map as an image.

Note: A Site Map will function only when you're working with a local site, not a remote site.

Defining and Viewing your Site Map Layout

Before you can actually work with, or even view, your Site Map layout, you first need to define a home page (the front door for your website, so to speak) from which the tree structure grows. The following steps assume you have already defined a local site using the procedure described earlier in this chapter. You certainly don't have to start with an already defined site. However, given the fact that newly defined local sites rarely have anything in them, they really don't have anything to visualize in a site map. Here's how to define a home page:

1. Choose Site > Manage Sites.
2. When the Manage Sites dialog box appears, select the site you want to work with and click Edit [Edit…].
3. When the Site Definition dialog box opens, click the Advanced tab and select Site Map Layout from the Category list (Figure 2.26).
4. Click the browse button 📁 to the right of the Home Page field.

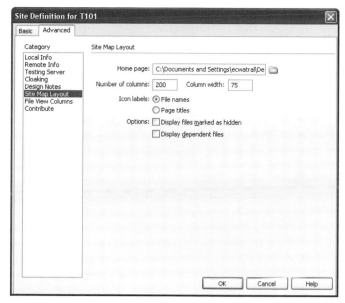

Figure 2.26 The Site Map Layout section of the Site Definition dialog box

5. When the Choose Home Page dialog box pops up, navigate to the file that will serve as the home page in your site map layout and click Open.

6. After you've selected the file that will act as the home page, click OK to exit the Site Definition dialog box and then Done to exit the Manage Sites dialog box.

> **Note:** Another neat thing about Dreamweaver is that, even if you haven't set a home page, it still tries to create a Site Map. In this event, it looks for an index.html or index.htm file on which to base your Site Map.

Now that you've established a home page, you can view your Site Map layout. To do this, follow these steps:

1. Make sure you are currently working in the local site for which you set the home page. Open the Files panel (Window > Files).

2. Click the Site panel's Expand/Collapse button 🔲 .

3. Click the Site Map button 🔳▾ (to the left of the Site Name drop-down menu). This will cause the Site Map to appear in the left-hand portion of the Site window (Figure 2.27).

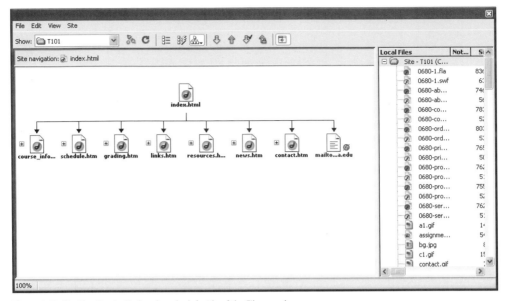

Figure 2.27 The Site Map is displayed on the left side of the Files panel

Note: To access your Site Map, you can also choose View > Site Map (in the Files panel drop-down menu). This automatically opens the Site window with the Site Map already visible, thereby saving you the step of having to click the Site Map button in the Site window.

Changing the Site Map Layout

You certainly aren't stuck with the default look of the Site Map. There are a number of operations you can perform to alter its appearance so it's easier for you to work with and interpret. Follow these steps manipulate the Site Map layout:

1. Choose Site > Manage Sites to open the Manage Sites dialog box.

2. Select the site whose Site Map you want to manipulate, and click Edit.

3. Click the Site Definition dialog box's Advanced tab. From the Category menu, select Site Map Layout.

4. From here, you can manipulate the Site Map's various options to alter its appearance:

Number Of Columns Sets the number of pages that are displayed in a single horizontal row in the Files panel. The higher the number, the fewer rows in the Files panel and the more your Site Map will look like a reverse branching tree.

Column Width Sets the width (in pixels) of each vertical column in the Files panel. A higher number results in more of any given filename or title being displayed. If you enter a lower number, filenames/titles will be truncated.

Note: The maximum column width is 1000, and the minimum is 70; you can have a maximum of 9999 columns and a minimum of 1.

Icon Labels When the File Names option is selected, each of the files in the Site window will be identified by its actual filename. Conversely, if you select Page Titles, the files in the Files panel will be identified by their page title.

Display Files Marked As Hidden By selecting this option, you can display files that have been hidden by the user (with the View menu). If this option is selected, hidden files are displayed in italics.

Display Dependent Files This displays all of the files (all non-HTML content) associated with any given HTML file in your local site.

Working with Files in the Site Map Layout

The Site Map is not just a simple tool for visualizing the structure of your site; it can also be used to carry out some limited editing tasks on the files in your local site.

To add a new file to the site (and automatically link it to an existing file in the hierarchy):

1. With the Site Map open, select the file to which you want to link the new file.

2. Using the File panel's drop-down menu, choose Site > Link to New File.

3. When the Link to New File dialog box opens (Figure 2.28), enter the filename of the new file into the File Name field.

Figure 2.28 The Link to New File dialog box

Note: Remember to include the proper file extension, either .html or .htm. If you don't, Dreamweaver will be unable to open the newly created file.

4. Enter a title for the page into the Title field. This sets the page's title just as if you were doing it in the Modify Page Properties dialog box (something you'll explore next chapter).

5. Enter some text into the Text of Link field. This text will serve as the hyperlink to the newly created file, which is inserted into the body of the selected file.

6. When you finish, click OK.

In addition to linking a newly created file to an existing file, you can also edit the page titles of the files in your Site window.

 Note: You won't be able to modify the page title in your Site window if you haven't selected the Page Titles option in the Site Map Layout section of the Site Definition dialog box.

To do this, follow these steps:

1. With the Files panel open and the Site Map visible, select the file whose title you want to modify.

2. From here, activate the file's name either by choosing File > Rename (Windows) or Site > Rename (Mac) in the Files panel or by clicking the filename itself. Once the selected file's title becomes editable, type in a new title and click your cursor anywhere off the file when you've finished.

3. The Update Files dialog box appears. Click the Update button, and all the files that reference the file whose name you changed will automatically update so you won't have any broken links.

Saving the Site Map as an Image

The Site Map is quite a handy little tool for visualizing the structure of your site. However, there is a distinct possibility that somewhere along the line you are going to want to be able to view the Site Map *outside* of Dreamweaver, say, to share it with a colleague or a team member. This is pretty easy, as Dreamweaver lets you save your Site Map as an image.

In Windows, to view the Site Map outside of Dreamweaver, open the Files panel and choose File > Save Site Map. When the Save Site Map dialog box opens, enter a name in the File Name field, select either .bmp or .png from File Type drop-down menu, navigate to the location on your hard drive to which you want to save the file, and click Save.

If you are using a Mac, the steps are a little different: Choose Site > Site Map View > Save Site Map > Save Site Map as PICT or Save Site Map as JPEG. You can then navigate to the location on your hard drive to which you want to image to be saved, enter a filename into the File Name field, and click Save.

Editing or Deleting an Existing Site

If you've already defined your site but you want to go back and change some of its information, choose Site > Manage Sites to open the Manage Sites dialog box. From the list of sites, choose the site you want to access and click Edit. This will open the Site Definition dialog box from which you can make any changes you want; when you're finished, click OK.

After you've established a local site (or a series of local sites), you may decide to delete it. If so, once again you would choose Site > Manage Sites to open the Manage Sites dialog box. From the list of sites, choose the site you want to delete and click Remove. A dialog box pops up, asking whether you indeed want to delete the selected site. If you wish to continue, click Yes; if you don't want to delete the site, just click No.

Note: If you delete a local site, you cannot undo your action.

Exporting and Importing an Existing Site

One of the biggest drawbacks to working with local sites is that the site definition information stays on the computer on which you originally set up the site and not with the files themselves. This means that each time you go to a new computer, you have to set up the local site again.

The good news is that you can actually export a site as an XML file and import it back into Dreamweaver, thereby allowing you to move sites between machines. To export a site, just follow these steps:

1. Choose Site > Manage Sites.
2. When the Manage Sites dialog box appears, select the site you'd like to export, and click the Export button [Export...].
3. When the Export Site dialog box appears, browse to the location where you would like to save the exported site file (an XML file with a .ste extension), enter a name into the File Name field, and click Save.
4. When you're returned to the Manage Sites dialog box, click Done.

   To import a site, just follow these steps:
1. Choose Site > Manage Sites.
2. When the Manage Sites dialog box appears, select the exported XML file corresponding to the site you'd like to import and click the Import button [Import...].
3. Browse to the location where where the site file resides, select it, and click Open.
4. Back in the Manage Sites dialog box, click Done.

Setting Page Properties

Before you add content in the Document window, you need to set the page's properties in the Page Properties dialog box (which is accessible by choosing Modify > Document). When you set the properties of a given element (text color, for example) with the Page Properties dialog box, you affect all those elements on that page.

 Note: Easily one of the coolest new features in Dreamweaver MX 2004 is that a huge amount of your document's properties are based on Cascading Style Sheets (CSS), not on HTML. As a result, you're going to have a far greater and far wider amount of control over your document's properties than in previous version of Dreamweaver.

In the following sections, you are going to explore how to give your page a title, change your page's background color, add a background image, set your page's text and hyperlink properties, and add a tracing image.

Giving Your Page a Title

Even though it may seem obvious, it's remarkably easy to forget to name your page. Naming your page is not the same as naming your file. The name of your page is displayed in the title bar of the browser. Leaving your page untitled will result in an unseemly "Untitled Document" in the title bar of a browser—something that should be avoided at all costs.

To title your page, follow these steps:

1. Open the Page Properties dialog box (Modify > Page Properties).
2. Select the Title/Encoding option in the Category list box (Figure 2.29).

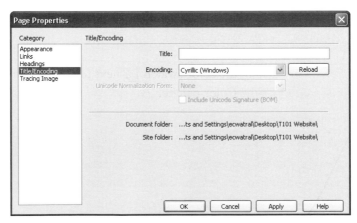

Figure 2.29 The Title/Encoding section of the Page Properties dialog box

3. Enter the title of your page in the Title field.

4. Click Apply, and then click OK.

Changing the Background Color

When you start a new document, the Document window has a white background. By default, this is the color that Dreamweaver sets as the background color for all new documents. Like background images (something we'll talk about next), you can easily choose the background color you want. Here's how to change the background color of your page:

1. Open the Page Properties dialog box (Modify > Page Properties).

2. Select the Appearance option in the Category list box (Figure 2.30).

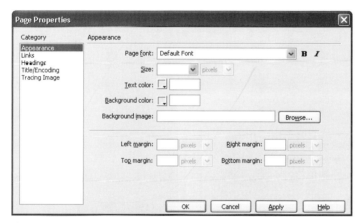

Figure 2.30 The Appearance section of the Page Properties dialog box

3. Open the Color picker by clicking the color swatch next to the Background Color field. Figure 2.31 shows the Color palette.

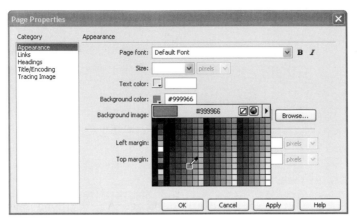

Figure 2.31 The Page Properties dialog box with the color picker open

4. From here, you can simply click the preset color you like in the color picker (and then move on to Step 5). Alternatively, you can mix your own color. To do so, just follow these sub steps:

    a. If you aren't satisfied with the colors offered in the Color picker, you can always use the Color dialog box to mix an alternate color. Click the Open Color Dialog Box icon ◉ (in the top-right corner of the Color picker) to open the Color dialog box (Figure 2.32).

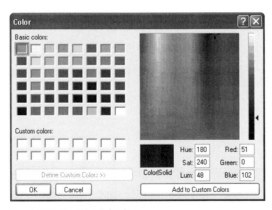

Figure 2.32 The Color dialog box

Note: Any color you use will automatically be added to the Colors section of the Assets panel (Window > Assets). This way, you don't run the risk of finding the perfect color only to lose it because you didn't write down its numerical code.

b. You can choose the color you want by clicking in the color picker or by entering its corresponding numerical RGB (red/green/blue) code. Alternatively, you can enter a numerical HSL (hue/saturation/luminosity) or adjust the shade slider.

c. When you are finished creating your custom color, click OK to return to the Page Properties dialog box.

5. Notice that the Color swatch in the Page Properties dialog box has changed to the color you've chosen. Click Apply and then OK.

Adding a Background Image to Your Page

You can spice up a web page by adding a background image. A background image can consist of either one large image or a smaller one that the browser tiles in a continuous pattern. If someone enlarges the browser window, the number of tiles will increase to fill all the available space.

> **Note:** You'll learn more about web graphics in Chapter 4, "Working with Images," but it's important to know that background images are no different from any other kind of web graphic. The only graphic files that can be displayed by a web browser are GIFs, JPEGs, and PNGs.

To add a background image to your page:

1. Open the Page Properties dialog box (Modify > Page Properties).

2. Select the Appearance option in the Category list box (shown back in Figure 2.30).

3. Click the Browse button [Browse...] to the right of the Background Image field to open the Select Image Source dialog box.

Web-Safe Colors

Even though most monitors out there can display at least 256 colors (most can display millions), there are really only 216 colors that all computers display exactly the same. These colors are part of what is called the web-safe color palette and make up the colors you'll find in the Dreamweaver Color palette. If you use a color outside the web-safe color palette, the browser will convert it to the closest color it can find in the system palette of your audience's computer. This means you run the risk of having your colors look slightly different from machine to machine if you stray from the web-safe color palette.

4.   Navigate to the location on your hard drive where your file is, click it once to select it, and click OK. Notice that a small thumbnail preview of the image appears in the Image Preview area when you select an image.

 Note: If you select an image that resides outside the structure of your current local site, Dreamweaver will prompt you to resave it to the root folder of your local site.

5.   When you return to the Page Properties dialog box, notice that the document's path appears in the Background Image field. Click Apply and then OK.

Setting Your Page's Text Properties

Remember, using the Page Properties dialog box to change the properties of your page's text affects all of the text on that page. However, this doesn't mean you can't change the properties of a specific character, word, or string of text. To learn how to do that, see Chapter 3, "Communicating Effectively with Text."

To change the properties of your page's text, just follow these steps:

1.   Open the Page Properties dialog box (Modify > Page Properties).

2.   Select the Appearance option in the Category list box (Figure 2.30).

3.   Choose your text formatting by setting the various options:

- To change the font of your page's text, select one of the options from the Page Font drop-down menu.

- If you want the text to be bold **B** or italic *I* , click the appropriate button to the right of the Page Font drop-down menu.

- To set the size of your text, select one of the options from the Size drop-down menu.

 Note: In previous versions of Dreamweaver, page properties were HTML based, but page properties in Dreamweaver MX 2004 are CSS based. As a result, you don't have to rely on HTML-based absolute and relative sizing for text. Instead, you can use point size.

- To change the text color, click the color swatch ⬛ next to the Text Color field. The Color palette will open, allowing you to immediately choose the color you wish. Alternatively, you can open the Color dialog box and mix your own color.

4.   Once you're done, click Apply and then click OK.

Setting Your Page's Hyperlink Properties

Changing the properties of your page's hyperlinks is almost identical to changing the page text; just follow these steps:

1. Open the Page Properties dialog box (Modify > Page Properties).

2. Select the Links option in the Category list box (Figure 2.33).

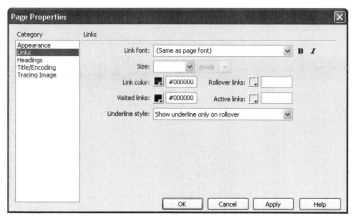

Figure 2.33 The Links section of the Page Properties dialog box

3. Choose your link text formatting by setting the various options:

- If you want the text of your links to have a different font, select one from the Link Font drop-down menu. If you want the links to have the same font as the rest of your page, select the Same as Page Font option.

- To make your links bold **B** or italic *I*, click the appropriate button to the right of the Link Font drop-down menu.

- If you want link text to be a different size than the rest of your page's text, select an option from the Size drop-down menu. If you don't select one of the options from the Size drop-down menu, the links will have the same text size as the rest of your page's text.

> **Note:** As with text properties, the properties of your links are now all controlled with CSS, thereby giving you access to some nifty new features—namely, underline style.

4. To set the color of your links, click the color swatch next to the Link Color field. When the Color palette opens, choose the color you wish. Alternatively, you can open the Color dialog box and mix your own color.

The Ins and Outs of Link Color

Link color refers to the color of a hyperlink before the user interacts with it. *Visited* link color refers to the color of a hyperlink after it has been clicked by the user. The *active* link color, which is probably the least important of the various hyperlink color "states," refers to the color that the link turns between the time the user presses their mouse button down and the time they release it (the click).

For the most part, the classic blue (which is the default color) underlined text is universally recognized as a link. If you change your link color to something else, there is the possibility that people might not even recognize it as a link. So unless there is some pressing design need to change the link color (or you detest the color blue), stick with the default.

5. Follow the same process for each of the other three types of links. To set the color of links after a user follows them, click the color swatch ⬛ next to the Visited Links field; for the color of a link while the user clicks it, click the Active Links swatch; and if you want your links to change color when the user moves their mouse over them, click the swatch next to Rollover Links. For each of these, as before, set the color in the Color palette or the color picker.

6. To set the underline style of your page's links, select one of the options from the Underline Style drop-down menu:

Always Underline All of the links in your page always have an underline.

Never Underline All of the links in your page never have an underline.

Hide Underline on Rollover The underline on all of your links will disappear when the user moves their mouse over them.

Show Underline Only on Rollover An underline will appear when the user moves their mouse over the link.

7. When you are finished, click Apply and then OK.

Using a Tracing Image

Remember back when you were a kid and you were really keen on drawing but weren't that confident about your skills? You'd sit down with a picture from a book and a piece of tracing paper and proceed to draw something that was just right. This approach to drawing by the young comes not so much from lack of skill, but from a desire to produce something that is *perfect*. Well, with tracing images, Macromedia has brought all of this into web design.

Despite all the electronic tools available, most interactive design (whether it is HTML based or rooted in another technology such as Macromedia Flash) is still conceived and fleshed out on paper before it goes anywhere near a computer screen.

The problem with this is that things on paper don't always translate to digital form exactly as the designer conceived. This is where tracing images come in. You can scan a hard copy design—say, your own hand-drawn art or storyboard—and stick it in the background of your web page. You can then line up elements on the page exactly (or as close as they can get) to the scanned image.

Note: A tracing image isn't the same thing as a background image. When you go live with your page (or preview it in a browser), the tracing image isn't seen. The only time it's ever visible is when you are working on your creation in the Document window.

Follow these steps to try it:

1. Open the Page Properties dialog box (Modify > Page Properties).
2. Select the Tracing Image option in the Category list box. (Figure 2.34)

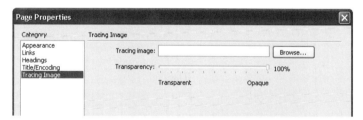

Figure 2.34 The Tracing Image section of the Page Properties dialog box

3. Click the Browse button, navigate to the appropriate file, and select it. Notice that a small thumbnail preview of the image appears in the Image Preview area of the file navigation screen.
4. Click Apply.
5. When you return to the Page Properties dialog box, you can adjust the transparency of the tracing image by using the slider.
6. When you are finished, click Apply, and then OK.

The Last Step: Saving Your Document

Obviously, the whole point of creating a web page is that you can keep it. This entails saving.

 Note: When a document contains unsaved changes, an asterisk (*) appears after the document name in the document title bar, the application title bar, and the document tab. When you save the document, the asterisk is removed.

To save your document, just follow these steps:

1. Open the File menu, and choose one of the Save options:

   Save Saves the document you are currently working on.

   Save As Saves a file that you've already saved under a new filename.

   Save All Saves all of the currently open documents.

   Save to Remote Server Select this if you've set up a Remote Site to which you want to save the document. (For more info on saving to a remote server, see Chapter 11.)

   Save As Template Saves your document as a Dreamweaver template. (For more information on templates, see Chapter 7.)

2. When the dialog box appears, navigate to the location in which you want to save the file, enter a filename into the File Name field, and click Save.

Communicating Effectively with Text

When Edward George Bulwer-Lytton penned the words "Beneath the rule of men entirely great, the pen is mightier than the sword" (in his 1839 play Richelieu)*, he couldn't have foreseen the digital age. Yet his words still ring true in the day of the World Wide Web. Despite the fact that the Web is becoming an increasingly more visual medium, the vast majority of the information is still textual.*

3

Chapter Contents

Creating and Styling Text

There really is no mystery to creating text in Dreamweaver MX 2004. Just click in the Document window and type. It's that easy! In fact, adding text in Dreamweaver's visual authoring environment (as opposed to its coding environment) is just like working in a word processor. The real fun comes when you get to change the text from its default size, font, and color into something that will fit with the design of your page.

Note: Easily one of the most exciting features in Dreamweaver MX 2004 is that all formatting is now controlled by Cascading Style Sheets (CSS) instead of HTML. As a result, you'll have far greater control over text creation and manipulation than in previous version of the program. For a more detailed explanation of CSS (and why it's so cool), check out Chapter 10.

Varying Your Page's Text Size

In previous version of Dreamweaver, when text formatting was controlled with HTML, web text size was not represented in the same way that digital text was. Instead of being measured by point size, the size of web-based text was represented using a sizing scale from 1 to 7, with 1 being the smallest size and 7 the largest. Previous versions of Dreamweaver offered two sizing systems: absolute and relative. I'll discuss them in detail in the following sections, but both systems are based on the 1–7 sizing system, which can be pretty limiting—especially for those who were used to sizing text using a point system.

This all changed in Dreamweaver MX 2004. As mentioned previously, Cascading Style Sheets (CSS), instead of HTML, is used for the purposes of formatting text. As a result, the old relative and absolute sizing systems have pretty much been thrown out the window, replaced with a far more intuitive (and flexible) system.

This having been said, let's take a look at how you go about changing the size of your text:

1. Select the text whose size you want to change.

2. If it isn't already, open the Property Inspector (Window > Properties).

3. Select one of the options from the Size drop-down menu.

Size drop-down menu ⌐   ⌐ Text Size Unit drop-down menu

4. Select the unit you would like to use for text size from the Text Size Unit drop-down menu.

Note: You'll notice that as you change the size of your text, a new option (that is actually a preview of the size you chose) appears in the Style drop-down menu. This is one of the great new features in Dreamweaver MX 2004. Whenever you change the properties of text, the program stores the formatting as a style in an embedded style sheet. As you add more (and different) text formatting to your document, the number of styles will increase. The whole point of the Style drop-down menu is that instead of applying the same formatting over and over again, you can simply select the text you want to change and then pick the appropriate style from the Style drop-down menu. For more information on CSS in Dreamweaver, see Chapter 10.

Changing Your Page's Text Color

When it comes to font color, you've got to take into consideration the legibility issues that were discussed in Chapter 1. Beyond those limitations, you've got a really nice palette of colors that you can apply to text.

Note: In Chapter 2, we discussed using the Page Properties dialog box to change the font color for all the text on a page; the following process changes the font color of specifically selected text only.

In Dreamweaver, changing text color is pretty easy, all you need to do is follow these steps:

1. Select the text whose color you want to change.
2. Open the Property Inspector (Window > Properties) and click the Text Color swatch ▢ to open the Color picker.

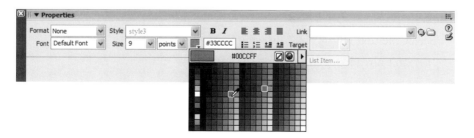

3. Move your cursor over a color you like and click it. The color of your text automatically changes. If you want to choose a color that isn't contained in the Color picker, follow the procedure described in the section "Changing the Background Color" in Chapter 2.

Avoiding "Hyperlink Blue"

Unless there is a really strong design reason, try to avoid using "hyperlink blue" for your fonts. Because that color has become so synonymous with a link, users might mistake your text for a link and get frustrated when they click it and there's no result.

To change text color with the Text menu, select the text whose color you want to change, choose Text > Color to open the Color dialog box, and make your choice.

Note: As in the case with all text formatting, when you change text color, a new style (containing all of the properties of the text whose color you just manipulated) will appear in the Property Inspector's Style drop-down menu. This style, which is saved in an embedded style sheet, can then be applied to any other text in the page, thereby saving you the trouble of having to manually restyle text (which might involve setting a bunch of different properties).

Altering Your Page's Font

One of the great things about type is that, because there are so many choices out there, you can always find one to suit your needs. When working with text in Dreamweaver, the good news is that you aren't limited to one font. The bad news is that, for all intents and purposes, you are limited to three. How will you ever survive with only three fonts? Don't worry, there is actually quite a bit you can do with them.

You might wonder how this happened. Well, it all comes down to the configuration of the computer that's opening the web page. Web browsers can display only fonts that are installed on the user's system. If a font that isn't installed on the user's computer is used in a web page, the browser substitutes a font that *is* installed. Now, as you can well imagine, this causes no end of trouble. The web designer (you) went to a lot of trouble to design something using a specific font, and it looked good. Then, along comes the web browser, and it displays the page using a totally different font. However, this sort of bothersome situation can be easily avoided.

Text, Typeface, and Fonts

When you work with text, you'll find that the words *text, font,* and *typeface* are often used interchangeably. Don't be fooled, however; there is a big difference between them. *Text* refers generally to any characters that combine to make up a written document of some sort (whether a word, a sentence, or this book). A font, on the other hand, is a complete set of characters in a particular size and style. This includes the letters, the numbers, and all of the special character you get by pressing the Shift, Option, or Command (Mac) or Ctrl (Windows) keys. Finally, *typeface* refers to a series of related fonts. For example, the typeface Arial contains the fonts Arial, Arial Bold, Arial Italic, and Arial Bold Italic.

Every computer in English-speaking parts of the world that was built since 1994 (and was loaded with a graphic user interface operating system) was shipped with what are called system fonts. These fonts consist of Times New Roman, Courier New, and Ariel (in Windows), and Times, Courier, and Helvetica (on the Mac). If you design with these fonts, you don't have to worry about them being substituted because everyone has them.

Note: Through the efforts of Microsoft and Apple, the fonts Verdana and Georgia are shipped with most desktop computers these days. As a result, you can add both of them to the list of fonts you can design with.

To change fonts in Dreamweaver, select the text whose font you want to change. Open the Property Inspector (Window > Properties) and choose the new font from the Font drop-down menu.

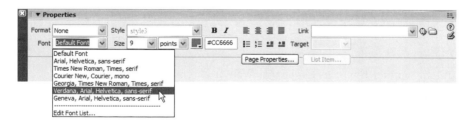

You can also change text fonts using the Text menu. Just select the text whose font you want to change, select Text > Font, and make your choice.

Note: You've probably noticed the Edit Font List option in both the Text > Font menu and the font list drop-down menu in the Property Inspector. By clicking this, you can add or subtract fonts to the list that is displayed. However, because of the browser limitation issues I just mentioned, unless you've got some solid design reasons, I strongly suggest that you leave the Edit Font List alone.

Changing Local Text Formatting

One of the other handy things you can do with text is change its formatting—which Dreamweaver refers to as style. By "style" here, I mean formatting such as **bold**, *italic*, and <u>underline</u> and not "style" in the sense of Cascading Style Sheets (CSS). As with many of Dreamweaver's features, there are two ways to change text style. The first way, which actually limits the amount of styles you can actually apply to text, involves the use of the Property Inspector:

1.   Select the text whose style you want to change.

2.   If it isn't already, open the Property Inspector (Window > Properties) and click either the Bold **B** or the Italic *I* button.

    To get a much wider range of possible text styles, you can use the Text menu. Just select the text and choose a style from the Text > Style submenu. It's a good idea to play around with all available styles so that you can get a general idea of how each looks with different text sizes and fonts.

Selecting a CSS Text Style

As I've already mentioned a few times already, one of the most exciting new features in Dreamweaver MX 2004 is that all text formatting (as well as many other page properties) is controlled through the use of Cascading Style Sheets (CSS) instead of HTML. As a result, you get a far greater degree of control over your designs. For a couple of reasons, this is especially useful when it comes to text. First, you can do things with text that was previously impossible (most notably when it comes to sizing text). Second, the Style drop-down menu stores text formatting as a style in an inline style sheet.

Note: A *style* can be a single property, such as color, or it can be a combination of many properties, such as font, color, and size.

As you add more (and different) text formatting to your document, the number of styles will increase. All of the styles that are created in this context are saved in an inline style sheet

Note: An *inline* style is information saved within the HTML document itself—opposed to a separate CSS file (which is called an *external* style sheet). For more information on the difference between embedded and external style sheets, see Chapter 10.

The whole point of the Style drop-down menu is that instead of applying the same formatting over and over again, you can simply select the text you want to change and then pick the appropriate style from the Style drop-down menu.

Note: It's important to remember that because the styles are saved in an embedded (internal) style sheet, they are available only in the document on which you are currently working. If you start working on a new document, you won't have access to those styles. In order to make styles available across multiple documents, you'll need to create an external style sheet—a process that will be covered in Chapter 10.

Formatting text with a stored style is really quite easy. All you need to do is follow these steps:

1. Select the text that you would like to format.

2. If it isn't already, open the Property Inspector (Window > Properties).

3. Select one of the styles from the Style drop-down menu.

Aligning and Indenting Paragraphs

Just as important as the appearance of individual characters and words in your page is the appearance of the blocks of text (paragraphs or lines). As with characters and words, there are a couple of different kinds of formatting that you can apply to blocks of text: indentation and alignment.

The most basic way you can lay out text is with the Alignment tool—which allows you to justify text to the left, to the center, and to the right. Like most features in Dreamweaver, there are two ways to align text: using the Property Inspector or using the Text menu. In either case, first place the cursor anywhere in the line of text you want to justify and then do *one* of the following:

- Open the Property Inspector (Window > Properties) and click one of the four Align buttons ≣ ≣ ≣ ≣ .
- Choose Text > Align and make your alignment selection from the submenu.

As with word processing, you might find the need to indent portions of your text. When you indent text in Dreamweaver, the line automatically wraps to accommodate the changes. As a result, the section of text that you indent will occupy more vertical space. To indent blocks of text, select the text that you want to indent or place your cursor somewhere on the line you are indenting. Then do *one* of the following:

- Open the Property Inspector (Window > Properties) and click the Text Indent button ≜ to indent one increment.
- Choose Text > Indent.

Note: The opposite of indenting is outdenting. If you want to outdent text, you can either click the Text Outdent button in the Property Inspector or choose Text > Outdent. But if text is already flush with the left edge of the Document Window, using the Outdent feature won't change anything.

Breaking Up Text with Horizontal Rules

Until now, all the things I've discussed have involved making an alteration to existing text. A horizontal rule, which is a great tool for breaking up blocks of text, is actually an HTML object that needs to be inserted into a document. Essentially, a horizontal rule is a straight line that extends across the Document window (Figure 3.1).

> Best known as the home of the exquisite ceremonial Palette of Narmer, so-called the first political document in history, and attributed to the first king of the first dynasty at about 3000BC, it contains far more.
>
> ―――――――――――――――――――――――――――――――――――
>
> Well before the construction of the pyramids, Hierakonpolis was one of the largest urban centers along the Nile -- a vibrant, bustling city containing many of the features that would later come to typify Dynastic Egyptian civilization. Stretching for over 3 miles along the edge of the Nile flood plain, already by 3500 BC it was a city of many neighborhoods and quarters.

Figure 3.1 A horizontal rule is a straight line that can be used to break up text.

Here's how to insert a horizontal rule:

1. Place the cursor where you'd like to insert the horizontal rule.

2. If it isn't already, open the Insert bar (Window > Insert).

3. Access the HTML section of the Insert bar (by clicking on the down-pointing arrow at the left side of the Insert bar and selecting HTML from the subsequent drop-down menu), and click the Insert Horizontal Rule button ▦ .

   Alternatively, you can choose Insert > HTML > Horizontal Rule.

Formatting Horizontal Rules

After you've inserted a horizontal rule, there are a few changes you can make to its appearance. Select the rule you want to edit, open the Property Inspector (Window > Properties), and change the rule's size, alignment, or shade as follows:

Size Type a value into the Width or Height field. If you want the horizontal rule to always occupy a certain width of the page (regardless of how large or small the Document window is), choose the percent sign (%) from the drop-down menu (to the right of the Width [W] field). If you want its width to remain fixed, choose Pixels.

Alignment Choose Left, Center, or Right from the Align drop-down menu.

Shading Select or deselect the Shading check box (depending on whether you want your rule shaded or unshaded, respectively).

Shaded horizontal rule

Unshaded horizontal rule

Organizing Text with Lists

You can format text into groups called lists. Essentially, lists are a good way to organize information that would be best presented as several separate items instead of "running" paragraph text. The program features two primary kinds of lists: ordered and unordered. Another list type, called a definition list, is not as widely used as the other list types, but it is useful in some situations.

Creating an Ordered (Numbered) List from Scratch

An *ordered list,* also referred to as a numbered list (Figure 3.2), presents information in a sequential, structured manner. To create an ordered list from scratch:

1. Place the cursor where you want the ordered list to begin.

2. Open the Property Inspector (Window > Properties) and click the Ordered List button ⦂☰ . The number *1* automatically appears.

3. Type the first item in your list.

4. Press Enter. The next number in the list automatically appears on the next line.

5. Repeat steps 3 and 4 until you've completed the list.

6. To terminate the list, press Return (Mac)/ Enter (Win) twice.

> 1. Dogs
> 2. Cats
> 3. Gerbils
> 4. Big Monkey

Figure 3.2 An ordered/ numbered list

Inserting an ordered list with the Text menu is just as easy. All you need to do is place the cursor where you want the ordered list to begin and choose Text > List > Ordered List. Then follow steps 3 through 6 as just described.

Creating an Ordered (Numbered) List from Existing Text

The previous process describes how you would go about creating an ordered list from scratch. However, I guarantee that you'll encounter a situation in which you'll need to take a block of existing text and turn it into an ordered list.

To do so, just select a series of lines or paragraphs that you want to turn into a list. Open the Property Inspector (Window > Properties) and click the Ordered List button ⦂☰ .

Note: Each item (line or paragraph) you select to be converted into a discrete list item must be separated by a paragraph break.

Creating an Unordered (Bulleted) List

Unlike an ordered list, where the items are organized in a systematic manner, an *unordered list* (Figure 3.3), which is often referred to as a bulleted list, is designed to present information that doesn't need to be in any specific sequence. To create an unordered list, follow these steps:

1. Place the cursor where you want the unordered list to begin.

2. Open the Property Inspector (Window > Properties) and click the Unordered List button ▤ . A bullet automatically appears.

3. Type the first item in your list.

4. Press Enter. Another bullet automatically appears on the next line.

5. Repeat steps 3 and 4 until you complete the list.

6. To terminate the list, press Return (Mac)/ Enter (Win) twice.

- Canada
- Mexico
- Egypt
- Australia
- Ireland

Figure 3.3 An unordered/bulleted list

You can also insert an unordered list by using the Text menu. Place the cursor where you want the unordered list to begin and select Text > List > Unordered List. Then follow steps 3 to 6 as just described.

Note: You can create an unordered list from already existing text by selecting the items of text and then clicking the Unordered List button ▤ . Each item must be separated by a paragraph break to be an individual item.

Creating a Definition List

Although not widely used (primarily because it isn't included as an option in the Property Inspector), the definition list still deserves a place in this discussion. A definition list is used to create a dictionary-like structure.

Say, for instance, you wanted to create a definition list in which the word *Menshevik* is defined. In the first line, the word itself would appear. In the second line, which would be indented slightly, the definition of *Menshevik* would appear, as shown in Figure 3.4.

Menshevik
A member of the moderate minority faction of the Russian Social Democratic Party which split (1903) from the Bolsheviks and was absorbed or liquidated after 1918 by the Russian Communist party.

Figure 3.4 A definition list

To create a definition list, do this:

1. Place the cursor in the Document window where you want the definition list to begin.

2. Choose Text > List > Definition List.

3. Type the term that will occupy the first line (the word to be defined) and press Return (Mac)/ Enter (Win).

4. Type the text that will occupy the second line (the definition of the word that appears in the first line).

5. To continue adding terms (and their associated definitions), just press Return (Mac)/Enter (Win) to move to the next line and repeat steps 2 and 3.

6. To terminate the list when you finish adding all the terms and their associated definitions, press Return (Mac)/ Enter (Win) twice.

Changing How Your List Looks

For the most part, the way Dreamweaver creates lists (whether ordered, unordered, or definition) is somewhat creatively confining. Despite this, you do have some degree of control over the way ordered and unordered lists look and behave. Through the List Properties dialog box, you can change the type of an already created list, alter the list style, change the number at which an ordered list begins counting, and fiddle with the properties of individual list members. Unfortunately, you can't alter the properties of a definition list.

To access the List Property dialog box for an ordered or unordered list, follow these steps:

1. Select any individual member of the list.

2. Open and expand the Property Inspector (Window > Properties).

3. Click the List Item button ⟨ List Item... ⟩. This will open the List Properties dialog box (Figure 3.5).

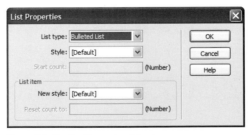

Figure 3.5 The List Properties dialog box

After the List Properties dialog box opens, you can alter the various properties of your list:

List Type This option lets you switch from your current type of list to another available type (bulleted, numbered, menu, or directory). In reality, both the menu and directory list types are nothing more than different names for an unordered (or bulleted) list.

Style Accessible only if you are working with a bulleted or numbered list type, this option lets you change the style of your list's bullets or numbers. This drop-down menu is dynamic—it will display the appropriate options depending on whether you've selected a bulleted or numbered list from the List Type drop-down menu.

Start Count Accessible only when you have a numbered list type, this option lets you choose where your numbered list will begin. For example, if you have an ordered list with five items and you set Start Count to 3, the items in the list will be numbered 3, 4, 5, 6, and 7 respectively.

List Item: New Style With this option, you can specify the style of an individual item within the list (as opposed to the entire list). To use this option, you must select the item whose style you want to change and select an option from the New Style drop-down menu. This menu is a dynamic tool, displaying only those options applicable to the list's current type (ordered or unordered). If you place your cursor next to an individual list item (instead of directly selecting it) and choose a style from the New Style drop-down menu, you'll change the style of that list item as well as all those that follow—but not those above.

List Item: Reset Count To This option lets you input a value to which the selected item's number will be reset. Note that changing the Reset Count To value not only affects the currently selected list item, but also all those that follow. For example, if you had a list of five items numbered from 1 to 5 and you reset the third item's Reset Count To value to 28, your list's numbering would be 1, 2, 28, 29, 30.

> **Note:** Once you finish manipulating the options in the List Properties dialog box, just click OK and the changes will be automatically applied to your list.

Inserting Characters That Aren't on Your Keyboard

What happens if you need to insert a character that doesn't appear on your keyboard? You might come across a situation in which you need to insert a pound sterling symbol (£), a copyright symbol (©), the euro symbol (€), or a trademark symbol (™), for example. Don't worry, the process by which you add characters that aren't on your keyboard is actually quite easy—just follow these steps:

1. Place the cursor where you want to insert the special character.

2. Open the Insert bar (Window > Insert) and select the Text category.

3. Click the Characters button 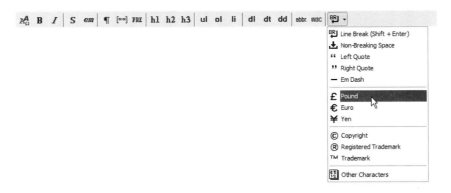, and select the character you want to insert from the subsequent drop-down menu.

Alternatively, you can choose Insert > HTML > Special Characters, and then make your selection from there.

 Note: If you want to insert a character that isn't in the Insert bar's Characters tab or on the Insert menu, click the Other Character option on the Characters drop-down menu. This lets you choose from a larger set of special characters.

Adding a Date to Your Page

In the process of creating a website, you'll find that you'll probably need to insert the current date at some point. Whether for use in a copyright statement or in a list of updates, it can get a little tedious having to constantly check the current date and then type it into your document. Dreamweaver MX 2004 helps you on this front with a handy labor-saving device that allows you to insert the current date into your document with a click of a button:

1. Place your cursor in the location where you want to place the current date.

 Note: Dreamweaver pulls the current date/time information from your computer. This means if your computer's date/time is wrong, the date that is inserted will be too.

2. Choose Insert > Date. This will cause the Insert Date dialog box to open.

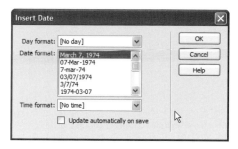

3. From here, choose the format in which you want the day displayed by selecting one of the options in the Day Format drop-down menu.

4. Select the way you want the entire date displayed by choosing one of the options in the Date Format list.

5. Select the way the time is displayed by choosing one of the options in the Time Format drop-down menu.

Note: It's extremely important to note that while most (if not all) U.S. institutions and individuals display the date as month/day/year, most other countries display the date as day/month/year. With this in mind, you might want to choose the appropriate format for websites that will be viewed by non-Americans. An alternative solution is to just spell out the date: for example, May 25, 2004.

6. If you want the date to automatically update whenever you save the document, check the Update Automatically on Save check box.

7. When you finish setting the date's properties, click OK.

Note: The date inserted into your web page is not dynamic—once it's uploaded to the server, it will not dynamically change to display the current date. To insert a dynamic date into your page, you'll have to use a custom behavior which, unfortunately, doesn't ship with Dreamweaver MX 2004 but can be downloaded from the Macromedia Exchange. For more information on behaviors, see Chapter 9, "Adding Interactivity with JavaScript Behaviors."

Avoiding Typos with the Spellchecker

Spelling errors are a surefire way to send people away from your site. Dreamweaver MX 2004 has made checking a document for spelling errors very easy by including a spell-check feature.

To use the spell-check feature, select Text > Check Spelling. Any errors will be picked up and you will get the option to make changes using the Check Spelling dialog box.

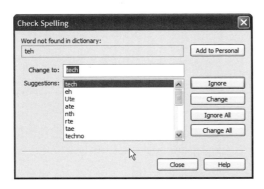

Adding Pizzazz with Flash Text

One of the coolest technologies to come down the pipe is Flash, Macromedia's vector animation program. Since objects in Flash are vector graphics, they look considerably smoother and crisper than graphics normally seen on the Web.

 Note: If you are particularly interested in Flash, check out *Flash MX 2004 Savvy* by Ethan Watrall and Norbert Herber (Sybex, 2004). (Wink wink.)

In Dreamweaver MX 2004, Macromedia gives you the ability to create editable vector text with the Flash Text feature. By using Flash Text, you can avoid the font and size limitations that discussed at the beginning of this chapter. In addition, if you use Flash vectors instead of an image for text, your graphics are scalable and smaller in file size and look good when they're printed.

 Note: Users must have the Flash plug-in installed on their computers to be able to view any Flash Text inserted into documents.

To use the Flash Text tool, follow these steps:

1. Place your cursor where you want to insert the Flash Text.

2. Open the Insert bar (Window > Insert) and then access the Common category (if it isn't already open).

3. Click the Media button , and then select the Flash Text option from the subsequent drop-down menu.

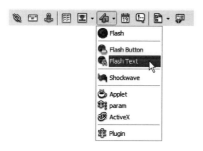

Note: If you haven't already, you will be prompted to save your page before you can add the Flash Text.

4. When the Insert Flash Text dialog box (Figure 3.6) appears, choose a font from the Font drop-down menu. The menu will include all the fonts you presently have loaded on your system.

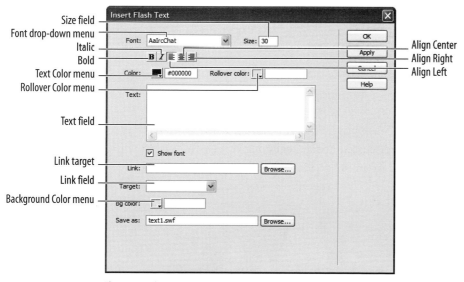

Figure 3.6 The Insert Flash Text dialog box

Note: You can also access the Insert Flash Text dialog box by choosing Insert > Interactive Images > Flash Text.

 Note: Because Flash can display fonts that aren't loaded on a user's machine, you don't have to limit yourself to using only the system fonts.

5. Enter the font size in the Size field.

6. Click the Color swatch to open the Color palette. From here you can choose the color you want your Flash Text to be.

7. Type your text in the Text field.

8. Enter a filename in the Save As field. You can use the default filename (text1.swf and so on), but you must enter something in this field. The file is automatically saved to the same directory as the current document.

9. Click Apply and then OK. Here is an example of what your text might look like.

Flash Text Rocks!

 Note: By setting the other properties in the Flash Text dialog box (such as rollover color, link, and target), you can change your Flash Text into an interactive button that links to another portion of your site.

Working with Images

We use images in many interesting ways to represent all sorts of online information. As you would expect, Dreamweaver MX 2004 makes including images in your web page a painless process. However, as in the case of web-based text, there are some issues you need to be aware of when dealing with web images. This chapter will begin by looking at some of these issues and then go on to discuss inserting and manipulating images with Dreamweaver.

Chapter Contents

Selecting the Image Format That's Right for You

One of the first and most important things about which you need to know is that, without the help of plug-ins, the Web supports only three types of images: GIF, JPEG, and PNG. Before we dive into how Dreamweaver MX 2004 deals with images, it's a good idea to become familiar with the strengths and weaknesses of each of the three image formats so that you can decide which is best for your creative purposes.

GIF Originally developed by CompuServe during the late '80s, GIFs (GIF stands for Graphics Interchange Format) are the workhorse images of the Web. Because the format itself can display a maximum of only 256 colors (8 bits), GIFs are best used for relatively simple images with flat colors and are generally smaller in size (in terms of kilobytes) than files saved in other formats. One of the great things about GIFs is that they come in a few different forms: transparent GIFs, interlaced GIFs, and animated GIFs. Transparent GIFs allow the background upon which they are placed to be visible. When they are created, the user decides which color should be transparent in the image. Interlaced GIFs are structured in such a way that they come into focus slowly as the browser loads the image. Animated GIFs are simply series of images saved in the same file. When a browser loads this file, all the images in the file are displayed in sequence, creating an animation much like a digital flip book.

JPEG JPEG stands for Joint Photographic Experts Group. JPEGs came along sometime after GIFs and were designed specifically to display photographic or continuous-color images. Their main strength comes from the fact that they can display millions of colors. Because of this, JPEG files tend to be larger than GIF files—as the quality of the JPEG increases, so does its file size. Unfortunately, JPEGs come in only one "flavor": no transparency, no interlacing, and no animation.

PNG PNGs are a little less straightforward than GIFs or JPEGs. PNG stands for Portable Network Graphics. They were designed to combine the best of both GIFs and JPEGs; they can therefore support indexed color (256 colors), grayscale, true-color images (millions of colors), and transparency. The problem with PNGs is that they have spotty browser support. Microsoft Internet Explorer (4.0 and later) and Netscape Navigator (4.04 and later) only partially support the display of PNG images. Because PNG is the native file type of Fireworks, Dreamweaver MX 2004 has some fairly sophisticated tools that are geared specifically toward PNG manipulation and management.

A collection of stock images for your use has been included in the Chapter 4 folder of this book's companion CD.

Note: For Dreamweaver to recognize a PNG, the file must have the .png extension.

Inserting Images into Your Page

Now that you know the basic web image types, you can insert an image into the Document window. To do so, follow these steps:

1. Place the cursor where you want to insert the image.

2. Do *one* of the following:

- From the main menu bar, choose Insert > Image.
- From the Insert bar (Window > Insert), choose the Common category, click the Images button , and select Image from the drop-down menu.

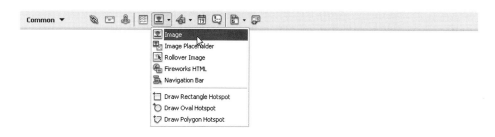

3. When the Select Image Source dialog box appears, navigate to where your image is located, select it, and click OK.

> **Note:** At this point, if you have not previously saved your web page, Dreamweaver displays a warning that it will use a file:// path until you save your page.

Inserting Image Placeholders

With Dreamweaver MX 2004, you can not only insert an actual image, but you can also insert an image placeholder, which serves as a generic graphic that can be used until final artwork is ready to be added to the page. To insert an image placeholder, just follow these steps:

1. Place the cursor where you want to insert the image placeholder.

2. If it isn't already, open the Insert bar (Window > Insert).

3. Select the Insert bar's Common category, click the Images button 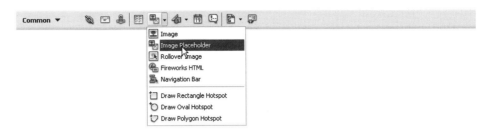, and choose Image Placeholder from the drop-down menu.

4. When the Image Placeholder dialog box (Figure 4.1) appears, enter a name for the placeholder into the Name field. The name simply acts as a label for the image placeholder.

Figure 4.1 The Image Placeholder dialog box

5. Enter the dimensions of the placeholder into the Width and Height fields.

 Note: The whole point of an image placeholder is that it occupies the same amount of space in the design as the "real" image. Because of this, the dimensions of the two should be exactly the same.

6. To set the color of the placeholder, which simply fills the area with a solid color, click the Color swatch and choose a color from the Color palette.

7. Enter the placeholder's ALT text into the Alternate Text field.

 Note: To learn more about ALT text, see the section "Making Images Accessible with the *alt* Tag" later in this chapter.

8. Click OK.

Aligning Images

One of the most basic things you can do with an image after it's been inserted into a Dreamweaver document is to align (or justify) it to the page. Because an image can't be moved around a document in Dreamweaver as it can in an image editing program like Fireworks or Photoshop, aligning it becomes an important part of your final design. Aligning an image is almost the same as aligning text:

1. Place your cursor anywhere along the line that contains the image (do not select the image itself).

2. Open the Property Inspector (Window > Properties).

3. Click one of the three alignment buttons: Left ≣ , Center ≣ , or Right ≣ .

Note: Most of the actions described in this chapter require the expanded Property Inspector. If you don't see the field or button mentioned, click the down arrow at the bottom-right corner of the Property Inspector to reveal more options.

Aligning Images in Relation to Text

It's a fair bet that when you create a web page, you're going to have more than just text or just images. You will ultimately want to combine the two in a pleasing visual form.

If you've already experimented with images and text in the same document, you've probably noticed that they don't integrate very well. In fact, images have the tendency to break up the flow of text, as illustrated in the image below.

GIF stands Originally developed by CompuServe during the late 80s, GIFs (which stands for Graphics Interchange Format) is the workhorse image of the web. for Graphics Interchange Format. Developed originally by CompuServe in the late '80s, GIFs are the workhorse image of the web. Because the format itself can display a maximum of only 256 colors (8 bits), GIFs are best used for relatively simple images with flat colors and are generally smaller in size (in terms of kilobytes).

Note: You cannot align an image placeholder to text using this process, only a regular image.

You can, however, exert some control over how the text on your page interacts with an image. Here's how to align an image to text:

1. Insert an image somewhere in a block of text.

2. Select the image you want to align by clicking it with your mouse.

3. Open the Property Inspector (Window > Properties).

4. Select an alignment method from the Align drop-down menu. Each setting here aligns text to an image in a different way, and the settings are explained next.

Note: Default generally means a baseline alignment. However, the default may differ depending on the browser that is being used to view the page.

Text Top and Top If you choose Text Top, the top line of the text aligns with the top of the image.

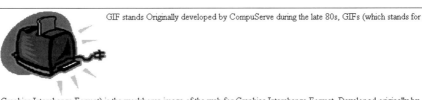

GIF stands Originally developed by CompuServe during the late 80s, GIFs (which stands for

Graphics Interchange Format) is the workhorse image of the web.for Graphics Interchange Format. Developed originally by CompuServe in the late '80s, GIFs are the workhorse image of the web. Because the format itself can display a maximum of only 256 colors (8 bits), GIFs are best used for relatively simple images with flat colors and are generally smaller in size (in terms of kilobytes).

Note: While it may appear that Text Top is the same as Top, there are some differences. Top aligns text with the highest item on the line, and Text Top aligns the tallest character in the line with the top of the image.

Bottom and Baseline These choices align the baseline of the first line of text to the bottom of the image.

GIF stands Originally developed by CompuServe during the late 80s, GIFs (which stands for Graphics Interchange Format) is the workhorse image of the web.for Graphics Interchange Format. Developed originally by CompuServe in the late '80s, GIFs are the workhorse image of the web. Because the format itself can display a maximum of only 256 colors (8 bits), GIFs are best used for relatively simple images with flat colors and are generally smaller in size (in terms of kilobytes).

Absolute Bottom This aligns the bottom of the image to the absolute bottom of the lowest characters (which includes descenders, as in the letters *g* or *j*).

GIF stands Originally developed by CompuServe during the late 80s, GIFs (which stands for Graphics Interchange Format) is the workhorse image of the web.for Graphics Interchange Format. Developed originally by CompuServe in the late '80s, GIFs are the workhorse image of the web. Because the format itself can display a maximum of only 256 colors (8 bits), GIFs are best used for relatively simple images with flat colors and are generally smaller in size (in terms of kilobytes).

Middle This choice aligns the text baseline with the middle of the selected object.

GIF stands Originally developed by CompuServe during the late 80s, GIFs (which stands for

Graphics Interchange Format) is the workhorse image of the web.for Graphics Interchange Format. Developed originally by CompuServe in the late '80s, GIFs are the workhorse image of the web. Because the format itself can display a maximum of only 256 colors (8 bits), GIFs are best used for relatively simple images with flat colors and are generally smaller in size (in terms of kilobytes).

Absolute Middle This choice aligns the image to the absolute middle of the current line.

GIF stands Originally developed by CompuServe during the late 80s, GIFs (which stands for

Graphics Interchange Format) is the workhorse image of the web.for Graphics Interchange Format. Developed originally by CompuServe in the late '80s, GIFs are the workhorse image of the web. Because the format itself can display a maximum of only 256 colors (8 bits), GIFs are best used for relatively simple images with flat colors and are generally smaller in size (in terms of kilobytes).

Left This places the image on the left margin and wraps the text around it to the right. If left-aligned text comes before the image on the line, it forces left-aligned objects to wrap to a new line.

 GIF stands Originally developed by CompuServe during the late 80s, GIFs (which stands for Graphics Interchange Format) is the workhorse image of the web.for Graphics Interchange Format. Developed originally by CompuServe in the late '80s, GIFs are the workhorse image of the web. Because the format itself can display a maximum of only 256 colors (8 bits), GIFs are best used for relatively simple images with flat colors and are generally smaller in size (in terms of kilobytes).

Right This places the image on the right margin and wraps the text around it to the left. If right-aligned text precedes the image on the line, it will force right-aligned objects to wrap to a new line.

GIF stands Originally developed by CompuServe during the late 80s, GIFs (which stands for Graphics Interchange Format) is the workhorse image of the web.for Graphics Interchange Format. Developed originally by CompuServe in the late '80s, GIFs are the workhorse image of the web. Because the format itself can display a maximum of only 256 colors (8 bits), GIFs are best used for relatively simple images with flat colors and are generally smaller in size (in terms of kilobytes).

 Note: Although the differences between standard alignment and an absolute alignment are sometimes difficult to detect, they do exist. An absolute alignment will use the entire height of a line of text (which is determined by the very top of the highest character and the very bottom of the lowest character) for alignment purposes.

Changing the Size of Images

Resizing an image in Dreamweaver is really quite easy, but there are some important things you need to know before you start. If you use Dreamweaver to increase the size of images, you'll see a marked loss in quality. The images will appear grainy and pixilated.

Think of it this way: if you draw a picture on a balloon and then blow that balloon up, what do you get? Well, the image, which looked great before you blew up the balloon, has gotten all stretched out of shape. If you resize an image that you've already placed in a Dreamweaver document, you'll get an effect along the same lines. So, unless you have some pressing design need, avoid changing the size of an image in Dreamweaver. Instead, make sure the image is the exact size you want it to be *before you insert it into a Dreamweaver document.*

Note: When you resize an image in Dreamweaver, you don't resize the actual image file itself. Instead, you are changing the HTML code so that the browser displays the image at a different size. To see how to edit the actual art file itself, see "Editing Images in Dreamweaver MX 2004" later in this chapter.

When you downsize an image, however, the image doesn't suffer the same loss of quality. The thing that you need to realize about downsizing an image is that, because you aren't changing the size of the actual image file, the time it takes to download the image will be exactly the same.

Resizing Images

When you resize an image, you aren't resizing the original file, you're just changing the way it looks in your Document window. To resize an image with the Property Inspector you've inserted into your Dreamweaver MX 2004 document, follow these steps:

1. Select the image you want to resize.

2. Open the Property Inspector (Window > Properties).

3. Enter a new width and height in the W and H boxes in the Property Inspector. Remember that all dimensions are in pixels, as opposed to another unit of measure like centimeters or millimeters.

4. The dimensions of the image will automatically update when you press Return/Enter or move the cursor out of either of the fields.

You can also resize an image by using the resize handles:

1. Click the image you want to resize.

2. Click and hold one of the resize handles.

Resize handles

3. Drag the resize handles until your image is the desired size and release your mouse button.

 Note: If you have the Property Inspector open while you are using the resize handles, you'll notice that the values in the W and H boxes will change dynamically to reflect the increasing size of the image.

 Note: If you hold down Shift while dragging the resize handles, your image will maintain the same proportions.

Resetting Images to Original Size

If you've increased the size of an image and aren't happy with the result—and you've forgotten its original dimensions—there is an easy way to revert to the original size of the document. Select the image you've resized by clicking it with your mouse. Then, in the Property Inspector (Window > Properties), click the Reset Size button ↻.

Making Images Accessible with the *alt* Tag

The alt (alternative) tag is probably one of the most overlooked features you can use in creating an image. Essentially, the alt tag is designed to provide extra information about an image when the image isn't visible. This handy feature provides information for text-only browsers (browsers that can't display images) or for browsers that are set to download images manually. One of the cool features about alt tags is that they will display a pop-up (which is similar to a Tool Tip) when the user moves their mouse over an image.

To add an alt tag to your image, first select the image. Open the Property Inspector (Window > Properties) and enter your text in the Alt field.

Integrating Low Source Images for Low-Bandwidth Users

A Low Source image is a helpful feature if you're designing a site that you know will be viewed by people with slower Internet connections. With this feature, you're essentially designating a temporary, alternative image to load before the main image. Many designers use a small black-and-white version of the main image because it loads more quickly than the main image and gives visitors an idea of what they're waiting to see.

Designing for Accessibility

In recent years, there has been a growing desire to make web content accessible to everyone, including individuals with a variety of disabilities. One of the most pressing issues in designing accessible content is that images can't be interpreted by a screen reader, a type of software that "reads" the contents of a computer screen and then "speaks" it back to a visually impaired user. This problem derives from the fact that visual information, unlike text, involves a subjective interpretation. One person's description of an image will probably differ from another individual's description of the same image. Because of this, screen readers, which are simple pieces of software, are completely incapable of describing visual imagery and visually impaired individuals are not only cut off from visual content, but they are often also cut off from navigation schemes—many of which depend heavily on graphical interface elements (buttons, menus, and so on). One of the best solutions to the problems is to use alt tags for all of your images because they provide a textual alternative that can be "read" by the screen reader.

Here's how to add a Low Source image:

 Note: The Low Source image must have the same dimensions as the regular image it is associated with.

1. Click the main image for which you want to set the Low Source image.
2. Open the Property Inspector (Window > Properties).
3. Click the browse button to the right of the Low Src field (its official name is Browse for File).

4. When the Select Image Source dialog box opens, locate the file you want to set as the Low Source image and select it. Then click OK.

Adding Borders around Images

During the creative process, you may need to add a solid border around an image; for instance, you may want to set off an image from the surrounding material on the web page. However, remember to use image borders sparingly, as overuse can result in a very unattractive design. To add a border to an image in Dreamweaver MX 2004, first select the image. In the Property Inspector (Window > Properties), enter a value (the width in pixels) in the Border field.

Editing Images in Dreamweaver MX 2004

Easily one of the coolest new features in Dreamweaver MX 2004 is that it provides some basic image editing capabilities. Now, we're not talking about Photoshop- or Fireworks-level image editing here. The new image editing tools in Dreamweaver are designed to provide you with what you need to do some very common (and simple) image editing tasks without having to turn to an external image editor.

In the following sections, you are going to explore how to use Dreamweaver's new image editing tools to crop, resample, adjust brightness/contrast, and sharpen.

Note: Any changes you make to an image file using Dreamweaver's image editing tools overwrites the original file.

Cropping Images

When you crop an image, you are reducing the overall area of the image in order to to place more emphasis on different aspects of the image or remove unwanted portions of the image.

To crop an image in Dreamweaver, just follow these steps:

1. Select the image that you would like to crop.

2. Do *one* of the following:

   • Click the Crop button in the Property Inspector ⬚.

   • Choose Modify > Image > Crop from the main menu bar.

3. Drag the crop handles that appear along the edges of the bounding box around the crop area to adjust the size of the crop.

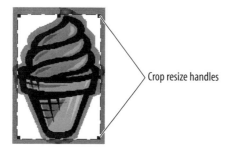

Crop resize handles

4. Drag within the bounding box to move the crop location.

5. When you've finished adjusting the dimensions of the crop, either double-click within the crop area or press Enter.

6. You will get an alert informing you that the changes will be saved to disk. If you are happy with the changes, click OK and the image will be cropped.

 Note: If you want to undo the crop, you can simply choose Edit > Undo. If you close down the document with the cropped image (and then reopen it), you will no longer be able to undo the crop.

Resampling Images

Earlier in this chapter, we discussed the process by which you resize an image in Dreamweaver. I said that, due to the low resolution of images inserted into a Dreamweaver document, resizing often causes weird distortions and pixelation. The great news about Dreamweaver MX 2004 is that you can partially mitigate this resolution-based problem by using the new resample image feature.

Image resampling adds or subtracts pixels from a resized JPEG and GIF image in an attempt to match the appearance of the original image as closely as possible. Granted, image resampling rarely results in an image whose quality matches that of the original. However, the image quality can be better when resizing than if you didn't resample at all.

 Note: Image resampling works only on an image that has been resized.

To resample a resized image, select the image and do *one* of the following:

- Click the Resample button in the Property Inspector .
- Choose Modify > Image > Resample from the main menu bar.

A dialog box will appear, telling you that the changes to the image will be saved to disk. Click OK.

 Note: If you want to undo the resampling, you can simply choose Edit > Undo. If you close down the document with the resampled image (and then reopen it), you will no longer be able to undo the resampling.

Adjusting Image Brightness/Contrast

The Brightness/Contrast feature, as the name suggests, allows you to change the contrast or the brightness of an image that is either too dark or too light for your needs.

To adjust an image's brightness or contrast in Dreamweaver MX 2004, just follow these steps:

1. Select the image whose brightness or contrast you would like to adjust.

2. Do *one* of the following:
   - Click the Brightness and Contrast button in the Property Inspector .
   - Choose Modify > Image > Brightness/Contrast from the main menu bar.

3. When the dialog box telling you that any changes you make will be saved to disk appears, click OK

4. When the Brightness/Contrast dialog box (Figure 4.2) appears, drag the sliders to adjust the image. Alternatively, you can enter a value (from -100 to 100, where -100 results in the darkest possible image and 100 results in the lightest possible image) into the numeric fields.

Figure 4.2 The Brightness/Contrast dialog box.

5. If you want to see the changes immediately, make sure the Preview check box is selected.

6. When you are finished, click OK.

> **Note:** If you want to undo the change in brightness or contrast, you can simply choose Edit > Undo. If you close down the document with the changed image (and then reopen it), you will no longer be able to undo the change.

Sharpening Images

When you sharpen an image in Dreamweaver MX 2004, you increase the contrast of the pixels around the edge of shapes within the image, thereby bringing out the details and increasing its overall definition.

To sharpen an image in Dreamweaver MX, just follow these steps:

1. Select the image you want to sharpen.

2. Do *one* of the following:

   - Click the Sharpen button in the Property Inspector .

   - Choose Modify > Image > Sharpen from the main menu bar.

3. When the dialog box telling you that any changes you make will be saved to disk appears, click OK

4. When the Sharpen dialog box (Figure 4.3) appears, drag the slider to adjust the image's sharpness. Alternatively, you can enter a value (from 0 to -10, with 0 resulting in the dullest effect and 10 resulting in the sharpest effect) into the numeric field.

Figure 4.2 The Sharpen dialog box.

5. If you want to see the changes immediately, make sure the Preview check box is selected.

6. When you are finished, click OK.

Note: If you want to undo the sharpening, you can simply choose Edit > Undo. If you close down the document with the sharpened image (and then reopen it), you will no longer be able to undo the sharpening.

Using an External Image Editor from Dreamweaver

One of the neat things about Dreamweaver MX 2004 is that it integrates well with external editors. Whether you're using an image editing program (such as Fireworks MX 2004 or Photoshop) or an HTML text editing program (such as BBEdit or Home-Site), Dreamweaver lets you define a series of editors. These editors allow you to open a given object (in the case of this section, an image), edit that object, exit the external editor, and immediately view the changes you've made.

In the following sections, you are going to first see how to define an external image editor. From there, you'll go on to explore how to launch an image in your external image editor.

Defining an External Image Editor

To define an external image editor, follow these steps:

1. Choose Edit > Preferences.
2. Select File Types/Editors in the Category list box (Figure 4.4).

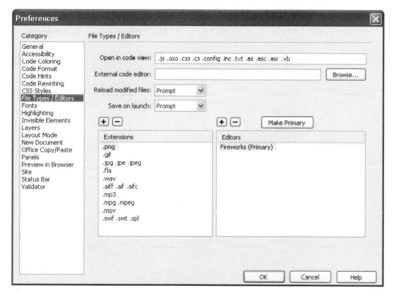

Figure 4.4 The File Types/Editors section of the Preferences dialog box

3. In the Extensions list, select the extension of the specific image type for which you want to define an external image editor.

4. Click the plus button above the Editors list.

5. When the Select External Editor dialog box appears, locate and select the program file of the editor you want to associate to the file type.

6. Click OK.

Launching an External Image Editor

Once you've associated a specific image editor with a specific file type, you can launch the editor by following these steps:

1. Select the image you want to launch in the external image editor.

2. Do *one* of the following:

   • Click the Edit button in the Property Inspector (Window > Properties).

> **Note:** If Fireworks MX 2004 (or a previous version of Fireworks) has been set as the external image editor for that specific file type, the Edit button will feature the funky Fireworks logo.

   • Right-click (Windows) or Control-click (Macintosh) the image, and select the Edit With option from the context menu.

> **Note:** If you haven't already set an external image editor, you can right-click/Control-click the image and choose Edit With > Browser from the context menu. This opens the Select External Editor dialog box with which you can locate the program file of the specific external editor you would like to use.

3. Once you've made changes to the image in the external editor, save it and exit. The image in Dreamweaver will be automatically updated to reflect the changes. After the changes are saved in the external image editor, Dreamweaver might prompt you to update the page. Click Yes if you want your image to be updated.

   If the external image editor you defined for that specific file type happens to be Fireworks, you'll get a specialized document window in Fireworks that indicates you are editing an image from Dreamweaver.

   When you are finished editing the image, all you need to do is click the Done button and Fireworks will automatically re-export the image, close down Fireworks, and return you to Dreamweaver.

Optimizing Images in Fireworks

If you have Fireworks MX 2004 (or Fireworks MX) installed, you can optimize images directly from within Dreamweaver. To do so, just follow these steps:

1. Select the image you want to optimize in Fireworks.

2. Do *one* of the following:

   - Click the Optimize in Fireworks button in the Property Inspector 🖫.

   - Choose Modify > Image > Optimize in Fireworks from the main menu bar.

3. From here, Fireworks will launch and ask whether you want to use the original Fireworks PNG version of the file (if you have one) or simply optimize the version of the file in the Dreamweaver document. Click the appropriate button.

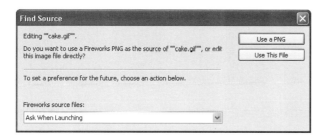

4. When the Optimize File dialog box appears (Figure 4.5), make any changes you want and click the Update button.

Figure 4.5 The Optimize File dialog box

Creation and Care
of Hyperlinks

*Early in your design project, you're going to want
to start creating links between documents and
other types of media. This is where hyperlinks
come into the picture. Hyperlinks are really the
core of HTML. They allow the user to move
effortlessly between documents, regardless of
whether they're on the same server or another
server entirely. Dreamweaver MX 2004 allows
you to create links between HTML documents,
inline multimedia files, images, and downloadable
files. In this chapter, you'll start off by learning
how to add hyperlinks to both images and text.
From there, you'll explore how to manage some
of the finer points of link manipulation.*

Chapter Contents

Creating Links

Using Named Anchors to Link to
   Points on a Page

Defining Where Linked Files Load

Creating E-Mail Links

Adding Image Maps to Your Pages

Building Jump Menus

Adding Flash Buttons to Your Pages

Creating Links

One of the great things about Dreamweaver MX 2004 is that you can create a link to an absolute URL very easily. You can create a link to a relative URL with the same ease—a process that is a lifesaver in situations where you might be unsure about the exact relative path of the file to which you are linking.

Absolute Links vs. Relative Links

An absolute link—or path—provides a complete URL. For example, http://www.macromedia.com/dreamweaver is an absolute URL. It's important to include the http:// protocol designationat the beginning of absolute URLs. If you don't, Dreamweaver MX will think that the document to which you are linking resides on your computer. The general rule is that absolute links are used to link to a document that sits on another server. You can certainly use absolute links for documents on the same server, but it's much easier if you use relative links instead.

Relative links are a little less straightforward than absolute links. Essentially, they are a cross between an instruction and shorthand. *Instruction* refers to the idea that the link itself contains information that uses the current folder on the server as a reference point for finding the document (HTML file, image, and so on) to which the URL refers. These instructions are called the path. *Shorthand* refers to the notion that a relative link doesn't need the same sort of strict use of structure and protocol (for example, http://) that an absolute link does. As a result, relative links can only be used to refer to documents that reside on the same server.

For example, if you were linking to a document that was in the same folder, all you would have to do would be to enter the name of the file (welcome.html). Now, if the welcome.html file was in a folder above the current folder in which the file from which you are linking , you would have to enter in the relative URL as ../welcome.html. The ../ in the relative URL instructs the browser that the file can be found one folder above the current folder. If the file to which you were linking was two folders above the current one, you would need to enter the relative link as ../../welcome.html.

Creating Text Links

Let's start off by looking at how you can create a link to a relative URL.

1. Select the text that you want to turn into a link.

2. Open the Property Inspector (Window > Properties).

3. Click the Browse for File icon 📁.

4. When the Select File dialog box appears, locate and select the file to which you want to link.

5. If you haven't saved the file in which the link resides, Dreamweaver will tell you that until you save it, an absolute URL will be used, like the following:

```
File:///C|/Program Files/Macromedia/Dreamweaver MX 2004/Samples/
GettingStarted/1-Design/layout.html
```

6. If the file to which you are linking is not located in the local root folder of your Local Site, Dreamweaver will ask you whether you want it copied to your Local Site.

If you are working from within a Local Site, it's wise to copy the external file to your local root folder. If you do so, when you move your files to your Remote Site, you won't have to worry about having to search for all of your assets; they will all be located in your local root.

7. Once you've located the file to which you are linking, you'll notice that the link, complete with the necessary path, has appeared in the Link field.

8. If it hasn't been already, you can activate the link by pressing Return (Mac) or Enter (Win) or click anywhere off the Property Inspector in the Document window.

 Note: To change the color of links (including visited and active links), see "Setting Page Properties" in Chapter 2.

The process by which you add an absolute link is similar; all you need to do is follow these steps:

1. Select the text that you want to turn into a link.
2. Open the Property Inspector (Window > Properties).
3. In the Link field, type the full URL of the document you're linking to.
4. To activate the link, press Return (Mac) or Enter (Win) or click off the Property Inspector anywhere in the Document window.

 Note: If the full absolute URL is long and easily forgotten, you can open the file in a browser, copy the full URL from the Address field, and paste it into the Link field of the Property Inspector

In Dreamweaver, you can also insert a text hyperlink using the Hyperlink command:

1. Place the cursor in the location in the Document window where you would like to insert the hyperlink.
2. If it isn't already, open the Insert bar (Window > Insert), make sure you are within the Common section, and click the Hyperlink button ✎. Alternatively, you can choose Insert > Hyperlink.
3. When the Hyperlink dialog box (Figure 5.1) appears, enter the text for the link into the Text field.

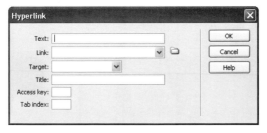

Figure 5.1 The Hyperlink dialog box

4. Click the Browse button to the right of the Link field. When the Select File dialog box appears, locate and select the file to which you want to link and click OK.

> **Note:** If you haven't saved your page yet, a dialog box will pop up telling you that, until you save the page, an absolute path will be used.

You'll notice that the link, complete with the necessary path, has appeared in the Link field. Alternatively, you can simply enter an absolute URL into the Link field.

5. Choose the link target from the Target drop-down menu. A link's target determines where the document will load. For more information on this, see "Defining Where Linked Files Load" later in this chapter.

6. Enter a title for the link into the Title field. The title itself has no bearing on how the link will look. Essentially, the name (which is not a requirement for creating a link using the Hyperlink command) is a unique identifier that you can use when you want to manipulate the hyperlink using Dynamic HTML.

7. Enter a value into the Access Key field. This value (which can only be a single key) will serve as a shortcut that your users can use to select the hyperlink in the browser.

8. Enter a value into the Tab Index field. The Tab Index value determines the sequence in which links on your page will be highlighted when the user presses the Tab key.

9. When you're finished, click OK.

Creating Image Links

The process by which you create an image link is almost identical to that of creating a text link.

> **Note:** Although you can create an image link using both a relative and absolute URL, the process is exactly the same as described in the previous section. Therefore, to reduce redundancy, I'll only cover the process by which you create an image link using an absolute URL.

Let's take a look at how:

1. Select the image that you want to turn into a link.

2. Open the Property Inspector (Window > Properties).

3. In the Link field, type the full URL of the document you're linking to.

4. To activate the link, press Return (Mac) or Enter (Win) or click off the Property Inspector anywhere in the Document window.

Removing the Border from Linked Images

Often, when you create an image link, you'll notice that the image itself has a blue border around it (Figure 5.2). In most cases, this is an unintended side effect of creating a linked image and can be easily remedied.

Figure 5.2 Linked images sometimes appear with a thin blue border around them.

To remove the border, follow these steps:

1. Select the linked image that has a blue border around it.

2. If it isn't already, open the Property Inspector (Window > Properties)

Border Field

3. In the Border field, if it isn't already, set the value to 0.

Note: Any Border value of more than 0 on a linked image will result in the blue border.

Using the Point to File Icon to Create Links

The Point to File icon is a handy tool that works in tandem with the Files panel to provide a visual way to link to files within your site. Be forwarned, however the Point to File icon can prove to be a little frustrating at times.

1. Make sure you've established a Local Site and that you are working within it.

Note: For more information on setting up a Local Site, see "The Fine Art of Local Sites" in Chapter 2.

2. Open the Files panel by choosing Window > Files.

3. With the Files panel open, select the text (or image) in the Document window that you want to turn into a link.

Note: If the Files panel disappears, use your toolbar to maximize the Files window (which brings it back into view). Alternatively, if you are working on a Mac, press Alt+Tab.

4. If it isn't already, open the Property Inspector (Window > Properties).

5. As illustrated in Figure 5.3, drag the Point to File icon ⊕ to the file in the Files panel to which you want to make a link.

6. Release your mouse button over the desired file. The relative URL automatically appears in the Link field.

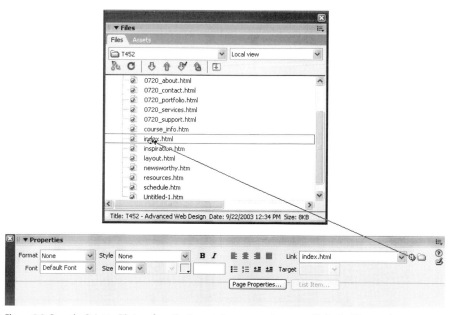

Figure 5.3 Drag the Point to File icon from the Property Inspector to the correct file in the Files panel.

Note: Dreamweaver will set a self link target by default if one isn't specified.

To determine where a link loads, just follow these steps:

1. Select either the text or image that you want to turn into a link.

2. Open the Property Inspector (Window > Properties).

3. Click the Browse for File icon to the right of the Link field 📁.

4. When the Select File dialog box appears, locate and select the file to which you want to link, and click OK.

5. In the Property Inspector, open the Target drop-down menu and choose _blank.

6. To activate the link, press Return (Mac) or Enter (Win) or click off the Property Inspector anywhere in the Document window.

 Note: We'll spend ample time exploring the other types of link targets in Chapter 6.

Creating E-Mail Links

An e-mail link is a link that opens a blank message window in the e-mail program of the user's browser. When the blank message window appears, it contains the e-mail address that was included in the link. To insert an e-mail link, all you have to do is follow these steps:

1. Click where you'd like to insert the e-mail link in the Document window.

 Note: If you want, you can also select some existing text that you'd like to use for the link. In this case, the selected text automatically appears in the Email Link dialog box's Text field.

2. If it isn't already, open the Insert bar (Window > Insert). Make sure you are in the Common section, and click the E-Mail Link button 📧. Alternatively, you can choose Insert > E-Mail Link.

3. When the Email Link dialog box opens, enter the text for the link in the Text field.

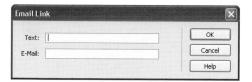

4. In the E-Mail field, enter the appropriate e-mail address.

5. Click OK.

You can also add an e-mail link manually by using the Property Inspector:

1. Select either the text or image that you want to turn into a link.

2. Open the Property Inspector (Window > Properties).

3. In the Link field of the Property Inspector, type **mailto:** followed by the appropriate e-mail address.

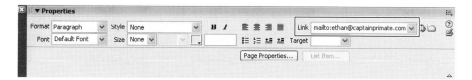

Note: For the e-mail link to work properly, there cannot be any spaces in the text you manually enter in the Link field.

4. To activate the link, press Return (Mac) or Enter (Win) or click off the Property Inspector anywhere in the Document window.

Note: Nowadays, it's standard practice to show the actual e-mail address rather than random text that says something like "e-mail me." By doing this, your audience can copy and paste it into an alternate e-mail client or write it down for future use.

Creating E-Mail Links with a Subject Line, CC, BCC, and Even Message Text

In the preceding section, you learned how to create an e-mail link (either manually or with the Insert Link command). But what if you wanted to create an e-mail link that, once clicked upon, not only opens up a blank message window (containing the e-mail that was included in the link), but also sticks something in other parts of the blank message window (such as a CC e-mail address, a BCC e-mail address, or text from the body of the message. Unfortunately, Dreamweaver doesn't provide a terribly quick and easy way to do this. But it is possible; let's take a look at how:

1. Select either the text or image that you want to turn into a link.

2. Open the Property Inspector (Window > Properties).

3. In the Link field of the Property Inspector, add the following code:

```
mailto:ethan@captainprimate.com?subject=Dreamweaver%20MX%202004%20Soluti
ons&cc=info@captainprimate.com&bcc=ethan@vonflashenstein.com&body=
Dreamweaver MX 2004 Solutions is the best book I've ever read!
```

This string of code not only opens up a message window in the user's default e-mail program, but it also includes a CC address (info@captainprimate), a BCC address (ethan@vonflashenstein.com), and some text in the body of the message.

There are a couple of things of which you should be aware about the code. First, individual elements of the e-mail (BCC address, CC address, etc.) must be separated by a question mark (?). Second, because there can be absolutely no spaces in any of the code that falls outside of the quotation marks, you must use %20 to represent spaces.

Adding Image Maps to Your Pages

An *Image Map* is a fusion of a link and an image. You've probably noticed that when you add a link to an image, the entire image becomes a link. With an Image Map, you can designate portions of an image (using hotspots) as links.

 Note: Before you start inserting hotspots and defining links, you should decide which areas of your image you want to attach links to.

You can even have multiple hotspots in the same image, each linking to a different page. Creating an Image Map involves two different processes: inserting the image and defining hotspots and links.

1. If you haven't already inserted the image you want to map, do so by following the procedure outlined in Chapter 4 in the section "Inserting Images into Your Page."

2. Select the image to which you want to add an Image Map.

3. If it isn't already, open the Property Inspector (Window > Properties). In the lower-left corner, you'll see the Image Map tools.

Image Map tools

4. In the Map field, enter a unique name for your Image Map.

> **Note:** If the name you choose is also used by another Image Map on the same page, neither will work. Also, try to not use spaces in the name

Now you must define your hotspots.

Defining Hotspots

Depending on the general shape of the area that you want to turn into a hotspot, you have three tools to choose from: Rectangular Hotspot, Circular Hotspot, and Polygon Hotspot (Figure 5.5). The Circular Hotspot and Rectangular Hotspot tools are self-explanatory. The Polygon Hotspot tool, on the other hand, is designed to create an irregular hotspot that is neither a circle nor a rectangle.

Figure 5.5 Left to right: rectangular, circular, and polygon hotspots

Depending on the shape of the hotspot you want to define, do one of the following:

- Click the Rectangular Hotspot button □ or Circular Hotspot button ○, move the crosshair (+) over the place in the image where you want the hotspot, and click and drag until you've covered the area you want. When you're finished, release the mouse button.

- Click the Polygon Hotspot button ▽, place the crosshair along any edge of the irregular area, and click once. A light blue point appears where you click. Move the crosshair to the next point along the edge of the irregular area and click again. A line appears between the two points. Continue clicking, adding points along the edge of the irregular area until it's fully outlined (and shaded) with the hotspot.

Once you successfully define a hotspot, the Hotspot view of the Property Inspector will appear (Figure 5.6).

Figure 5.6 The Property Inspector's Hotspot view

Adding the Image Map Links

Now you can integrate the actual hyperlink into your Image Map:

1. Select the hotspot to which you wish to attach the hyperlink.

2. Click the Browse for File icon 📁 to the right of the Link field.

3. When the Select File dialog box appears, locate and select the file to which you want to link, and click OK. Alternatively, you can manually enter an absolute URL into the Link field.

4. Choose a link target from the Target drop-down menu.

5. Enter any ALT text that you want associated with the hotspot in the Alt field.

6. To activate the Image Map, click anywhere off the Property Inspector in the Document window.

Once you create the Image Map, you can edit it by clicking the hotspot you want to edit (represented by the pale blue area on the image) and making any changes in the Property Inspector. To move a hotspot around, click and drag it with the Pointer Hotspot tool.

 Note: If you create two overlapping hotspots, the area of overlap will be associated with the final hotspot created (as opposed to the first one created).

Building Jump Menus

A Jump Menu is a handy little widget that allows you to create a special kind of drop-down menu populated with a series of options, each of which serve as a hyperlink (Figure 5.7).

Figure 5.7 A Jump Menu

A Jump Menu is really nothing more than a standard menu object to which the Jump Menu Go behavior has been attached. However, because Jump Menus are easily created without having to go anywhere near the Behavior panel, this chapter is a good place to discuss them.

Note: For more on menu objects, see see Chapter 14; for more on behaviors, see Chapter 9.

To create a Jump Menu, follow these steps:

1. Place your cursor in the location where you want to insert the Jump Menu.

2. If it isn't already, open the Insert bar (Window > Insert), make sure you are in the Forms section, and click the Jump Menu button 🔲. Alternatively, you can choose Insert > Form > Jump Menu. This will open the Insert Jump Menu dialog box (Figure 5.8).

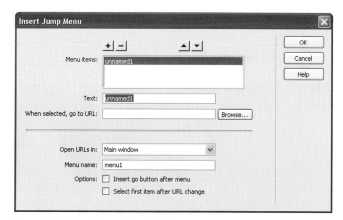

Figure 5.8 The Insert Jump Menu dialog box

3. In the Text field, enter the text you want for the first menu item.

4. In the When Selected Go to URL field, enter either the relative or absolute URL you wish to open when the user clicks the menu item. Alternatively, you can click the Browse button ⌈ Browse… ⌉. When the Select File dialog box opens, locate the file you wish to open when the user clicks the menu item, and click Select.

5. Select the location where you want the URL to open from the Open URLs In drop-down menu. If the document in which the Jump Menu is located doesn't contain frames, the only option available in the Open URLs In drop-down menu will be Main Window. If, however, your document contains frames, the drop-down menu will contain their names.

Note: To learn about frames, see Chapter 6.

6. To add additional menu items, click the Add Item button ⌈ + ⌉ and repeat steps 3 to 5. When you finish adding all the menu items to the Jump Menu, go to the next step.

7. Enter a name into the Menu Name field. The name can contain spaces and any special characters you want.

8. To add a Go button, select the Insert Go Button After Menu option. If you do this, the user will have to click the Go button after selecting one of the options from the menu itself. If a Go button isn't added, the link will load automatically when the user selects it from the Jump Menu.

9. When you finish adding all of the menu items, click OK.

Note: Jump Menus have a peculiar little bug you should be aware of: once a user has selected a menu item, they cannot return to the page on which the Jump Menu is located and reselect the same menu item. To bypass this glitch, insert a Go button. The user will be able to revisit any of the Jump Menu links by selecting one and clicking the Go button.

Editing Jump Menus

Once you build a Jump Menu using the previous steps, you aren't stuck with what you've created. You can quite easily go back and make changes and modifications. The only hitch is that you can't make changes with the Insert Jump Menu dialog box (which fulfilled all your Jump Menu needs in the previous section); you must use a somewhat less-streamlined tool accessible through the Property Inspector. Here's how to edit a Jump Menu:

1. Select the Jump Menu that you want to edit.

2. Open the Property Inspector (Window > Properties).

3. Click the List Values button [List Values...] to open the List Values dialog box (Figure 5.9).

Figure 5.9 The List Values dialog box

4. You'll see that all the menu items (whose names you set by entering text into the Insert Jump Menu dialog box's Text field) are in the Item Label column. Each menu item's associated URL is located in the Value column. From here you have two options:

   • To change a menu item's text, select it in the Item Label column. The text will automatically change into a live field into which you can type some new text.

   • To change a menu item's associated URL, select it in the Value column. When it turns into an editable field, just type in a new URL.

5. When you finish editing the Jump Menu items, click OK.

Adding Flash Buttons to Your Pages

Back in Chapter 3, you learned that Dreamweaver MX 2004 allows you to insert Flash text into your document. In this section of the chapter, you are going to explore how you can insert a Flash button into your document. Although Flash buttons in Dreamweaver are a cool feature, they may not be as exciting as you think. Unfortunately, you can't create any kind of button you want; you are restricted to choosing from a series of preset buttons. The upside to this is the fact that you have some control over how the preset button looks.

To add a Flash button to your page, follow these steps:

1. Place your cursor in the location where you want to insert the Flash button.

2. If it isn't already, open the Insert bar (Window > Insert) and make sure you are in the Common section.

3. Open the Media drop-down menu, and select Flash Button. Alternatively, you can choose Insert > Media > Flash Button. Either action will open the Insert Flash Button dialog box (Figure 5.10).

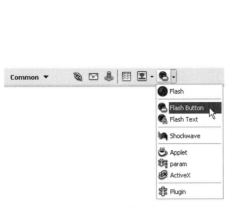

Figure 5.10 Opening the Insert Flash Button dialog box

 Note: If the document into which you are inserting the Flash button is unsaved, Dreamweaver will prompt you to save it.

4. Select one of the preset buttons from the Style list box. Notice that you get an interactive preview of the particular style in the Sample section at the top of the Insert Flash Button dialog box.

5. Enter the text that you would like to appear on the button into the Button Text field.

6. Select the button text's font from the Font drop-down menu.

 Note: Because Flash embeds the font in the file itself, you are free to use any font you want.

7. Enter the size of the button's text into the Size field.

8. Enter the button's link into the Link field. Alternatively, you can click the Browse button to the right of the Link field ⟨Browse...⟩ and locate the specific file to which you would like to link.

9. Select a link target from the Target drop-down menu.

10. From here, click on the Bg Color swatch , and select a color from the color picker. This color acts as the background of the Flash movie and will display if the movie isn't playing.

11. Enter a filename in the Save As field. You can use the default filename (text1.swf, text2.swf, and so on), but you must enter something in this field. The file is automatically saved to the same directory as the current document.

12. When you are finished, click OK, and the button will be inserted into your document.

Note: You might be tempted to use the Get More Styles button as a way to increase the number of presets available. Clicking the button only opens up the Macromedia Exchange website (www.macromedia.com/exchange), where Macromedia had big plans of making more buttons available but never did. However, if you are comfortable with making your own buttons in Flash, you can stick their SWF files in the Flash buttons subfolder in the Flash Objects folder—which is located in the Configuration subfolder of the folder in which you installed Dreamweaver MX 2004. Then, they'll be available in the Insert Flash Button dialog box.

The Ultimate

Dreamweaver MX

Color Gallery

This section is a gallery of websites that illustrate the possibilities of interactive design and provide inspiration for your own work. Although these sites have been built with a variety of tools, the common thread is that all use their particular medium to its fullest extent in order to create compelling and interesting interactive experiences.

Doug Chiang Studios

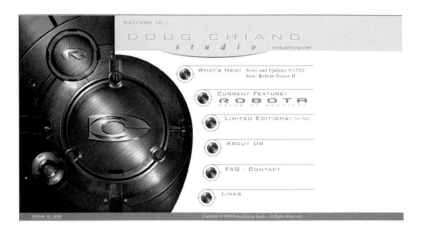

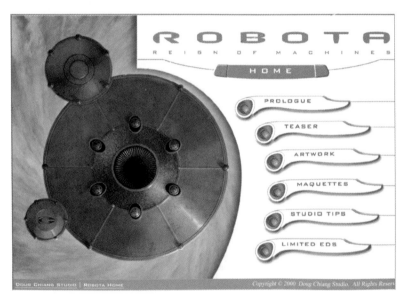

Founded by Doug Chiang, head of the art department and design director for the *Star Wars* prequels, Doug Chiang Studios recently completed work on a film/book project called *Robata: Reign of Machines*. The website is intended to cater to those fascinated by the incredible work of Doug Chiang as well as publicize and explore the *Robata: Reign of Machines* project.

www.dchiang.com

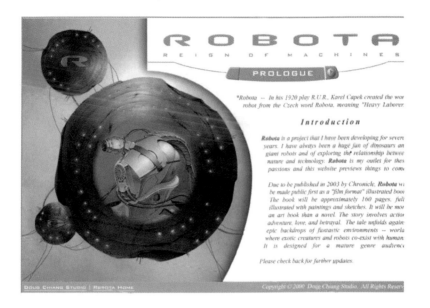

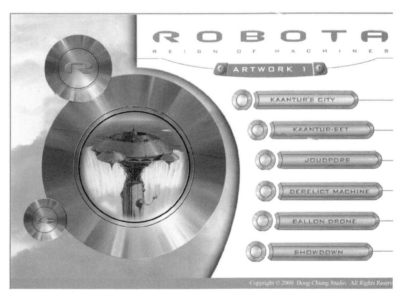

TOP: Designed using a combination of both Dreamweaver and Fireworks (along with several other software packages), the website combines Doug Chiang's beautiful and compelling style of illustration with a highly intuitive navigation scheme to create an exceptionally immersive experience.
BOTTOM: *Robota: Reign of Machines* is a 160-page "film format" illustrated book, published in the fall of 2003, that explores the relationship between technology and nature against the backdrop of a futuristic society. The *Robota* section of the Doug Chiang Studios site combines incredible illustration and immersive navigation to allow the user to explore the world of *Robota*.

Playdo Community

Not to be mistaken for that weird doughy stuff you used to play with as a kid, Playdo Community is an extremely entertaining and engaging virtual online community (with free membership) that lets you interact and communicate with other "citizens" in your choice of either a 2D or 3D environment, both of which are very cool.

www.playdo.com

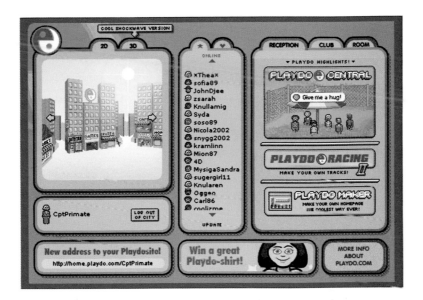

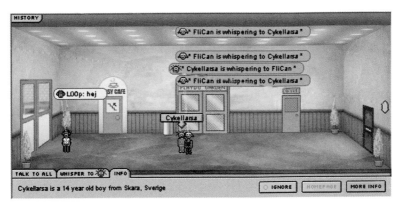

At playdo.com, you can create a unique online character by choosing from over 40,000 different appearance combinations. Your character then plays a role as a citizen in Playdo City, where you can gossip over a cup of coffee, send your mail, get challenged in an online game, and meet (and interact with) fellow Playdo citizens.

Rustboy

Created by XL5 Design (www.xl5design.com), Rustboy is a promotional site for a forthcoming short film of the same name that will ultimately be distributed online by Brian Taylor. Rustboy (the primary character of the film) originally began life as a simple 2D creation but has since been thrust into the glorious world of 3D—and is now a book as well!

www.rustboy.com

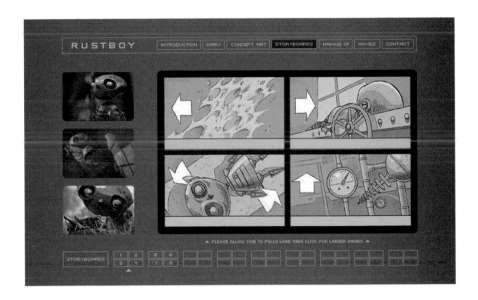

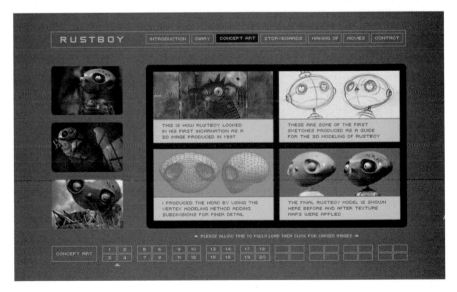

The site, which is a great example of simple but stylish design, features a constantly updated diary on the current Rustboy milestones, beautifully illustrated storyboards and concept art, short QuickTime teasers, and insights into the creation of the film. The site perfectly captures the slightly dark feeling of Rustboy and the world in which he lives.

The Theban Mapping Project

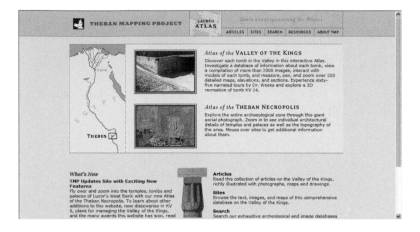

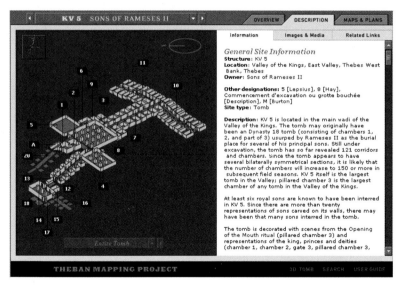

TOP: Created by Second Story Interactive (www.secondstory.com), this site is designed to support and publicize the efforts of the Theban Mapping Project, an Egyptological expedition (based at the American University in Cairo) dedicated to preparing a comprehensive archaeological database of Thebes (an area that includes the Valley of the Kings) and conserving and preserving an incredible archaeological resource for study and education of future generations. **BOTTOM:** Beyond an incredibly rich resource for those wanting to learn more about ancient Egyptian history and archaeology, the site features an extraordinary example of interactive Flash edutainment (the Atlas of the Valley of the Kings) that lets people explore the valley where, from 1500 B.C. to 1000 B.C., ancient Egyptian pharaohs were buried in expansive underground complexes.

www.thebanmappingproject.com

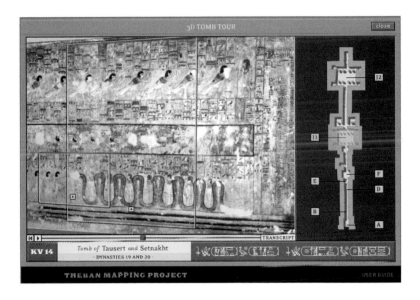

TOP: From professional Egyptologists to school children, this site serves the needs of a wide and diverse audience. Visitors unfamiliar with the Valley of the Kings can go on a virtual tour of a 3D tomb or watch narrated movies. For experienced academics, the site offers the opportunity to research the architecture and decoration of every chamber in every tomb in the Valley of the Kings. **BOTTOM:** The Interactive Atlas, a stand-alone multimedia experience, displays compelling movies, dynamic information, and gripping images in context with detailed maps and measured drawings of the tombs within the Valley of the Kings.

Daring Planet

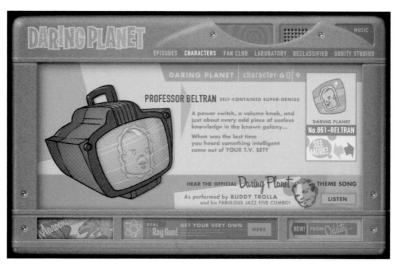

TOP: Woohoo, more fun than a barrel of psychic monkey girls! Created by the insanely talented Paul Corrigan, Daring Planet is easily one of the most creative and entertaining uses of Flash in the universe. Designed as a promotional site (and future platform) for a campy retro sci-fi serialized Flash animated toon, Daring Planet is an interactive (and outright enjoyable) feast for the eyes. **BOTTOM:** Drawing inspiration from old B-movie sci-fi/horror posters from the '50s and '60s and pop culture/subculture advertising and references from the '40s, '50s, and '60s, Daring Planet's design features an authentic retro look reminiscent of period comic books and magazines. If you look closely at the site's design, you'll notice subtle visual touches that give it a true retro style—like cheap paper, bad registration, sub-par printing procedures and colors that bleed.

www.daringplanet.com

TOP: One of the goals of the Daring Planet project is to create an "immersive" online environment for fans and casual visitors alike. Complete with a developer's journal, animation samples, how-to tutorials, and regular character-specific features, Daring Planet provides much more than the anticipated episodes and storylines. It's also meant to be a destination that combines expert illustration, copy writing, storytelling, and design in a way that both surprises and delights. **BOTTOM:** The individual Daring Planet episodes (which are currently in production) will be serialized, self-contained plots that fit within a larger, continually evolving saga. They will include components of sequential, frame-based art that is punctuated with animated sequences, sound effects, and a background musical score. Ultimately, the storytelling mechanism is designed to make the most of traditional comic-book pacing, animated embellishments, and online interactivity.

America on the Move

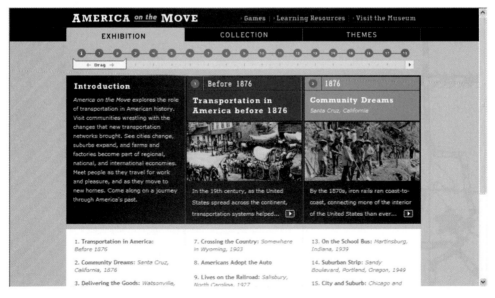

Created by Second Story Interactive (www.secondstory.com) as the dynamic companion website to the largest exhibition to ever be installed in the National Museum of American History, America on the Move explores the past two centuries of how Americans took to the rails, roads, and water in the past two centuries, driving the economic and cultural life of the nation.

www.americanhistory.si.edu/onthemove

The heart of the site consists of three main sections. In the Exhibition section, visitors get an historical overview that is designed to give context to the themes. A dynamic search features in the Collection section provide access to over 1,500 transportation-related artifacts and photographs. In the Themes section, diverse viewpoints on a variety of related topics are explored. The addition of learning resources and three fun games makes the entire site a wonderful rich resource for collectors, enthusiasts, teachers, and students.

The Halifax Explosion

December 6, 1917, dawned clear and sunny in Halifax, Nova Scotia. Before darkness fell, more than a thousand people would die in the largest man-made explosion the world had ever seen, with another thousand to die later as a result. Nine thousand more were injured and maimed. Caused by the collision of two ships in the Halifax harbor, one of which was carrying munitions bound for the battlefields of WWI Europe, the devastating explosion left scars on the city that are visible even today. Created by the Canadian Broadcasting Company (CBC), the Halifax Explosion website was designed not only in remembrance for those who lost their lives on that fateful day, but to allow the exploration of how the tragic event shaped and influenced the lives of people throughout Canada.

www.cbc.ca/halifaxexplosion

The site itself is a phenomenal historical and educational resource that allows visitors to explore not only all aspects of the event itself, but also the historical, geographic, and social context in which the event occurred. Numerous interactive modules (such as a Flash-based timeline of the collision and numerous interactive historical docu-comics) are meticulously created in order to provide a rich and vivid window into the explosion and the events that followed.

Kaliber10000

Based in Denmark, Kaliber10000 is your one stop center for all things cutting-edge digital. Originally created as a place where a few select digital designers could display their work, the site has evolved into a deign hub that revolves around special regularly published "issues" that feature anything that strikes the creators' collective fancies: pages of weird typography, shocked sound and video stuff, freaky animation pieces, an interactive murder mystery, random Flash weirdness, straightforward graphic design pieces, photo montages, and Java applets.

www.k10k.net

Laying Out Tables and Frames

HTML was not conceived as a way to create intricate layout and design. But the Web blossomed into a medium to which designers have flocked. As a result, new methods developed that allow designers to bypass HTML's inherent limitations. Tables provide you the opportunity to lay out your content with a high degree of control. Frames allow you to display multiple HTML documents in one browser window, thereby increasing the control you have over your page's interface and content.

Chapter Contents

Adding Tables

Dreamweaver MX 2004 lets you insert and manipulate tables in two different modes: Layout view and Standard view. Standard view, which has been around since Dreamweaver was first released, is best for creating tables to organize tabular data and do some light page layout. Layout view, because of its very malleable authoring environment, is best for more complex page designs. Throughout this chapter, I'll point out where you can accomplish something in either view and where the two views provide different power and functionality.

To move back and forth between Layout and Standard views, all you need to do is open the Insert bar (Windows > Insert), make sure you are working in the Layout section, and click either the Layout button `Layout` or the Standard button `Standard`.

Adding Tables in Standard View

As with many tasks in Dreamweaver, there are two ways to insert tables in Standard view:

1. Place your cursor at the location in the Document window where you want to insert the table.

2. Do *one* of the following:

    *   Choose Insert > Table.

    *   Open the Insert bar (Windows > Insert), make sure you are within either the Layout or the Common section, and click the Table button ⊞.

3. Set the table's initial characteristics in the Table dialog box (Figure 6.1). These properties are briefly described shortly.

4. When you're done, click OK.

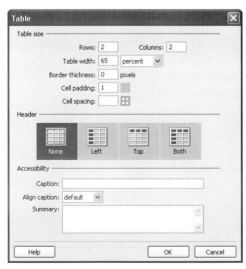

Figure 6.1 The Table dialog box

Tables in Expanded View

You'll probably notice that besides the Layout and Standard buttons in the Layout section of the Insert Bar, there is also a third button, called Expanded . A new feature to Dreamweaver MX 2004, Expanded view *temporarily* adds cell padding and spacing to all tables in a document, thereby increasing the tables' borders. This allows you to select table items with greater ease or to better and more precisely place insertion points.

From here, you can go ahead and set the initial properties of the table. You can leave the properties at their defaults or make changes now. But *almost* all of the options here can also be altered later.

Note: Unfortunately, the only time you can create a header or set the accessibility options is when you initially create the table.

You can modify these properties, and many other characteristics of your table, using the Property Inspector, Insert bar, and other methods described throughout this chapter. What Dreamweaver has included in the Table dialog are the most basic settings to get your table started:

Rows and Columns When you enter the number of rows and columns, you are essentially setting the structure of your table.

Table Width There are two types of width values you can choose from: pixels and percent. As with horizontal rules (which were discussed in Chapter 3), if you choose pixels, the width of your table will be fixed regardless of the size of the user's browser window. As a result, if the width of the table is larger than the browser window, the user will have to scroll to see the entire table. On the other hand, if you choose percent, your table will always resize dynamically.

To set the width of your table, click the drop-down menu to the right of the Table Width field and select either Pixels or Percent. Then click in the Table Width field itself and enter a value for the width of your table.

Border Thickness This property sets the thickness of the solid edge that runs around the perimeter of the table (Figure 6.2). Enter a value in pixels. The default border color is gray, but you can change that after you've set the initial table properties.

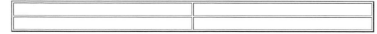

Figure 6.2 Table with solid border

Note: If you want the borders of your table to be invisible, a common strategy for laying out your content is to set the border thickness to 0.

Cell Padding and Cell Spacing These can be tricky to get a handle on. Basically, cell padding refers to the number of pixels between the wall of the cell and the object within the cell, and cell spacing is the number of pixels between each cell. Enter values for cell padding and cell spacing in pixels.

Header The ability to add a header to your table is a feature that is new to Dreamweaver MX 2004. Basically, when you turn any cell, row, or column into a header, a special <th> tag is inserted. The <th> tag is accessible by screen readers and allows the screen reader to keep track of content within the table. You can have a table without a header, but to set a header, click the specific option that best suits your needs:

None	No portion of the table is set as a header.
Left	The first column is set as a header, allowing you to enter a heading into each cell in that column.
Top	The first row is set as a header, allowing you to enter a heading into each cell of that row.
Both	The left column and the top row of the table are set as headers, allowing you to enter a heading into any cells within those areas.

Note: The minimum size of a table is determined by objects contained within the table itself. For example, a table whose sizing is set to percent that contains an image measuring 200 pixels by 200 pixels will not be able to shrink any smaller than 200 × 200.

Accessibility options Dreamweaver MX 2004 includes several new features that allow you to make your table accessible to those who are visually impaired or blind. In the Caption field, enter descriptive text that will display outside of the table and can be read by a screen reader. Select a setting from the Align Caption drop-down menu to determine where the caption is located in relation to the table. Enter a description for your table into the Summary field; this text is not visible in a browser but acts to provide extra information about the contents of your table to a screen reader.

Note: You can also choose to create a new table based on a library of presets. To do this, choose File > New. When the New Document dialog box appears, select Page Designs from the Category list box. From there, select one of the available table-based designs from the Page Designs list box.

CHAPTER 6: LAYING OUT TABLES AND FRAMES ■

Adding Tables in Layout View

Layout view is probably one of the most useful features in Dreamweaver MX 2004—at least when it comes to tables. With Layout view, you create tables with a much higher level of control than you have in Standard view. Layout view allows you to actually draw tables and cells (called layout tables and layout cells) and then manipulate them. The result is a page laid out with far more precision than is possible in Standard view. The cool thing (and this is the whole point of creating tables in Layout view) is that once you draw a layout table or a layout cell in Layout view, Dreamweaver MX 2004 automatically takes care of the underlying table structure, thereby allowing you to focus on your creative endeavors instead of wrestling a table into the exact form you want.

When you insert a layout table, you are essentially drawing the *external* structure of your table. A layout table, however, doesn't have any internal structure until you draw layout cells within it. Think of a layout table as a frame within which you create the internal structure (rows, columns, and cells) of your table. Here's how insert a layout table:

1. Open the Insert bar (Windows > Insert) and access the Layout section.

2. Click the Layout button Layout .

> **Note:** When you click the Layout view button, the Getting Started In Layout View dialog box will appear. Don't worry about this—it is designed purely to give you some quick information on Layout view and can be immediately closed down. To stop the dialog box from popping up every time you enter Layout view, click the Don't Show Me This Message Again check box.

3. Click the Layout Table icon .

4. Move the cursor off the Insert bar; it will automatically change into a plus (+) symbol. Position the plus (+) cursor where you want to start your layout table.

5. Click and drag until the outline is the size that you want for your layout table.

6. When the outline is the size you want, release your mouse button. The layout table is automatically created (Figure 6.3).

> **Note:** A layout table must be justified to the top-right corner of your Document window. However, as you've probably noticed, Dreamweaver MX 2004 lets you draw a layout table anywhere on your page. So how can you stick one anywhere you want? Dreamweaver cheats a little by placing the layout table that is not justified to the top-right corner inside another layout table (which it automatically generates) that *is* justified to the top-right corner.

Figure 6.3 A layout table

Layout tables have some unique characteristics and tools that are not available in Standard view. To see what you can do specifically with a layout table, be sure to read the section "Manipulating Layout Tables" later in this chapter.

If you just create a layout table and do nothing else, what you have is essentially a table consisting of a single cell. To add more cells, see "Drawing Layout Cells" later in this chapter.

Manipulating Table Size and Shape

Tables, regardless of whether they were created in Layout view or Standard view, have a host of properties that you can manipulate in order to get them looking the way you want. In the following sections, we'll explore the properties that determine how large your table is and its row/column structure.

Many properties that are accessible in Standard view are not accessible in Layout view. This doesn't mean that if you create a table in Layout view, you can't access one of these properties. You can simply switch back into Standard view, manipulate the particular property, and then switch back to Layout view.

Note: Many of the following sets of steps end with the instruction to apply your changes by pressing Return/Enter or by clicking off of the Property Inspector. However, you can certainly set multiple table properties at once; if you choose to do so, ignore that step and wait until you've set all of your properties before "locking in" your changes.

Configuring Rows and Columns

A table certainly wouldn't be much use if you were allowed to work only with a fixed number of rows and columns, so even after you create a table you can go back later and change these.

To change the overall row and column structure of your table, follow these steps:

1. Select the table that you want to configure.

2. Open the Property Inspector (Window > Properties).

3. Enter a value into the Rows field for the total number of rows you want your table to have.

4. Enter a value into the Cols field for the total number of columns you want your table to have.

5. Apply your changes: either press Return/Enter, or click off of the Property Inspector anywhere in the Document window.

If you want to make a change in only one place in the table, you can add or delete rows or columns at the cursor location by using the main menu. Place your cursor at the point in the table that you want to modify (do not select the entire table as you did previously) and then do *one* of the following:

To insert a single row above the cursor position, choose Modify > Table > Insert Row.

To insert a single column to the left of the cursor position, choose Modify > Table > Insert Column.

To delete a single row, click in a cell of the row you want to delete (do not select the entire row) and choose Modify > Table > Delete Row.

To delete a single column, click in a cell of the column you want to delete (do not select the entire column) and choose Modify > Table > Delete Column.

To insert multiple rows or columns at once, choose Modify > Table > Insert Rows Or Columns to open the Insert Rows Or Columns dialog box (Figure 6.4), from which you can set the number of rows or columns to be inserted and whether they are inserted above or below the current position of your cursor in the table.

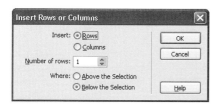

Figure 6.4 The Insert Rows Or Columns dialog box

Finally, you can also quickly add or remove a single row or column using the Insert bar (Window > Insert). Make sure you are in the Layout section of the Insert bar and then click the appropriate button:

	Inserts a row above the cursor position
	Inserts a row below the cursor position
	Inserts a column to the left of the cursor position
	Inserts a column to the right of the cursor position

Combining and Splitting Table Cells

When you're working with tables in Standard view, you aren't stuck with a symmetrical layout of columns and rows. It's quite easy to turn any number of contiguous cells into one "megacell," thereby allowing you to exert far more control over using a table to lay out content:

1. Place your cursor in the first cell you want to include in your multicell selection.
2. Shift-click in the next cell that you want to include in your selection. A black selection box appears around both cells.
3. With Shift still held down, click any other cells you want to include in your selection.

> **Note:** Besides being contiguous, the cells you want to merge must also be in the shape of a rectangle. If they aren't, Dreamweaver MX 2004 will automatically expand the selection to make it a rectangle.

4. If it isn't already, open the Property Inspector (Window > Properties).
5. Click the Merge Selected Cells Using Spans icon ▣ in the bottom-left corner of the Property Inspector. The selected cells will automatically combine into one cell.

While you can easily merge two or more contiguous cells into a larger cell, you can also take a single cell and split it into multiple rows or columns:

1.   Click your cursor in the cell that you would like to split.

2.   If it isn't already, open the Property Inspector (Window > Properties).

3.   Click the Split Cell button ⊞ in the lower-left corner of the Property Inspector.

4.   When the Split Cell dialog box appears (Figure 6.5), select either the Rows or Columns radio button, depending on whether you want to split the cell up into rows or into columns.

Figure 6.5 The Split Cell dialog box

5.   Enter the number of rows or columns into which you want to split the cell.

6.   Click OK.

Changing Table Dimensions

You certainly aren't stuck with the initial table width you set in the Table dialog. You can modify a table's size either numerically or visually. You can make these changes in either Standard or Layout view.

To change the size of your table using pixel dimensions or a percentage of the window width, follow these steps:

1.   Select the table you want to resize.

2.   Open the Property Inspector (Window > Properties), shown in Figure 6.6.

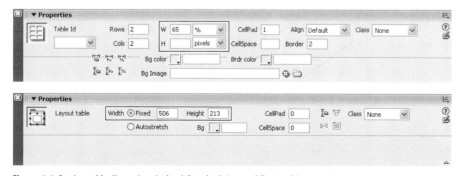

Figure 6.6 Setting table dimensions in (top) Standard view and (bottom) Layout view

3. In Standard view, open the drop-down menu to the right of the Width (W) field to choose either Pixels or Percent; then enter a value into the Width (W) field itself. In Layout view, you can enter only pixel dimensions.

Note: The Autostretch option is explained later in this chapter.

4. Do the same (choose Pixels or Percent then enter a value) for the table height.

5. To apply your changes, press Return/Enter or click anywhere off the Property Inspector in the Document window.

Note: It isn't as important to set the Height value as it is to set the Width value because a table will expand vertically to fit the content in its cells. However, you might want to create a table with a specific height so that it fits perfectly into a custom-sized browser window.

As an alternative to resizing your table numerically, you can do it manually using resize handles:

1. Select the table you want to resize; resize handles appear on the bottom edge, right side, and bottom-right corner of the table, as shown in Figure 6.7.

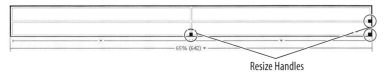

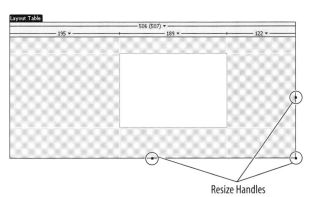

Figure 6.7 Resize handles in (top) Standard view and (bottom) Layout view

2. Click and drag any of the handles to manually resize the selected table:

   - Dragging the handle on the bottom resizes the table vertically.
   - Dragging the handle on the right resizes the table horizontally.
   - Dragging the corner handle resizes the table both horizontally and vertically at the same time.

3. When you've reached the desired size, release the mouse button and the table will automatically resize.

Aligning Tables to the Page

Like most elements in Dreamweaver (such as images and text), you can align a table to your page. However, as with any other alignment, you are limited to left, center, and right justification.

Note: If your table width is set at 100 percent, aligning it won't make any difference.

To align your table to the page, just follow these steps:

1. Select the table you want to align.
2. Open the Property Inspector (Window > Properties).
3. Open the Align drop-down menu and choose one of the options: Default, Left, Center, or Right.

4. To apply your changes, either press Return/Enter, or click off of the Property Inspector anywhere in the Document window.

Manipulating Layout Tables

The tables you create in Layout view are essentially the same as those created in Standard view (they both use the exact same HTML tags). However, some procedures and properties, because of the nature of layout tables and layout cells, are unique to Layout view. The next few sections will explore how you carry out these procedures and manipulate these unique properties.

Drawing Layout Cells

Layout cells cannot exist without a table. If you want to insert a layout cell, you can first create a layout table, as described earlier in this chapter, and then create a layout cell within it. Alternatively, you can draw a layout cell in Layout view, and Dreamweaver MX 2004 automatically creates a layout table as a container for the cell.

 Note: When you draw a layout cell without a layout table, the layout table that is created by Dreamweaver automatically occupies the entire width of your Document window.

To insert a layout cell, just follow these steps:

1. Make sure you are working in Layout view.

2. Click the Draw Layout Cell button 🔲 in the Layout panel.

3. Your cursor will automatically change into a plus (+) symbol when you move it off the Insert bar. Position the plus (+) cursor where you want to start your layout cell.

4. Click and drag until the outline is the size that you want for your layout cell.

5. When the outline is the size you want, release your mouse button. The layout cell (and, if necessary, its underlying layout table) will be automatically created (Figure 6.8).

 Note: When you create a layout cell, faint lines are added to the layout table. This is the underlying structure (rows and columns) that Dreamweaver creates to accommodate your newly created cell.

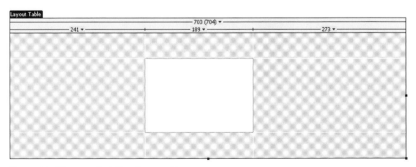

Figure 6.8 A layout cell within a layout table

Resizing and Moving Layout Cells

One of the great strengths of Layout view is that layout cells and layout tables are far more malleable than they are in Standard view. You can effortlessly (and radically) change the structure of your table by resizing or moving a layout cell—something that is impossible in Standard view.

Here's how to resize a layout cell:

1. Select the cell you want to resize by clicking its edge. (The edge of this layout cell will change color from blue to red when you move your mouse over it.)

2. After you click the cell's edge, the resize handles will appear.

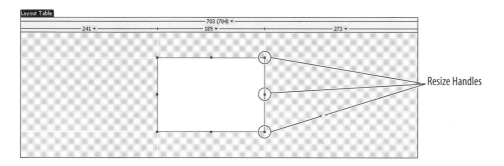

3. Click and drag one of the handles.

4. Release your mouse button when the cell has reached the desired size.

Note: You can't increase the size of a layout cell beyond the edge of the layout table.

You can also easily move a layout cell around the layout table in which it resides (thereby quickly changing the overall structure of the table); here's how:

1. Select the cell you want to move by clicking its edge. (The edge of this layout cell will change color from blue to red when you move your cursor over it.)

Note: You can't move the layout cell outside the confines of the layout table. In addition, you cannot move one layout cell over another.

2. With your cursor still on the cell's edge, click and drag to where you want to move the cell (Figure 6.9).

3. When the layout cell is where you want it, release your mouse button.

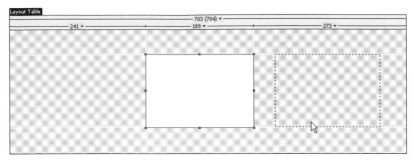

Figure 6.9 Moving a layout cell

Making Columns Autostretch

You may have noticed that in Layout view, the Property Inspector displays an Autostretch option that isn't visible when you are working in Standard view. As opposed to the Width: Fixed option—which gives you a cell (and therefore a column) with a specific numerical width that doesn't change—Autostretch allows you to define a column that will dynamically resize when the user changes the size of the browser window.

Note: When you use Autostretch, the table will always take up the user's entire browser window.

You can create a table that has a mixture of fixed-width columns and one Autostretch column. This way, when the user resizes their browser window, the Autostretch column will expand or contract so that the table always occupies the entire width of the window. The fixed-width columns maintain their predetermined width and the Autostretch column takes up the space not taken up by the fixed-width columns.

Note: You can only have one Autostretch column in any given table.

By default, all columns created in Layout view (including those columns created by Dreamweaver MX 2004 when you construct layout cells) are fixed width. To convert a column to Autostretch, follow these steps:

1. In Layout view, select a layout cell that resides in the column you wish to convert to Autostretch.

2. Open the Property Inspector (Window > Properties) and select the Autostretch option.

3. When the Choose Spacer Image dialog box appears, select one of the options and click OK.

> **Note:** For more information on working with a spacer image, see the following section.

After the column has been converted to Autostretch, the width value normally displayed in the header area at the top of each column is replaced by a squiggly line. This indicates that the column is now Autostretch.

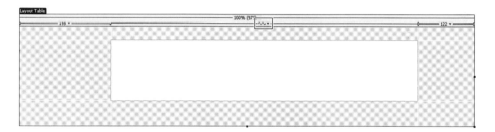

You can also convert a fixed-width column to Autostretch using the drop-down menu that's accessible in the header area at the top of each column:

1. Open the Column Header drop-down menu by clicking on the column's Width value.

2. Select Make Column Autostretch.

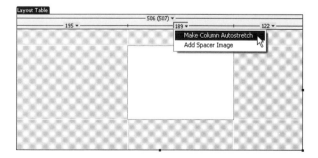

3. When the Choose Spacer Image dialog box appears, select one of the options and click OK. The spacer image options are discussed next.

Using Spacer Images with Autostretch

One of the drawbacks of creating a table in which there is an Autostretch column is that any other columns (despite the fact that they are fixed width) have a tendency to collapse entirely and effectively disappear. The only way to avoid this is to add content to the non-Autostretch columns so that they are, in effect, "propped open." But what if you aren't keen on adding visible content just to avoid losing fixed-width columns when you add an Autostretch column? This is where a *spacer image* comes in.

A spacer image is a tiny transparent image that serves to maintain the width of a non-Autostretch column—it acts as a digital shim that props open the column.

Note: You can insert and manage spacer images only in Layout view. However, they stay in your document when you switch back to Standard view.

As mentioned in the preceding section, when you convert a fixed-width column to an Autostretch column, the Choose Spacer Image dialog box (Figure 6.10) opens. You have several options:

Create A Spacer Image File Opens the Save Spacer Image File As dialog box. Navigate to the location on your hard drive where you want to save the spacer image (which by default is a GIF image).

Note: Dreamweaver MX 2004 names the spacer image spacer.gif by default, but you can change the name. The image format, however, must remain a GIF so that it can be transparent.

Use An Existing Spacer Image File Opens the Select Spacer Image File dialog box. Locate the spacer image you wish to use and click Select. For the most part, you'll choose this option if you've already created a spacer image and don't want to create an additional one.

Don't Use Spacer Images For Autostretch Tables Prevents Dreamweaver MX from using a spacer image to prop open the non-Autostretch columns in your table.

Note: As mentioned before, if you decide not to use a spacer image, any non-Autostretch columns in your table will probably collapse to such a degree that they will effectively disappear.

Figure 6.10 The Choose Spacer Image dialog box

As illustrated in the image below, after making the appropriate choice in the Choose Spacer Image dialog box, the presence of a spacer image will be represented by a double bar in each non-Autostretch column's header area.

Using Spacer Images without Autostretch

In addition to automatically inserting a spacer image into all non-Autostretch columns when converting a fixed-width column to an Autostretch column, you can manually insert a spacer image into any selected column:

1. In Layout view, select a layout cell in the column to which you wish to add a spacer image.

2. Open the Column Header drop-down menu by clicking the column's Width value (or its Autostretch symbol, if you previously converted that column into Autostretch).

3. Select Add Spacer Image.

   A spacer image will be automatically inserted into the column of the selected cell.

Removing Spacer Images

Manually removing spacer images is just as easy as adding one:

1. In Layout view, select the layout cell in the column from which you wish to remove a spacer image.

2. Open the Column Header drop-down menu by clicking the column's Width value (or its Autostretch symbol if you previously converted that column into Autostretch).

3. Select Remove All Spacer Images.

A spacer image will be automatically removed. The header area goes back from showing two bars (indicative of the presence of a spacer image) to showing a single bar (indicative of a standard fixed-width column).

Manipulating Table Contents and Appearance

Once you have actually created and refined the structure of your table, you are all set to manipulate it so that it looks exactly as you want it to look and then add your content. In this section, you will not only explore how to add content to your table, but also how to manipulate the appearance of your table and the properties of individual cells.

Note: Many properties that are accessible in Standard view are not accessible in Layout view. This doesn't mean that if you create a table in Layout view, you can't access one of these properties. Simply switch into Standard view, manipulate the particular property, and then switch back to Layout view.

For many of these property changes, you must first select a table. Doing so is as easy as clicking anywhere on its edge with your cursor. When you move your mouse over the edge, the table will highlight with a very thin red line—which is handy for making sure that you are about to select the entire table as opposed to a single cell within it.

Adding Content to Table Cells

The process by which you add content to your table, either in Standard view or Layout view, is really quite easy.

To add text to a table, just follow these steps:

1. Click in the cell where you want to add text.

2. Type the text you want to add. The cell automatically expands to accommodate what you're typing.

Note: You'll find that as your text expands, the cell in which it resides will horizontally resize itself. This results in the adjacent cells resizing as well.

3. To move to the next cell, click in the desired location.

To add an image to your table, follow these steps:

1. Click in the cell where you want to add an image.

2. If it isn't already, open the Insert bar (Window > Insert).

3. Make sure you are in the Insert bar's Common section, click the down-arrow, and select Image from the subsequent drop-down menu.

4. When the Select Image Source dialog box appears, navigate to where your image is located, select it, and click OK.

Aligning Content within Table Cells

Because a table cell is a unit unto itself, you have a few more alignment options than you normally would if you were aligning something to the page. You can align content horizontally to the left, center, or right, and you also can align content vertically to the top, middle, bottom, or baseline. This is handy when you want to exert a little more control over how the content in your table looks.

When working in either view, follow these steps to align content within a cell:

1. Select the cell:
   - In Standard view, place your cursor in the cell whose contents you want to align. Make sure that your cursor is visible in the cell before you continue.
   - In Layout view, click the edge of the layout cell whose content you want to align. The edge will change color from blue to red when you move your cursor over it.

Note: There is no need to select the object you want to align. You simply need to place your cursor in the cell you want to work with and Dreamweaver MX 2004 will do the rest.

2. Open the Property Inspector (Window > Properties) shown in Figure 6.11.

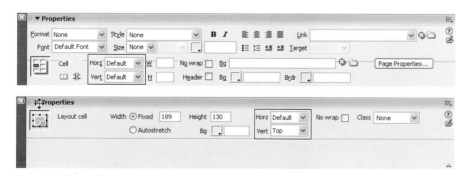

Figure 6.11 Table cell alignment in (top) Standard view and (bottom) Layout view

3. Click the down-arrow to the right of the Horz field and choose Default, Left, Right, or Center according to your page's needs.

4. Click the down-arrow to the right of the Vert field and choose Top, Middle, Bottom, or Baseline according to your page's needs.

 Note: Once you set a cell's alignment (whether horizontal or vertical), all future content that you add to that particular cell will also be aligned this way.

Arranging Content with Cell Padding and Cell Spacing

As mentioned earlier, cell padding is the distance (in pixels) between the end of an object in a cell and the wall of the cell. Cell spacing, on the other hand, is the distance (in pixels) between individual cells. Manipulating your table's cell padding and cell spacing is a great way to control the distance between elements in your table's cells.

To change the cell padding and cell spacing of your table in either view, just follow these steps:

1. Select the table, and open the Property Inspector (Window > Properties) shown in Figure 6.12.

2. Enter a value (in pixels) into CellPad field to change the table's cell padding.

3. Enter a value (in pixels) into the CellSpace field to change the table's cell spacing.

4. To apply your changes, either press Return/Enter or click anywhere off the Property Inspector in the Document window.

 Note: If you don't have any layout cells in your layout table, your changes will not be visible until some are added.

Changing Table Border Thickness

Back when you set the initial properties of your table, you had control over border thickness. You certainly aren't stuck with your initial decision, it can easily be changed—here's how:

1. Select the table whose border thickness you want to edit.

2. Open the Property Inspector (Window > Properties).

3. Enter a value (in pixels) into the Border field.

   If you want the borders of your table to be invisible, a common strategy for laying out your content is to set the border thickness to 0.

4. To apply the changes, either press Return/Enter or click anywhere off the Property Inspector in the Document window.

Note: Setting the thickness of a table border is a feature available only in Standard view.

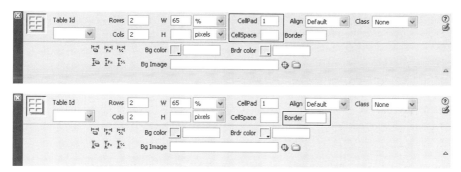

Figure 6.12 Setting cell padding and spacing in (top) Standard view and (bottom) Layout view

Changing Table Border Color

Along with changing a table's border thickness, you can also change the border color as well:

1. Select the table whose border color you want to change.

Note: Changing your table's border color is a feature available only in Standard view.

2. Open the Property Inspector (Window > Properties).

3. Click the Brdr Color swatch to open the Color palette.

4. Click a color. The color of your table's border automatically changes.

Note: If your border thickness is set to 0, changing the border color won't have any visible effect. If you have your border thickness set to more than 0, you'll still be able to see the rows and columns after you've changed the table's background color. If you want your entire table to be one solid color, you can either set your table border thickness to 0 or set your border color to the same color as the background of the table.

Changing Table Background Color

Changing the background color of a table works pretty much the same as changing the background color of your page except that the color is confined to the table itself. If you resize the table (a process you'll look at shortly), the background color will automatically increase to fill the entire table. To change the background color of your table in Standard view, follow these steps:

1. Select the table whose color you want to change. If you are working in Layout view, simply click the layout table's tab.

2. Open the Property Inspector (Window > Properties), shown in Figure 6.13.

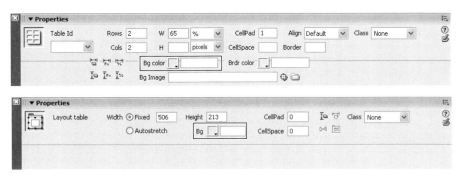

Figure 6.13 Changing a table's background color in (top) Standard view and (bottom) Layout view

3. Click the Bg Color swatch to open the Color palette.

4. Move your cursor over a color you like and click it. The background color of your table automatically changes.

Changing Cell Background Color

While you can change the background color of an entire table (either in Layout view or Standard view), you can also change the background color of individual cells.

To do this, just follow these steps:

1. Select the cell whose color you want to change:

- In Standard view, place your cursor in the cell. Alternatively, you could simply select the entire cell outright (by Ctrl-clicking/⌘-clicking the cell).

- In Layout view, click the edge of the cell. The edge will change color from blue to red when you move your cursor over it.

2. Open the Property Inspector (Window > Properties) shown in Figure 6.14.

3. Click the Bg Color swatch to open the Color palette.

4. Click a color. The background color of the selected cell automatically changes.

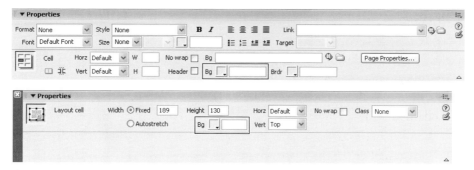

Figure 6.14 Changing background color of a single cell in (top) Standard view and (bottom) Layout view

Adding a Table Background Image

As in the case of your web page, you can add a background image to a table. The only difference, obviously, is that the image is confined to the table itself. If you resize the table (as you'll learn how to do shortly), the background image will automatically fill its increased size. Note that when you add a background image to a table, the image tiles to fit the available space, just as when you add a background image to a web page.

Note: Adding a background image to your table is a feature available only in Standard view.

1. Select the table to which you want to add a background image.
2. Open the Property Inspector (Window > Properties).
3. Click the browse icon to the right of the Bg Image field 📁.
4. When the Select Image Source dialog box appears, locate and select the file you want to use as a background image in your table, and then click OK.

Note: If you have both a background image and a background color set for your table, the background image will always cover the background color.

Importing Tabular Data

As I mentioned before, tables created in Standard view are particularly good for displaying tabular data. The great thing about Dreamweaver MX 2004 is that if you have a tabular document (such as a Microsoft Excel file), you can import it directly into your document and Dreamweaver will automatically re-create the table complete with all of the tabular data.

To import tabular data, make sure you are working in Standard view, and then follow these steps:

1. Place your cursor in the location where you want to import the data.

2. Choose *one* of the following:
    *   Click the Tabular Data button 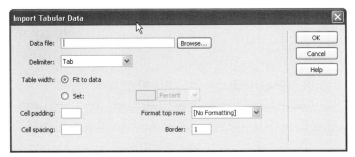 in the Layout section of the Insert bar.
    *   Choose Insert > Table Objects > Import Tabular Data.
    *   Choose File > Import > Tabular Data.

3. After the Import Tabular Data dialog box (Figure 6.15) appears, click the Browse button `Browse...` to the right of the Data File field.

Figure 6.15 The Import Tabular Data dialog box

4. When the Open dialog box appears, locate and select the file you want to import, and then click Open.

5. From the Delimiter drop-down menu, select the specific type of delimiter that was used in the tabular data file you are importing.

 Note: If you do not select the type of delimiter that was used when the file was saved, the table won't be created properly.

6. Set the width of the table—you've got two choices:

    Fit To Data Makes each column wide enough to fit the longest text string in the column.

    Set Specifies a fixed table width in pixels or as a percentage of the browser window's width.

7. Enter values for the Cell Padding and Cell Spacing fields.

8. If you want the first row in your table to be specially formatted, select one of the options from the Format Top Row drop-down menu.

9. Set the table's border thickness by entering a value (in pixels) into the Border field.

10. When you are finished, click OK.

Creating and Manipulating Frames Pages

When you create a frames page, you essentially combine a series of discrete HTML files into one entity that is displayed in a single browser window. Each HTML file is displayed in its own section of the browser window (called a frame) with its own discrete properties. One of the great benefits to using this technique is that different HTML documents can be dynamically loaded into one frame while the content of other frames are maintained within the document. As a result, generally speaking, frames are used to partition a document into several general areas such as content, navigational elements (like buttons), and static material (like banners and logos). You can think of a document that has been partitioned with frames as a television on which several channels are displayed using a split screen. While each channel contains different content, they are all being displayed in the same space (the television screen).

The way each frame looks and behaves is partially controlled by something called a *frameset file*, which is an HTML document that contains all the "guidelines" that set the location, size, and various other properties of each frame. If we were to extend the split-screen television analogy, the frameset file would be the television itself.

Note: To view a frames page with a browser, you load the frameset file, which based on its guidelines, locates and displays the appropriate additional HTML files, which then populate the discrete frames.

When you create a frames page, you are dealing with multiple files. For instance, say you had a page that was broken up into four equal quarters using frames. Not only would you have four HTML files (each of which would be displayed in one of the frames), but you'd also have the frameset file—which is not visible, so you would actually be dealing with five discrete files.

In Dreamweaver MX 2004, there are two ways to partition a single document into several frames. The first, splitting, lets you manually set the number and position of frames in your document. The second method, using the Insert bar, lets you choose from a series of predetermined framesets, each with its own configuration.

Creating a Frames Document by Splitting

The first method of carving your page into a series of frames involves manually splitting it using Dreamweaver's Modify menu.

Note: The following steps will discuss how to create frames in a document with no other existing frames. The process of creating additional frames in a page with an already existing frameset, a nested frameset, will be discussed later.

To do so, just follow these steps:

1. Make sure your cursor is placed in the document you want to split into frames.

2. Choose Modify > Frameset. You have several options; each will carve up your existing document into different frames:

    Split Frame Left Creates two vertically parallel frames, shoving any existing content into the leftmost frame (Figure 6.16).

    Split Frame Right Creates two vertically parallel frames, shoving any existing content into the rightmost frame (Figure 6.17).

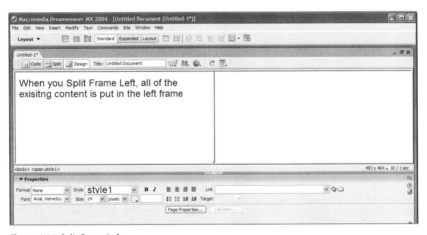

Figure 6.16 Split Frame Left

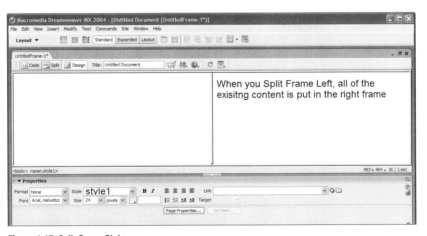

Figure 6.17 Split Frame Right

Split Frame Up Creates two horizontally parallel frames, shoving any existing content into the topmost frame (Figure 6.18).

Split Frame Down Creates two horizontally parallel frames, shoving any existing content into the bottommost frame (Figure 6.19)

3. At this point, you can save your frames page if you want. Later in the chapter, you'll be asked to begin with an already existing frames document, so it might as well be this one.

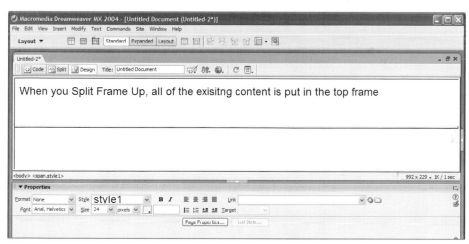

Figure 6.18 Split Frame Up

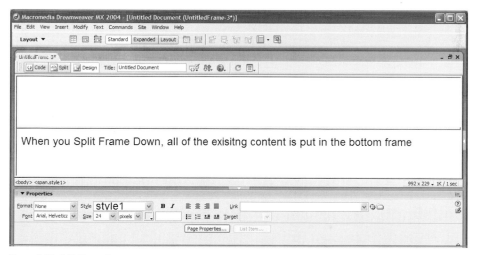

Figure 6.19 Split Frame Down

Note: Saving a frames page is slightly more complicated than saving a regular nonframes page. If you do decide to save the document you created in this section, see the "Saving Frames Pages" section later in this chapter.

Creating a Frames Document from a Preset Layout

The second method of carving a page into frames is by choosing from a group of preset framesets, each of which has its own frame configuration, from the Insert bar:

1. If it isn't already, open the Insert bar (Window > Insert).

Note: When you use the Insert bar to insert a frameset, the frames themselves look slightly differently than they do when you create them manually by splitting. This is primarily because, when you use the Insert bar, the properties of the available options have also been preset, something you'll learn how to do manually later in the chapter.

2. Make sure you are in the Layout section of the Insert bar. Click the Frames button, and select one of the options in the subsequent drop-down menu, which are explained in Table 6.1.

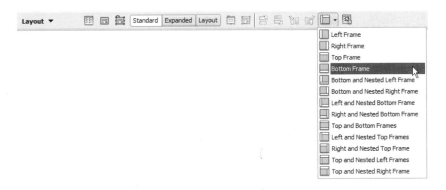

Note: To get a preview of how the preset frameset will look, look at its icon within the Frames drop-down menu. In the icon, the frame that holds any existing content is the one highlighted blue.

3. At this point, you can save your frames page if you want.

► **Table 6.1** Frame layout options

Button	Option	Description
	Left Frame	Your page will be split into two vertical frames: a narrow one along the left and a very wide one along the right. Any existing content will be shifted into the rightmost frame.
	Right Frame	Your page will be split into two vertically parallel frames: a narrow one along the right and a wide one along the left. Any existing content will be moved into the wide frame along the left.
	Top Frame	Your page will be split into two parallel horizontal frames: a narrow one running along the top and a wide one along the bottom. Any existing content will be shifted into the bottom frame.
	Bottom Frame	Your page will be split into two horizontally parallel frames: a narrow one running along the bottom and a wide one running along the top. Existing content will be shifted into the top frame.
	Bottom And Nested Left Frame	Your page will be split into three frames: one narrow frame that runs along the bottom from left to right and two others (one narrow and one wider) that vertically split the area left by the first frame. Any existing content will be shifted into the rightmost of the two vertical frames.
	Bottom And Nested Right Frame	Your page will be split into three frames: one narrow frame that runs along the bottom from left to right and two others (one narrow and one wider) that vertically split the area left by the first frame. Any existing content will be shifted into the leftmost of the two vertical frames.
	Left And Nested Bottom Frame	Your page will be split into three frames: one narrow frame that runs along the left from top to bottom and two others (one narrow and one wider) that horizontally split the area left by the first frame. Any existing content will be shifted into the topmost of the two horizontal frames.
	Right And Nested Bottom Frame	Your page will be split into three frames: one narrow frame that runs along the right from top to bottom and two others (one narrow and one wider) that horizontally split the area left by the first frame. Any existing content will be shifted into the topmost of the two horizontal frames.

Button	Option	Description
	Top And Bottom Frames	You page will split into three horizontal frames: two narrow frames running along the top and bottom and one wider frame running through the middle. All of the page's existing content will be moved into the center frame.
	Left And Nested Top Frames	Your page will be split into three frames: one narrow frame that runs from top to bottom along the left and two others (one narrow and one wider) that horizontally split the area left by the first frame. Any existing content will be shifted into the bottommost of the two horizontal frames.
	Right And Nested Top Frame	Your page will be split into three frames: one narrow frame that runs from top to bottom along the right and two others (one narrow and one wider) that horizontally split the area left by the first frame. Any existing content will be shifted into the bottommost of the two horizontal frames.
	Top And Nested Left Frames	Your page will be split into three frames: one narrow frame running from left to right along the top, one narrow frame running from the bottom of the first frame to the bottom of the window along the left side, and a wider one running from the bottom of the first frame to the bottom of the window along the right side. Any existing content will be shifted in the rightmost vertical frame.
	Top And Nested Right Frame	Your page will be split into three frames: one narrow frame running from left to right along the top, one narrow frame running from the bottom of the first frame to the bottom of the window along the right side, and a wider one running from the bottom of the first frame to the bottom of the window along the left side. Any existing content will be shifted in the leftmost vertically running frame.

Note: A nested frame results from a kind of frameset called a *nested frameset*. For more information on nesting frames and nested framesets, see the following section.

Note: Saving a frames page is slightly more complicated than saving a regular nonframes page. If you do decide to save the document you created in this section, see the section "Saving Frames Pages" later in this chapter.

Nesting Frames

Now you know how to take a fresh page and carve it up into several frames by either splitting it with the Modify menu or using the Insert bar. What if you want to take one of those frames and subdivide it further, creating a more complex frameset? This is where a *nested frameset* comes in. Essentially, a nested frameset is created when you take one of the HTML files occupying one of the previously created frames and convert it to a frameset file, complete with its own frames. This results in a frameset file nested within a frame of another frameset file.

To subdivide a frame into several additional frames (thereby creating a nested frameset), follow these steps:

1. Click anywhere in the frame you want to subdivide. Make sure your cursor is located in the frame before continuing.

2. Use either of the frame-splitting methods described previously to carve the frame into several additional frames.

You can continue to partition frames and create more nested framesets until your page is configured exactly as you want it to be.

Changing Frame Sizes

Frames wouldn't be that useful if you weren't able to resize them. Here's how to resize your existing frame:

1. Move your cursor over the border of the frame that you want to resize. Notice that your cursor will change to two arrows pointing in opposite directions. The directions the cursor arrows point depend on whether the border you've moused over runs horizontally or vertically.

Note: If you move your cursor over the spot where two borders intersect, it will change to four small arrows pointing in the four cardinal directions. If you click and drag (as is described in the next few steps), you'll move both borders, as opposed to just one.

2. When the cursor changes, click and drag the border so that the frame either increases or decreases in size (Figure 6.20). Notice that you get a ghost-like preview of the position of the frame's border as it's dragged.

3. When the border is located where you want and the frame is the size you want, release the mouse button. *Voilà!* Your frame has been resized.

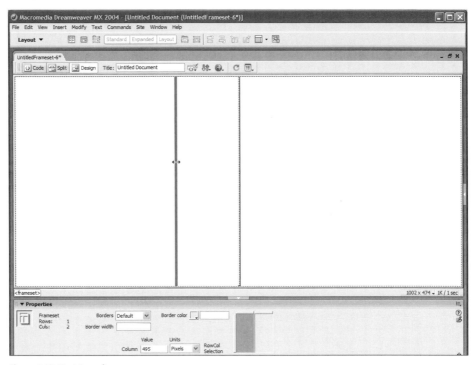

Figure 6.20 Resizing a frame

Deleting Frames

Unfortunately, the process involved in removing individual frames from your document is somewhat counterintuitive. You'd think that you could select the frame in the Frames panel and simply press Delete—unfortunately, it doesn't work that way. When you need to delete a frame, you must drag it out of existence: Move your cursor over the border of the frame that you want to delete, and then click and drag the frame border to the edge of the screen.

Note: If you are dealing with one frameset, you must drag the border to the edge of the screen to delete the frame. However, if you are dealing with nested frames (one frameset embedded within another frameset), you only need to drag the border of the frame that you wish to delete to the edge of the parent frameset.

As you might have guessed, the direction you drag the border determines the frame that is removed. For example, if a page has two horizontally running frames and you click and drag upward, the top frame will be deleted. On the other hand, if you drag downward, the bottom frame will be deleted.

Editing Individual Frames

Each individual frame in your frames document has a set of properties that affect the way in which your document appears. As a result, you should become familiar with them so that you can exert total control over your frames page.

Naming Frames

It's no exaggeration to say that when it comes to working with framesets, assigning names to individual frames is probably one of the most important things you can do. As in many other cases, Dreamweaver creates functional HTML code based on unique names you assign to objects. In the case of frames, a unique name allows you to specify the exact frame in which you want a link to load. For instance, you can have a link in one frame that, when clicked, loads a file into a totally different frame. This is all made possible by a simple process:

1. Open the Frames panel (Figure 6.21) by choosing Window > Frames. This panel contains a miniature schematic of your current frameset. If you created your frameset by splitting, any previously unnamed frames are given a default name of (no name). However, if you created your frameset using the Insert bar, all of your frames are given more specific—yet still generic—names.

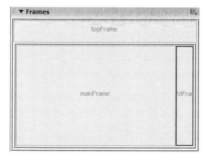

Figure 6.21 The Frames panel

2. In the Frames panel, click the frame that you want to name. When selected, the frame in the Frames panel will be highlighted with a black border.

Note: To select a frame without having to open the Frames panel, you can also Alt+click (Windows) or Option+Shift+click (Mac) anywhere within the frame itself in the Document window.

3. With the frame still selected, open the Property Inspector (Window > Properties). Notice that the Property Inspector displays a bevy of options specific to frame properties.

4. Type a name into the Frame Name field.

Note: It's wise to keep your frame names simple yet descriptive and avoid using spaces or characters other than letters, numbers, periods, dashes, and underscores.

5. When you finish entering the desired name, either click anywhere off the Property Inspector or press Return/Enter. The name of the frame in the Frames panel will update to reflect the change you made.

Changing the Source of a Frame

As you've already learned, a frames page is composed of multiple discrete HTML documents each displayed in individual frames, whose configuration is controlled by the frameset file. When you initially create some frames, Dreamweaver MX 2004 automatically generates most of the HTML files that are displayed. You can go right ahead and add content directly to these files from within the Document window. However, you can also take the HTML files with which Dreamweaver has populated the frames and replace them with already-existing documents. To do this, you need to change the frame source:

1. In the Frames panel (Window > Frames), select the frame whose source you want to change. Remember that when any given frame is selected, it will be displayed with a black border.

2. Open the Property Inspector (Window > Properties).

3. With the frame still selected in the Frames panel, do *one* of the following in the Property Inspector:

   • Type an absolute URL into the Src field.

   • If you want to change the frame's source to a file within your local site (thereby using a relative link), you can click the browse icon to the right of the Src field. When the Select HTML File dialog box appears, locate and select the file to which you want to link.

4. When you finish changing the frame's source, either press Return/Enter or click anywhere off the Property Inspector.

> **Note:** If you are loading an external file (using an absolute URL) into a frame, text will appear in the Document window indicating this, such as, for example, Remote File: http://www.captainprimate.com.

Alternatively, you can change a frame's source directly from within the Document window:

1. In the Document window, click in the frame whose source you wish to change—make sure your cursor is blinking away in the desired frame.

2. Choose File > Open In Frame.

3. When the Select HTML File dialog box opens, navigate to the file you want to stick into the frame, select it, and click Select.

Turning Frame Borders On and Off

By default, the borders in any frames page have a somewhat simulated 3D beveled appearance. While the presence of the border itself might seem desirable when you first start working with frames, you'll quickly find that it serves no serious design function. In fact, in the world of web design, they are pretty undesirable because they break the visual flow of your design. It's in your best interest to learn early on how to turn your borders on and off:

> **Note:** Beyond turning the visibility of frame borders on and off, you can also set the border visibility for an entire frameset (something you'll learn how to do in "Working with Framesets" later in this chapter). However, choosing a border visibility option for individual frames overrides border settings defined for the frameset.

To turn frame borders on and off, just follow these steps:

1. In the Frames panel (Window > Frames), select the frame whose borders you want to turn on or off.

2. If it isn't already, open the Property Inspector and choose one of the options from the Borders drop-down menu: Yes will make the frame's border visible, No

will make the frame's border hidden, and Default will automatically switch the frame's borders to the browser's default (most browsers default to Yes).

3. Repeat step 2 on any frames that share a border with the frame whose border visibility you just manipulated.

Note: If you don't synchronize the border visibility settings on all frames that share a common border, you won't see any change.

Changing Frame Border Color

While frame borders, for the most part, are pretty undesirable, you might feel the need (if they are visible in your creation) to change their color. While the process involved with changing border color is quite easy, the result is often somewhat perplexing. When you change the border color of a given frame, all the borders of that frame (even if they are shared with another frame) will change color. The result is that, while you can change the color of any given frame's border, you run the risk of affecting other, totally unrelated frames.

Note: As with changing a border's visibility, you can change border color for an entire frameset (something you'll learn how to do in "Working with Framesets" later in this chapter) as well as for individual frames. Changes to an individual frame's border color will override any change you make to the entire frameset's border color.

Here's how change a frame's border color:

1. In the Frames panel (Window > Frames), select the frame whose border color you want to change.

2. If it isn't already, open the Property Inspector (Window > Properties).

3. Click the Border Color swatch to open the Color palette. Select the color you want.

Creating Non-Resizable Frames

By default, users will be able to drag the borders of your frames page around in their browser—much like you did when you went through the process of manually resizing frames earlier in this chapter. This is quite annoying and arguably one of the biggest drawbacks of frames. You've spent a great deal of time getting your page to look exactly right; why would you want the user to come along and fiddle with it?

Note: The user can resize frames only if the borders are visible (they have to click and drag the frame border to resize the frame). This means frames whose border visibility has been turned off cannot be resized in the browser.

Don't worry too much, however, because locking your frames so the user can't drag them around is easy:

1. In the Frames panel (Window > Frames), select the frame that you want to lock.

2. If it isn't already, open the Property Inspector (Window > Properties).

3. Select the No Resize check box.

Making Frames Scrollable

A scroll bar is an integral part of any HTML document. As the document's content increases beyond the scope of the browser window, a scroll bar (either vertical or horizontal, depending on the direction in which your content exceeds the browser window) will automatically be added.

Horizontal Scrolling

Because of the way web pages have developed, we have been conditioned to absorb information vertically (from top to bottom). So, while vertical scroll bars are quite common, horizontal scroll bars are usually (unless they are explicitly desired) the mark of bad design.

If you think about a frame as a mini browser window, it's only natural to assume that a frame will react to content in the same way as a window—by adding a scroll bar.

While necessary, however, the frame scroll bar is ironically one of the biggest problems with frames. Think of it this way: If you have three frames, all of which have content that requires scroll bars, you are not only eating up a good chunk of screen real estate, but you are also adding a huge confusion factor for the user. On top of that, it just looks plain messy! Thankfully, in Dreamweaver, you can set whether a given frame gets a scroll bar:

1. In the Frames panel (Window > Frames), select the frame whose scroll bar properties you want to set.

2. If it isn't already, open the Property Inspector (Window > Properties).

3. Choose one of the options from the Scroll drop-down menu.

Yes Will make a scroll bar (both horizontal and vertical) appear in the frame regardless of whether it requires it or not.

No Will make no scroll bar appear in the frame even if it is required. The problem with this is that any content that would normally have to be scrolled down to will be inaccessible to users.

Auto Will automatically force the browser to add a scroll bar only when it is needed.

Default Will let the browser decide whether or not to add a scroll bar based on its own rules—for the most part, the browser default for a scroll bar is auto.

4. To apply your changes, either press Return/Enter or click anywhere off the Property Inspector in the Document window.

> **Note:** Unfortunately, when it comes to scroll bars and frames, it's all or nothing. You either have them or you don't. There is no real way to specify whether you want a horizontal scroll bar but not a vertical one—or vice versa.

Working with Framesets

While each frame has a series of properties you can manipulate, the frameset itself also has properties that can be manipulated. In some cases, such as border visibility, frames and framesets have similar options. However, the difference is that when you set the value of a given frameset property, it overrides individual frame properties.

Before you move forward and explore how you manipulate the properties of a frameset, however, a word needs to be said about how you select the frameset in the Frames panel. Upon close inspection of a frames page in the Frames panel, you'll notice that some of the lines (which serve to either outline or break up frames) are solid, while others have a beveled 3D look. The difference between them is that the solid lines represent the border between frames in the same frameset, while the beveled lines represent the frameset itself.

When you select a regular frame, it is highlighted in black. However, as illustrated in Figure 6.22, when you select a frameset (by clicking the beveled 3D border), it is highlighted in a thicker black line.

> **Note:** The Property Inspector will indicate whether you've selected a frame or a frameset.

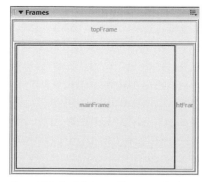 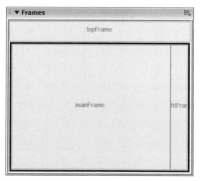

Figure 6.22 The left image illustrates what happens when you select a frame. The image on the right illustrates what happens when you select the frameset—note the darker highlight.

Selecting the frameset in the Frames panel can be a little tricky—especially when the frameset border is sometimes indistinguishable from the inner edge of the Frames panel itself. It's really in your best interest to have an agile mouse finger and become adept at selecting framesets.

Note: You can also select the frameset by clicking on any border within the Document window. This, however, will select only the frameset associated with the selected border. If you have a nested frameset, you'll need to select it manually before you can gain access to its properties.

This having been said, why don't we move forward and explore the various frameset properties with which you can fiddle.

Making Borders Visible or Invisible

As you learned earlier in the chapter, you can easily set the border visibility between frames. So, what exactly is the difference between the visibility of a frame's border and the visibility of a frameset's border? Well, when you set the border visibility of a frameset, all the borders, as opposed to just those associated with the selected frame, are affected.

To set the border visibility for a frameset, follow these steps:

1. In the Frames panel (Window > Frames), select the frameset whose border visibility you want to set. Remember that when a given frameset is selected, it will be displayed with a thick black border (as opposed to the light one displayed when you select an individual frame).

2. If it isn't already, open the Property Inspector (Window > Properties).

3. Choose one of the options from the Borders drop-down menu:

Yes Makes the frameset's border visible.

No Makes the frameset's border lose its 3D beveled look. You will still be left with a small gap (whose default is 6 pixels wide) that will show up as gray in Netscape Navigator and white in Internet Explorer.

Default Automatically switches the frameset's borders to the browser's default—most browsers default to Yes.

> **Note:** To lose the border altogether, not only must you set the border visibility to No, but you also have to set the border width to 0—a process we'll look at shortly.

Setting Frameset Border Thickness

When you are working with a frames document, you have control over the thickness of the border itself.

> **Note:** The default thickness of a frameset's border is 6 pixels—if you set it to anything less than 5, you'll lose the 3D look.

Here's how to set the frameset's border thickness:

1. In the Frames panel (Window > Frames), select the frameset whose border width you want to set. Remember that when a given frameset is selected, it will be displayed with a thick black border (as opposed to the light one displayed when you select an individual frame).

2. If it isn't already, open the Property Inspector (Window > Properties).

3. Enter a value into the Border Width field.

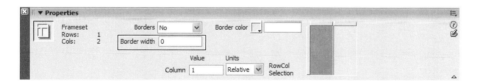

4. When you've entered the desired value, press Return/Enter or click anywhere off the Property Inspector.

Changing Frameset Border Color

Changing the color of a frameset's border is just as easy as setting its visibility. Let's take a look at how:

1. In the Frames panel (Window > Frames), select the frameset whose border you want to change color.

2. If it isn't already, open the Property Inspector (Window > Properties).

3. Click the Border Color swatch to open the Color palette. From there, select the color you want.

Note: As you'd expect, if you have the visibility set to No or the thickness set to 0, changing border color will have absolutely no effect.

Linking to Specific Frames with Targets

One of the great things about working with frames is that, by employing *link targets,* you can create a link in one frame that, when clicked, loads up a file in a totally different frame. This means, for example, that you can create a frames page in which one frame consists of a navigation bar whose elements, when clicked, load different documents into a primary content frame, thereby leaving the frame in which the navigation elements reside completely unchanging.

Note: Back in Chapter 5, we looked briefly at link targets. A link target is an instruction to the browser relating to the location where you want a hyperlink loaded.

Overall, this is a pretty handy technique that is rather easy to put into play. The only caveat is that to successfully create hyperlinks that call files into other frames, you have to have previously named each of your frames in your frameset—a process covered earlier in the section "Naming Frames." Beyond this, the process is about as straightforward as they come:

1. First, make sure you've named all of the frames in your frameset.

2. In one frame, include the hyperlinks (either text or images) that will load the desired HTML documents.

3. Select the hyperlink to the document that you want to load up in another frame.

4. Open the Property Inspector (Window > Properties).

5. With the desired link still selected, open the Target drop-down menu (notice that it's populated not only with the standard link targets, but also with the names of the frames in your frameset), and choose the name of the frame into which you want the document to load.

Note: By default, if you don't set a target for a link when working in a frames document, the file will load in the same frame in which the link itself resides—something you don't necessarily want to happen.

Beyond any named frames, you also have access to four additional link targets in the Target drop-down menu. It's a good idea to become familiar with each:

_blank This option loads the link in a totally new browser window, maintaining the window in which the hyperlink was located just below the newly opened window.

_parent The document, when loaded, will occupy the entire area of the frameset document in which the link resides.

_self The default link target, it opens the document in the frame where the link resides.

_top The document will be loaded into the uppermost (hierarchically speaking) frameset, wiping out all frames and nested framesets.

Saving Frames Pages

It's no great intellectual leap to say that you need to save your pages often! However, when you're working with frames pages, primarily because you are dealing with multiple discrete HTML documents, you need to go through several different steps to get everything safely saved.

The first technique involves manually saving each file (after this procedure, I'll tell you how to save everything all at once):

1. With the frames page open which you want to save, click in the first frame—make sure the cursor is blinking in the frame before you continue.

2. Choose File > Save Frame.

3. When the Save As dialog pops up, enter a filename for the frame into the Filename field, navigate to the location where you want the file to be saved, and click Save.

Note: A frames page can contain anywhere from three to, well, a lot of files, so it's a really good idea to give the HTML file a descriptive filename. This means you'll easily be able to locate and identify any given file in your frameset and edit it independently.

4. Repeat steps 1 through 3 on all the remaining frames in your document.

5. Once you've saved all the frames, you need to save the frameset file itself. To do this, make sure the frames page whose frameset file you want to save is currently open the Document window.

6. In the Frames panel (Window > Frames), select the frameset you want to save.

7. Choose File > Save Frameset.

8. When the Save As dialog pops up, enter a filename for the frameset into the Filename field, navigate to the location where you want the file to be saved, and click Save.

Note: Unless you tell Dreamweaver that the source for the HTML file displayed in any given frame is located in another location (by using the procedure described earlier in "Changing the Source of your Frame"), you'll need to make sure all frames and the frameset file are saved in the same directory.

Manually saving each and every frame can be a little tedious. There is, however, a way in which you can save all the frames in one fell swoop:

1. Make sure the frames page you want to save is open in the Document window.

2. Choose File > Save All.

3. When the Save As dialog pops up, enter a filename for the frame into the Filename field, navigate to the location where you want the file to be saved, and click Save.

4. After you click the Save button, Dreamweaver will prompt you to save the next frame by re-opening the Save As dialog box—repeat the actions in step 3.

5. During the process, Dreamweaver will also prompt you to save the frameset file—you'll be able to tell which prompt refers to the frameset file because the default name assigned in the Save As dialog box will be called UntitledFrame (as opposed to Frame or Untitled).

Note: As you go through the process of saving each frame, the frame currently being saved will be highlighted in the Document window by a hatched border.

Creating Content for Browsers That Don't Support Frames

Although frames are supported by the major browsers out there (Netscape Navigator and Internet Explorer), other browsers don't support them. For the most part, these are text browsers, such as Lynx, but they are used far more widely than one would expect.

If you are trying to deliver your content to the widest audience possible, you need to take these non-frames-enabled browsers into account. Thankfully, Dreamweaver lets you integrate content specifically geared for non-frames-enabled browsers into your frames page. This content, called NoFrames (after its HTML tag) will automatically be loaded by the non-frames-enabled browser when it encounters a frames page.

To add NoFrames content to a frames page, follow these steps:

1. Choose Modify > Frameset > Edit NoFrames Content.

2. Dreamweaver will open a special Document window where you can create the content that will be displayed by a browser that doesn't support frames. Note the there is a bar along the top of the screen indicating that you are currently working on the NoFrames content.

3. Add any content you'd like. Remember, however, that if you are targeting your NoFrames content at a text browser, you'll be limited to text and hyperlinks. If, on the other hand, you are targeting your content at an older browser that is limited only by the fact that it doesn't support frames, you can add images and any other HTML elements that that specific browser supports.

4. When you're finished creating your NoFrames content, choose Modify > Frameset > Edit NoFrames Content to return to the main frames component of the document.

Using Templates, Library Items, and Digital Assets

7

As you've probably figured out by now, web design is a time-consuming process that gets even more time consuming as your sites grow in size and sophistication. To fully realize your site, you need many disparate digital assets such as text, images, and multimedia elements. Any tools that provide you with an efficient manner of streamlining the production process or help you manage your ever-increasing cornucopia of digital elements are definitely a boon. Enter Dreamweaver MX 2004's reusable elements: Library Items, Templates, and other assets. Each provides you with invaluable ways to make time-consuming (and often tedious) website production a far more efficient, effective, and satisfying process.

Chapter Contents

Managing Digital Assets with the Assets Panel

Websites can be composed of lots of stuff: text, images, Flash movies, Shockwave movies, audio files, and digital video files, as well as lots of other less tangible things like colors, scripts, and hyperlinks. When you stop to think about it, the amount of resources you can use creating a website of any significant size is pretty staggering.

Even more staggering is the thought that the larger your web creations get, the more assets you use and the harder it gets to manage them. Short of keeping a running tally of all the colors, hyperlinks, image names and locations, scripts, and Flash files on an enormous piece of paper, it's terribly difficult to keep track of all this stuff. Or is it?

It seems natural that there should be an integrated tool within your visual web design software whose sole task is to help you manage all of your various digital assets. This is exactly what Macromedia created back in Dreamweaver 4, when the Assets panel was introduced. Acting as a central repository for all sorts of digital resources, the Assets panel lets you manage and manipulate many different types of digital assets for an entire Local Site.

Note: Because digital assets are associated with a Local Site, you'll need to define a Local Site (and create a local cache) before the Assets panel will be of any use to you.

In the following sections, I'll show how to manage and manipulate all manner of digital assets using the Assets panel. It is, however, important to note that although Templates and Library Items are digital assets like any other (and are managed using the Assets panel), they are essential enough to the design process to warrant their own unique coverage later in this chapter.

Adding Assets to Your Page

The whole point of the Assets panel is that once a digital asset is used, it can be almost instantly re-accessed and reused without having to go through the steps you underwent the first time it was integrated into the document.

Note: Templates are a special case of asset. See the sections on Templates later in this chapter for details on how to make and apply Templates.

To add assets to a page, follow these steps:

1. Open the Assets panel (Window > Assets).

2. Click the button corresponding to the specific type of asset you would like to add to your page (Figure 7.1).

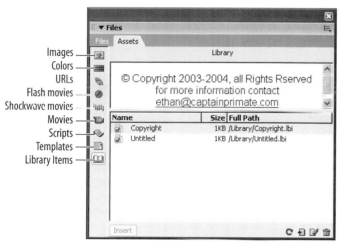

Images
Colors
URLs
Flash movies
Shockwave movies
Movies
Scripts
Templates
Library Items

Figure 7.1 Choose an asset type to display.

3. Select the asset you want to add to the page.

4. At this point, the steps to take differ depending on the type of asset you want to use:

   Images, Flash files, video files, and shockwave files. To add an image, Flash movie, Shockwave movie, digital video, or Library Item to your page, place the cursor where you want to insert the asset. Then either click the Insert button `Insert` or select Insert from the panel options menu. Library Items have special features and are described in much more detail later in this chapter.

   Colors and URLs To apply a color or a URL to something on your page, first select the text or image you want to modify, and then either click the Apply button `Apply` or select Apply from the panel options menu.

Note: Sometimes, even though you have a color selected in the Assets panel and some text or a link selected in the Document Window, the Apply button will be inaccessible. If this happens, select another color and click back to the originally selected color. The Apply button should then be accessible.

Scripts To insert a script, choose View > Head Content to view the location in which scripts reside. Then either click the Insert button [Insert] or select Insert from the panel options menu.

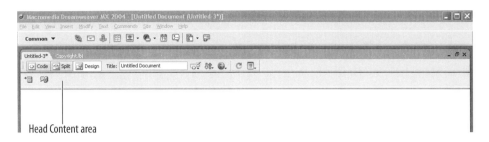

Head Content area

Note: To insert a script into the head section of the HTML document, the Head Content area, located along the top of the Document Window when you choose View > Head Content, must be white (as opposed to the gray color it turns when you click your cursor anywhere within the Document Window's normal working area).

Templates A Template is a document upon which you can base multiple files with the same design. While Templates will be covered in great detail later in this chapter, you can access all of your current Local Site's Templates by clicking the Templates button

Library Item A Library Item is any element (image, text, etc.) or combination of elements that you store in the Library section of the Assets panel for future use. Once stored there, they can be placed on any page without having to re-create them over and over again. While the Library and Library Items will be discussed n detail later in the chapter, you can access them for the Local Site in which you are working by clicking the Library button .

Working with the Favorites List

As your site gets larger, you'll find that the number of assets displayed in the Assets panel can get a little overwhelming. Why wade through a list of colors or images, most of which you've used only once or twice, when you are looking for something you use more frequently? This is where the Favorites list comes into the picture. Essentially, the Favorites list is a catalog of your most commonly used digital assets.

Note: Neither Library Items nor Templates can be added to a Local Site's Favorites list.

To view or work in the Favorites list, open the Assets panel (Window > Assets). If it isn't already selected, click the Favorites radio button ○ Favorites .

Adding and Removing Assets in the Favorites List

The Favorites list will be empty until you manually add digital assets to it.

To add a site's asset to your Favorites list, make sure you are currently in the site list by clicking the Site radio button in the Assets panel. Select the asset you want to add and either click the Add To Favorites List button or choose Add To Favorites List from the panel options menu.

> **Note:** A single item can be added to the Favorites list more than once.

You can easily remove assets from your Favorites list as well. To do so, make sure you are currently in the Favorites list by clicking the Favorites radio button in the Assets panel. Select the asset you want to remove and either click the Remove From Favorites List button or choose Remove From Favorites List from the panel options menu.

Organizing Assets in the Favorites List with Folders

One of the great features of the Favorites list is that you can organize assets into folders:

1. Open the Assets panel (Window > Assets).
2. Make sure you are currently in the Favorites list by clicking the Favorites radio button.
3. Either click the New Favorites Folder button or choose New Favorites Folder from the panel options menu.
4. When the new folder appears, type a title into its name field. When you finish, either click your cursor anywhere off the Assets panel or press Enter/Return.
5. Click and drag any asset into the folder.

Click a folder to expand it (see image below). To collapse an open folder, click it again.

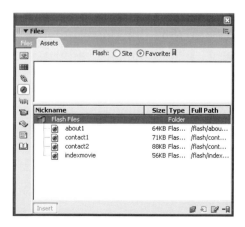

MANAGING DIGITAL ASSETS WITH THE ASSETS PANEL

Copying Favorite Assets to Another Local Site

Just like assets in your regular site list, assets in the Favorites list are bound to a particular Local Site. However, you can easily copy them to the Favorites list of another Local Site:

1. Open the Assets panel (Window > Assets).

2. Make sure you are currently in the Favorites list by clicking the Favorites radio button.

3. Select the asset you want to transfer and select Copy To Site from the panel options menu.

4. Choose the target site from the list of previously defined Local Sites.

    You can copy entire folders from one Local Site's Favorites list to another Local Site's Favorites list.

Editing Assets

Once an asset has been included in the Assets panel, it can easily be changed to suit your needs. There is, however, a little wrinkle you should be aware of when it comes to editing assets. You can edit Flash movies, Shockwave movies, digital video, and images directly from the general site list of the Assets panel. However, URLs and colors must first be added to the Favorites List before they can be edited.

Editing Assets That Require Other Applications

To edit files that require an external editor to manipulate (such as images, Flash movies, Shockwave movies, and digital video), follow these steps:

1. Open the Assets panel (Window > Assets).

2. Select the asset you want to edit and either click the Edit button 📝 or choose Edit from the Assets panel options menu. From here, the external editor for the particular file type opens.

3. Make any changes you want to the file and save it.

4. After you finish, close the external editor.

5. Click the Refresh Site List button ⟳ or select Refresh Site List from the Assets panel options menu.

Editing Dreamweaver-Based Assets

Before editing assets that don't need an external application (such as colors or URLs), you must first add them to the Favorites list. Once you've done that, follow these steps to edit such assets:

1. Open the Assets panel (Window > Assets).

2. Make sure you are working within the Favorites list by clicking the Favorites radio button located along the top of the Assets panel.

3. Select the asset you want to edit and either click the Edit button 📝 or select Edit from the panel options menu.

4. If the asset you selected is a URL, type a new URL into the URL field of the Edit URL dialog box and then type a nickname (if you so wish) into the Nickname field. A nickname is a name you can give to any URL to more easily identify the asset when it appears in the Assets panel.

   If the asset you selected is a color, simply choose a new color from the Color palette. If the color you want is not located in the Color palette, click the Color Wheel icon to open the color picker, where you can mix your own custom color.

5. When you've made the changes to the selected asset, either click the Refresh Site List button or select Refresh Site List from the panel options menu.

Making and Editing Templates

If you are doing your job well as an interactive designer, all of the pages in your site will be closely related variations of the same visual theme. This means you'll be creating page after page with the same basic layout and design. This is especially true with very large websites. The only real distinction between the pages is their content.

Wouldn't it be cool if you could create a framework HTML file and then dump content into it to create each new page? Don't worry; this isn't just wishful thinking. Such a thing exists in Dreamweaver: it's called a Template. A Template is a document upon which you can base multiple files with the same design. When you create a Template in Dreamweaver, you create a web page and define areas that are both editable and uneditable (locked). When the Template is applied to a blank document, the areas that were locked cannot be fiddled with, while the areas that were marked as editable can be filled with any kind of content. One of the best things about Templates (much like Library Items) is that they create a parent/child relationship between the file to which the Template is applied and the Template itself. When you change the parent Template, all of the associated linked documents will automatically update to reflect the changes.

Not convinced about the power of Templates? Here's a real-world example: Say, for instance, that you are part of a web team at a small university. In the effort to update your university's Web presence, the website, which has grown rather haphazardly over the past few years, is to be completely overhauled. One of the primary goals of this endeavor is to bring the websites of all the university's offices and academic departments under the same design umbrella. Without Templates, each person on the web team would have to manually create each department's website after an overall design had been developed. However, with Templates, you only have to create the overall design once, convert it into a Template, and add content, thus guaranteeing a far more streamlined production process. You could also be sure that, because they were all based on the same Template, each department's websites would have the same look—instant design continuity!

 Note: Templates are saved within their own special directory in the local root folder of your Local Site; they are saved as DWT files.

Creating Templates from Scratch

There are actually two different ways to create a Template: from scratch and from an existing document. Which you choose depends completely on your own needs and workflow.

Here's how to create a Template from scratch:

1. Make sure you've got a blank document open in the Document window.
2. Choose Window > Assets and click the Templates button . This gives you access to the Templates section of the Assets panel (Figure 7.2), which should be completely empty.

 Note: When you are working with Templates (as well as with Library Items), you'll be using the Assets panel. In previous versions of Dreamweaver, there was a discrete Templates panel—but not anymore.

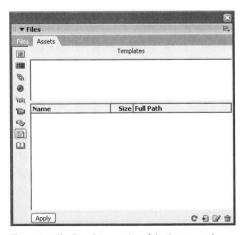

Figure 7.2 The Templates section of the Assets panel

3. Choose New Template from the panel options menu. Alternatively, you can click the New Template button  at the bottom of the Assets panel.

4. A new, blank Template will be added to the Templates section of the Assets panel. Type a name into the Templates' Name field (by default, any new Template is named Untitled). Because this Template is blank, nothing shows up in the preview window (other than directions on how to fill the blank Template).

5. Select the newly created blank Template and either click the Edit Template button or choose Edit from the panel options menu.

6. A new Document Window (we'll call it the Template Editor—it really doesn't have an official name) opens up. This is where you create your Template. The tricky thing is that the Template Editor looks almost identical to any other blank document in a Document window. The only real difference is that the name of the Template appears in the window's title bar as well as in the document's tab.

7. Now you need to create the structure of Template itself. Add images, tables, text, hyperlinks, multimedia—anything you can add to a regular document, you can add to a Template. Remember to think about which areas to make editable and which to leave locked.

Note: The elements you place in a Template are limited to those things normally integrated into the <body> section of an HTML document. This means that Cascading Style Sheets, some behaviors, and timeline-based animations can't be included in your Template because their information is stored in the <head> section of the HTML document.

When you finish creating the structure/design of the Template itself, you need to add editable regions and then save the Template. For the sake of organization, we'll cover these steps in the upcoming sections.

Creating Templates from Existing Documents

While it's quite easy to create a Template from scratch, you may want to turn a document that you've already created (through hours of careful planning and digital sweat) into a Template:

1. Make sure you have the document that you want to convert into a Template open in the Document Window.

2. Choose File > Save As Template; the Save As Template dialog box opens (Figure 7.3).

Figure 7.3 Saving an open document as a Template

3. From the Site drop-down menu, choose the Local Site to which you want to save the Template.

When you change the site you want the Template saved to using the Site drop-down menu, a list of all Templates associated with that particular site will pop up in the Existing Templates list.

4. Type the name for the Template into the Save As field. This name will serve as both the DWT filename and the name listed in the Templates section of the Assets panel.

Note: Remember, Templates are saved in a Templates subfolder (which Dreamweaver MX 2004 creates) in your local root folder as files with a .dwt extension.

5. Click Save.

Note: If the page that you are converting to a Template has some existing links, Dreamweaver will prompt you to update them. Remember, if you do choose to update the links, they will automatically be changed to reflect the path from the Template file to the linked file. If you then apply that Template (something we'll talk about shortly) to another file in another location, you are going to have to go through and check all of your links to make sure they work (and possibly manually change them)

6. The Template will automatically open up in the Template Editor, and you'll be able to set editable and locked regions (something we'll discuss in the following section).

Adding Editable Regions to Templates

Once you create the actual Template (either from scratch or by converting an existing document), you need to set the regions that will be editable when the Template is applied to a page. It's no exaggeration to say that editable regions are the heart of any Template.

Note: Remember to mark any areas you want to work with in a Template as editable. By default, any area that you don't mark as editable will be locked when the Template is applied to a document. Locked regions, whether they contain text, images, or any other combination of elements, cannot be manipulated in any way, shape, or form—that is, they can't be deleted, moved, or changed.

Follow these steps to set editable regions in a Template:

1. With the Template open in the Template Editor, select the components (text, images, and so on) that you want to make editable.

2. Choose Insert > Template Objects > Editable Region.

3. When the New Editable Region dialog box (Figure 7.4) appears, type a unique name for the editable region into the Name field. You cannot use angled brackets (<>), single or double quotation marks (' "), or ampersands (&) in an editable region name. The name is used by Dreamweaver to label the editable regions in a document to which the Template has been applied.

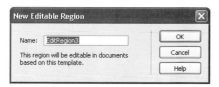

Figure 7.4 Creating an editable region

4. After you've entered a name for the new editable region, click OK. You'll notice that, in the Template Editor, the object (whether it be a block of text, an image, or some other element) that you converted into an editable region is surrounded by a thin border attached. Attached to the border is a tab with the region's name (Figure 7.5).

> **Text Region**
> Lorem ipsum dolor sit amet, consectetuer adipiscing elit. Donec purus massa, bibendum nec, interdum et, scelerisque ac, lacus. Duis ullamcorper, odio vel laoreet aliquet, sapien lorem euismod mi, quis hendrerit velit mauris pulvinar justo. In accumsan nonummy risus. Praesent pharetra ante eu leo. Maecenas leo. Aenean laoreet egestas lectus. Aenean eget eros vitae nunc semper pellentesque. Nunc mattis luctus quam. Nam auctor nonummy ante. Curabitur a tortor nec orci cursus viverra. Duis tellus. Pellentesque habitant morbi tristique senectus et netus et malesuada fames ac turpis egestas. Suspendisse sapien. Mauris venenatis leo id nisl. Sed vitae pede a lacus aliquam dictum. Suspendisse potenti. Sed id massa vel ante ornare convallis. Donec mauris sem, varius eget, facilisis nec, ullamcorper sed, nunc. Sed nibh sem, dictum consectetuer, facilisis et, hendrerit quis, diam.

Figure 7.5 In the Template Editor, editable regions are surrounded by a border. In addition, a tab indicates the editable region's name.

While these steps cover the process of creating editable regions based on existing blocks of text or other elements, you can just as easily create an empty editable region. An empty editable region will appear blank and ready to be filled with content when the Template is applied to a document. A filled editable region, on the other hand, will include the elements you originally selected when you first created the Template in the Template Editor. But don't worry—even if the filled version of an editable region includes some text or other objects, they can be easily deleted when the Template is applied to a document.

To create an empty editable region, follow these steps:

1. With the Template open in the Template Editor, place your cursor in the area where you want the editable region to be located.

2. Choose Insert > Template Objects > Editable Region.

3. When the New Editable Region dialog box appears, type a unique name for the editable region into the Name field. The name is used by Dreamweaver to label the editable regions in a document to which the Template has been applied.

Adding Optional Regions to Templates

An optional region is a section of a Template that is designated to hold content that may or may not appear in the final document.

There are two kinds of optional regions. The first, a regular optional region, contains content that the content author (not the person who originally created the Template) can set as visible or invisible in the final Template-based document. The second type of optional region, the editable optional region, contains content that can be edited by the content author.

Let's take a look at a simple example. Say a designer creates a generic Template that has content that, depending on its subject, may or may not be appropriate for a specific page. However, the Template designer doesn't want the person in charge of adding the content to have to manually add any generic content to the page. So, the Template designer loads all of the generic content into the page's optional regions, thereby allowing the person in charge of adding the content to pick and choose which they want visible. If, on the other hand, the Template designer wanted the content author to be able to edit any of these blocks of generic content to the page, they could place them in *editable* optional regions.

Here's how to create an optional region:

1. With the Template open in the Template Editor, select the element (text, images, and so on) that you want to be optional or place your cursor in the area where you want the optional region to be located.

2. Choose Insert > Template Objects > Optional Region or Editable Optional Region.

3. When the New Optional Region dialog box (Figure 7.6) appears, type a unique name for the optional region into the Name field. The name is used by Dreamweaver to label the editable regions in a document to which the Template has been applied.

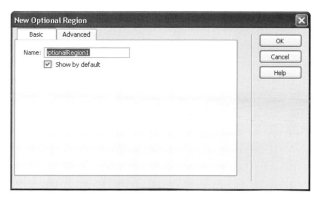

Figure 7.6 Creating an optional region

4. If you want the region to automatically be visible (as opposed to being hidden by default), click the Show By Default option.

Note: The options under the Advanced tab let you set the parameters of the optional region—a topic about which you can find out more by clicking the Help button in the New Optional Region dialog box.

5. Click OK.

Adding Repeating Regions or Tables

A repeating region lets you designate areas of your Template for content that repeats.

There are two kinds of repeating regions that you can create. The first, a regular repeating region, is a section of content that can be duplicated as often as desired in the final Template-based page. The kicker about a regular repeating region is that it cannot be edited unless the Template author has included an editable region within it. The second type of repeating region, a repeating table, is a table in which editable regions automatically occupy the individual cells.

Follow these steps to create a regular repeating region:

1. With the Template open in the Template Editor, select the elements (text, images, and so on) that you want to set as a repeating region or place your cursor in the area where you want the repeating region to be located.

Note: Elements that already appear in an editable region cannot be selected.

2. Choose Insert > Template Objects > Repeating Region.

3. When the New Repeating Region dialog box (Figure 7.7) appears, type a unique name for the repeating region into the Name field.

Figure 7.7 Creating a repeating region

4. Click OK.

To create a repeating table, follow these steps:

1. With the Template open in the Template Editor, place your cursor in the area where you want the repeating table to be located.

 Note: A repeating table cannot be placed in a region already designated as editable.

2. Choose Insert > Template Objects > Repeating Table to open the Insert Repeating Table dialog box (Figure 7.8).

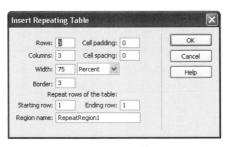

Figure 7.8 Creating a repeating table

3. Configure the table by filling in the number of rows and columns, the amount of cell padding and cell spacing, the table width, and the border thickness in pixels. Remember that you can set whether the table's size is represented in pixels or as a percentage of the web page's width.

4. Define which rows in the table are included in the repeating region. To do this, enter the row where the repeating region will start into the Starting Row field, and enter the last row to be included in the table's repeating region into the Ending Row field.

5. Finally, enter a name for the repeating element into the Region Name field.

6. Click OK.

Making Specific Tag Attributes Editable in a Template

Beyond entire areas, images, or blocks of text, you can also make the attributes of specific tags editable in your Templates. For example, what if you want an image in your Template to be editable but you want whatever image is used to be the exact same dimensions of the one you originally inserted in the Template? Well, you could set the image's src attribute as editable while leaving its width and height attributes uneditable—pretty snazzy, huh?

To make a specific attribute of a tab editable, just follow these steps:

1. Select an item whose tag you want to set an editable attribute for. Alternatively, you can select the specific tag from the Tag Selector.

2. From there, choose Modify > Templates > Make Attribute Editable to open the Editable Tag Attributes dialog box (Figure 7.9).

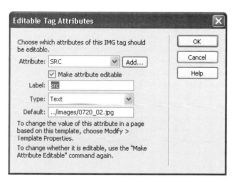

Figure 7.9 Choose the tag attribute you want to make editable.

3. Select the specific attribute you want to make editable from the Attribute drop-down menu.

4. Check the Make Attribute Editable check box.

5. Enter a unique identifier for the editable attribute into the Label field.

6. In the Type pop-up menu, select the specific type of value allowed for this attribute from the following options:

   • If you want the user to be able to enter a text value for the attribute, select Text. For example, you can use the Text option in concert with the align attribute. By doing this, the user can then set the attribute's value to "left", "right", or "center".

- To attach a link to an element, such as the path to an image, select URL.
- If you want a color picker to be available to the user, select Color.
- To allow a user to enter a numerical value for an attribute (such as the the height or width values of an image), select Number.

 Note: Choosing URL from the Type drop-down menu allows Dreamweaver MX 2004 to automatically update the path used in a link. If the user moves the image to a new folder, the Update Links dialog appears, prompting them to enter the updated path.

7. The Default text box displays the value of the selected tag attribute in the Template. Enter a new value in this text box to set a different initial value for the attribute in the Template-based document.

8. When you are finished, click OK.

Changing the Template Region Highlight Colors

When a Template is applied to a page, each individual editable region is highlighted in pale green in Dreamweaver. In addition, the entire document is highlighted in pale yellow. Although this is a superficial property, you can easily change these colors to suit your own tastes. Here's how:

1. Choose Edit > Preferences.

2. Select Highlighting from the Category list (Figure 7.10).

3. Click the Editable Regions Color swatch to open the Color palette. From there, select the color in which you want your editable regions highlighted.

4. Click the Locked Regions Color swatch to open the Color palette. From there, select the color in which you want your locked regions highlighted.

5. If you don't want your editable or locked regions highlighted, uncheck the Show option (to the right of the Editable Regions and the Locked Regions fields).

 Note: Turning off the highlighting in a Template is usually not the best idea because the color helps show that a given element is an editable region. These kind of indications help you keep a handle on the design process, especially if you are working on a large site.

6. Click OK.

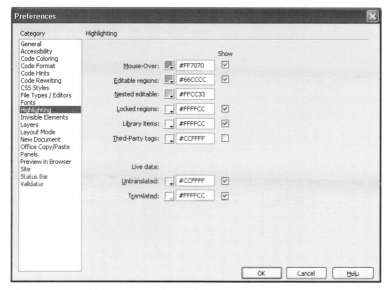

Figure 7.10 The Highlighting section of the Preferences dialog box

Editing Existing Templates

Once you've created a Template, it wouldn't do you much good if you weren't able to go back and edit it. To edit a Template, just follow these steps:

1. Make sure you are currently working in the Local Site where the Template you wish to edit is located.

2. Choose Window > Assets and click the Templates button .

3. Select the Template you wish to edit and choose one of the following options:

   - Click the Edit button .
   - Choose Edit from the panel's options drop-down menu.
   - Double-click the selected Template.

4. The Template opens in the Template Editor, where you can make any changes you wish to make, including adding additional editable or optional regions.

5. When you finish editing the Template, choose File > Save and then File > Close.

6. As soon as you resave the Template, Dreamweaver will prompt you to choose whether you want to update all the documents based on the Template.

Saving and Managing Templates

After you've actually created a Template with editable regions, you need to save it. Remember, when you save a Template, it is stored as a DWT file in the Template directory located in your site's local root folder.

Follow these steps to save a Template:

1. Make sure the Template you want to save is open in the Template Editor.

2. Choose File > Save As Template.

3. When the Save As Template dialog box (Figure 7.11) appears, select the site to which you want the Template saved from the Site drop-down menu. Remember that when you select a site, its Templates will appear in the Existing Templates list box.

Figure 7.11 Saving a Template (There are two Templates here Home Template and Home.)

4. Enter the name of the Template in the Save As field.

5. Click Save.

6. After saving the Template, choose File > Close to return to the main Document window.

> **Note:** If you save a Template without setting any editable regions, you'll get a warning about possible dire consequences. Actually, the consequences aren't that dire. If you apply the Template to a page, you won't be able to add any content. However, it's remarkably easy to go back and edit the Template so that it has some editable regions.

Renaming Templates

As your digital creation gets larger, you'll probably accumulate more and more Templates, so it's a good idea to give each a fairly descriptive name. As the size of your site increases, your plans might change and you might need to rename an existing Template. To rename your Template, follow these steps:

1. Make sure you are currently working in the Local Site in which the Template you wish to edit is located.

2. Choose Window > Assets and click the Templates button 📄 .

3. Select the Template you wish to rename and either choose Rename from the panel options menu or click the Template's name.

4. When the name field becomes editable, type a new name.

5. When you finish typing the name, press Enter (Win)/Return (Mac) or click anywhere off the Templates section of the Assets panel.

Deleting Templates

Templates are files that are saved in a special directory in your Local Site's root folder. As such, they do take up a certain amount of memory, though it's pretty insignificant in the grand scheme of things. Still, it's worthwhile, for the sake of both organization and space conservation, to keep the Templates in the Templates section of the Assets panel limited only to those that are in use. Here's how to delete a Template:

1. Make sure you are currently working in the Local Site where the Template you wish to delete is located.

2. Choose Window > Assets and click the Templates button 🖹 .

3. Select the Template you wish to delete and either click the Delete button 🗑 or select Delete from the panel options menu.

4. When prompted, select Yes if you want to delete the Template and No if you don't.

Once you've deleted a Template from the Templates section of the Assets panel, you cannot undo the action with the Edit > Undo command—it's a permanent deletion. The funny thing is that documents that were based on a deleted Template retain the structure and editable regions that the Template had before it was deleted.

Copying Templates to Another Local Site

All Templates are unique to a given Local Site. However, there will probably be a point when you'll want to use a certain Template in another existing Local Site. There are a couple ways to do this. You can copy the actual Template's DWT file to the Templates subfolder in the intended Local Site's root folder, but this can be cumbersome. To copy a Template more efficiently, follow these steps:

1. Make sure you are currently working in the Local Site that contains the Template you want to transfer to another Local Site.

2. Choose Window > Assets and click the Template button 🖹 .

3. Select the Template you want to transfer.

4. Select Copy To Site from the panel options menu, and then choose the target site from the list of previously defined Local Sites. The selected Template will automatically be copied to the target site's Templates folder.

If you copy a Template that has hyperlinks relative to the Local Site in which it was originally created, they won't work properly in the Local Site to which it is copied.

Using Templates

So, you've gone to all the trouble of creating a Template, and now it's time to start using them. In this section, you'll explore how to apply a Template to a blank page, how to create a page based on a Template from scratch, how to apply a Template to an existing page, and how to detach a Template from a page.

Applying Templates to Blank Pages

Follow these steps to apply a Template to a page:

1. Open a blank document in the Document window.
2. Choose Window > Assets and click the Templates button 🗋.
3. Select the Template you wish to apply to the document and choose from the following options:
   - Click the Apply button [Apply].
   - Choose Apply from the panel options menu.
   - Click and drag the Template from the Templates section of the Assets panel into the Document window.
4. The Template, complete with editable regions, will be automatically applied to the blank document. Note that the editable regions are contained within a colored border identified by a unique name.

Creating Template-Based Pages from Scratch

Now that you've learned how to apply a Template to a blank document, let's look at how to create a Template-based page from scratch:

1. Choose File > New.
2. When the New Document dialog box appears, click the Templates tab.
3. From the Templates For list box (Figure 7.12), select the specific Local Site from which you want to draw the Template.
4. After you select the site, you'll notice that the list box to the right of the Template For list box (whose name is dynamically generated based on the site you selected) is populated with all of the Templates for that site. Select the one you want to use. A preview of the Template will appear in the Preview section of the New Document dialog box.
5. Click the Create button [Create].

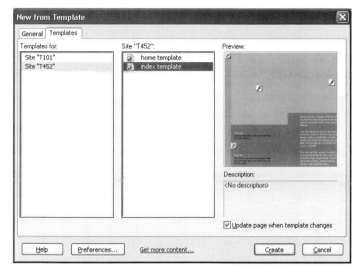

Figure 7.12 Creating a new document based on a Template

Applying Templates to Pages with Existing Content

You don't have to start off with a blank document when applying a Template—you can also apply one to an existing document. The real difference is that you need to figure out what happens to the page's existing content—something that is managed by the Inconsistent Region Names dialog box.

Let's take a look at how to apply a Template to a page with existing content:

1. Open the existing document to which you want to apply the Template.

2. Choose Modify > Templates > Apply Template To Page.

3. When the Select Template dialog box opens (Figure 7.13), choose the Local Site where the Template you want to use is located from the Site drop-down menu.

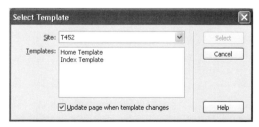

Figure 7.13 Select the Template you want to apply to your document.

4. After selecting a site, a list of Templates for that Local Site will appear in the Templates list; select the appropriate one.

5. If you want the page to update when the Template itself changes, select the Update Page When Template Changes option.

6. Click Select.

7. When the Inconsistent Region Names dialog box opens (Figure 7.14), choose the regions into which you want to place the document's existing content.

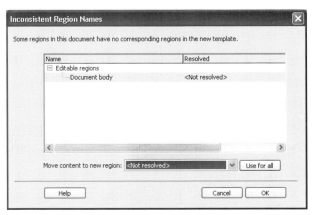

Figure 7.14 The Inconsistent Region Names dialog box allows you to tell Dreamweaver how to handle existing content when a Template is applied.

8. If you aren't interested in keeping the page's existing content, choose Nowhere from the Move Content To New Region drop-down menu and it will be all discarded.

9. Click OK. The Template will be applied to the existing document.

Detaching Pages from Templates

As I'm sure you've noticed, once you apply a Template to a page, the editable/locked regions that you define severely limit what you can do. This is part of the point of a Template. However, there will probably be a point when you decide that you want to change the editable/locked regions you initially defined in a Template. To do this, you much detach the page in question from the Template: Just open the page, and choose Modify > Templates > Detach From Template. The page will automatically detach from its parent Template, thereby making all areas editable.

Creating and Manipulating Library Items

As your websites get larger and larger, you'll incorporate more and more digital assets: more text, more hyperlinks, more multimedia, and more images. You'll also find that

many of these elements get used over and over again. Whether it's a copyright statement or a logo that appears on every page, creating (and re-creating) these repeating
elements every time they need to be employed can get very tiresome. This is where the
Library comes in—and, no, we're not talking about books and late fines.

Dreamweaver's Library, although it is called by that name, is actually just an
aspect of the Assets panel. Open the Library by choosing Window > Assets and then
clicking the Library button .

Essentially, the Library is a central repository in which you can place any object
for future use. What's supremely cool about anything you place in the Library (called
Library Items) is that they can be any object (or combination of objects) you can place
in a Dreamweaver document.

Note: The only real limitation is that you can include only elements that would appear in the <body>
section of the HTML document into a Library Item. This means Timelines, Cascading Style Sheets, or behaviors
(because they are associated with the <head> section of the HTML document) cannot be Library Items.

Once you've converted something into a Library Item, the element can be easily
added to any page within the Local Site, thereby avoiding the need to manually re-create the element. For example, say you have a copyright statement that you have to add
to every page in a large site. Retyping it each time is a lengthy and time-consuming
process, even if the copyright statement itself is short. You also run the risk of mistyping something and introducing errors into your creation. If you use the Library, however, all you have to do is type out the copyright statement once, convert it to a Library
Item, and then add it to each desired page with a click of a button.

If the Library *only* served this purpose, it would still be quite useful. However, it
has some additional valuable uses. Whenever you add a Library Item to a
Dreamweaver document, it maintains a special parent/child relationship with its counterpart in the Library. Essentially, each Library Item (the child) in a document is really
just a representation (an instance) of its parent in the Library. As such, it is locked and
cannot be directly edited. However—and here comes the cool part—all instances of any
given Library Item in your Local Site can be changed by changing its parent in the
Library. For example, referring back to the copyright statement example, say you created a large site in which each page contains a copyright statement that is an instance
of a Library Item. The copyright statement, as most copyright statements do, contains
a date. What happens when the year changes and you need to update the date? Well,
because you created the copyright statement as a Library Item, all you need to do is

change the parent in the Library. All the associated children throughout your Local Site or Templates will automatically change.

Note: While my example sticks to the simplest use of the Library, you are not limited to turning simple text into a Library Item. You can turn an entire paragraph in which there are images and multimedia files into a Library Item—any element or combination of elements that you plan on using repeatedly can and should be turned into a Library Item.

Library Items are saved to a special directory (called Library) in the local root folder of your Local Site. Each exists as a discrete file with a .lbi extension. If you want to move a Library Item from one Local Site to another, simply copy the appropriate file and paste it into the Library folder in the target Local Site.

Making Library Items from Scratch

When you create a Library Item from scratch, you'll be working directly from within the Library itself.

Since Library Items are stored within the directory in the local root folder of a Local Site, you'll need to be working within a Local Site before you can create them. All of the examples in this chapter assume that you have already created and are working from a Local Site.

Follow these steps to create a Library Item from scratch:

1. Open the Library by choosing Window > Assets and then clicking the Library button 📖 .

2. When the Library section of the Assets panel pops up (it should be blank if you haven't created any Library Items for that Local Site), choose New Library Item from the panel's options menu or click the New Library Item button ⊞ .

3. A new (blank) Library Item will be added to the Library (Figure 7.15). Type a name into the Library Item's Name field (by default, any new Library Item is named Untitled). Because this Library Item is blank, nothing shows up in the preview window (besides directions on how to "fill" the blank Library Item.)

4. To "fill" the blank Library Item, select it and either click the Edit Library Item button 🖉 or choose Edit from the panel's options menu.

5. A new Document window (we'll call it the Library Item Editor—though, like the Template Editor, it really doesn't have an official name) opens up. The Library Item Editor looks very similar to the regular Document window—the only difference, which is slight, is that the name of the Library Item is displayed in the title bar and the document tab. (Figure 7.16). This is where you'll create the Library Item itself.

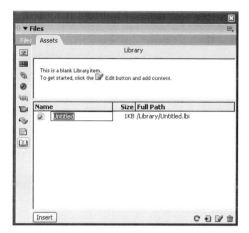

Figure 7.15 Name your new Library Item.

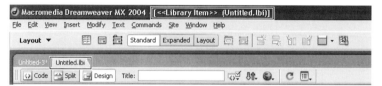

Figure 7.16 The Library Item Editor, which looks similar to the regular Document Window (except for the name of the Library Item displayed in the title bar and the document tab), is where you'll create Library Items.

6. With the Library Item Editor open, use any of Dreamweaver's tools to create the Library Item itself. Remember that you can use any element or combination of elements.

7. When you finished composing the Library Item, choose File > Save. The Library Item will automatically be saved to the Library directory of your Local Site's local root folder.

8. Choose File > Close to exit the Library Item Editor and return to the main Document window. Notice that when you now select the newly created Library Item in the Library, you see a preview in the Library's preview window.

Turning Existing Page Elements into Library Items

In addition to creating a Library Item from scratch, you can also take an existing element (or combination of elements) in your document and convert it into a Library Item. This is a useful technique, particularly if you have existing content you would like to add to a Library.

Follow these steps to convert an existing page element into a Library Item:

1. In the Document window, select the element (or elements) that you want to convert to a Library Item and open the Library (Window > Assets and click the Library button 📖).

2. Choose one of the following options to convert the selected elements into a Library Item:

    *   With the element (or elements) still selected, click the New Library Item button ⊞ .

    *   Drag the selected element (or elements) from the Document window into the Library.

    *   With the element (or elements) still selected, choose Modify > Library > Add Object To Library.

3. Type a name into the Library Item's Name field (by default, any new Library Item is named Untitled).

Renaming Library Items

It's quite possible that during the production of your digital marvel, you'll want to rename one (or perhaps more) of the items in your Local Site's Library. The process is quite easy:

1. Open the Library (Window > Assets and click the Library button 📖).

2. Select the Library Item whose name you wish to change and either choose Options > Rename or click the item's name.

3. When the Library Item's name becomes editable, type in a new one.

4. When you finish entering the new name, press Enter/Return or click your cursor anywhere off the Library.

Editing Library Items

After you've created a Library Item, you can easily go back and edit it. Here's how:

1. Open the Library (Window > Assets and click the Library button 📖).

2. Select the Library Item you want to edit and choose from one of the following options:

    *   Click the Edit Library Item button 📝 .

    *   Select Edit from the Library's options menu.

    *   Double-click the Library Item (either on its preview or its actual name).

3. The Library Item Editor opens. Make any changes you want to the Library Item.

4. When you finish making your changes in the Library Item Editor, choose File > Save.

5. Dreamweaver asks whether you want to update all the edited Library Item's instances. You have two choices:

   - If you want to update all the instances of the Library Item in the entire Local Site, click Update.

   - If you do not want to update all the instances of the Library Item, click Don't Update.

   While choosing Update will automatically change all the edited Library Item's instances throughout your Local Site, what if you clicked Don't Update and later decided you did want to update? Just choose Modify > Library > Update Current Page to update all the instances only on the currently open page, or choose Modify > Library > Update Pages (which will open the Update Pages dialog box) to update all the instances in the entire Local Site.

Note: Remember, the instances of Library Items on your page have a relationship with their "parent" in the Library. When you change the parent, all of the children will change accordingly.

Deleting Library Items

As your site gets larger and larger, you will probably accumulate more and more Library Items. Some Library Items are bound to fall out of use and become obsolete. Even though they take up very little space in the overall scheme of things, Library Items are files that are saved in a directory in the local root folder of your Local Site. As a result, if you are particularly storage-space conscious, you should always make sure your Library doesn't contain any unused items.

Note: Another good reason for keeping your Library stocked only with those items currently in use is purely organizational: as your site gets larger and your Library Items increase, the sheer number of Library Items can get confusing. Keeping your Library neat and up-to-date can save you a lot of grief.

To delete items from your Library, follow these steps:

1. Open the Library (Window > Assets and click the Library button).

2. Select the Library Item you want to delete and either choose Delete from the Library's options menu or click the Delete Library Item button 🗑 .

3. At the prompt, select Yes if you want to delete the item or No if you don't.

> **Note:** When you delete an item from the Library, the instances that you added to your document(s) are unaffected.

Copying Library Items to Another Local Site

All Library Items are unique to a given Local Site, but there will probably be a point when you'll want to use a certain Library Item in another Local Site. There are a couple ways to do this. You can copy the actual Library Items LBI file to the Library sub-folder in the intended Local Site's local root folder, but this can be cumbersome. To copy a Library Item more efficiently, follow these steps:

1. If you aren't already, make sure you are currently working in the Local Site that contains the Library Item you want to transfer to another Local Site.

2. Open the Library (Window > Assets and click the Library button) and select the Library Item you want to transfer.

3. Select Copy To Site from the Library's options menu and choose the target site from the list of previously defined Local Sites. The selected Library Item will automatically be copied to the target site's Library folder.

Changing the Library Item Highlight Color

When it's inserted into a page, the Library Item is highlighted in pale yellow. Here's how to change the color:

1. Choose Edit > Preferences.

2. Select Highlighting from the Category list.

3. Click the Library Items Color swatch to open the Color palette. From there, select the color in which you want your Library Items highlighted.

4. Click OK.

If you don't want your Library Items highlighted, uncheck the Show option (to the right of the Library Items color field). However, this is not the best idea because the color helps show that a given element is a Library Item. These kinds of indications help you keep a handle on the design process, especially if you are working on a large site.

Applying Library Items to a Page

The whole point of Library Items is that they are to be used in a document in order to save your precious time and energy. After you've created a Library Item (either from scratch or from an existing element), it's simple to add it to your document:

1.   Open the Library (Window > Assets and then click the Library button 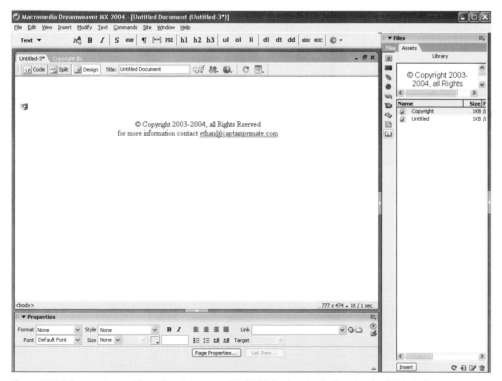).

2.   In the Document window, place your cursor in the location where you wish the Library Item to be inserted.

3.   In the Library, select the item you wish to insert and choose one of the following options:

   •   Click the Insert button [Insert].

   •   Choose Insert from the Library's options menu.

   •   Click and drag the Library Item from the Library into the Document window.

Once inserted into the document, the Library Item is locked (Figure 7.17); the only actions you can take are to change its position within the Document window or delete it. To edit the Library Item, you'll either have to edit its parent or detach it from the Library.

Figure 7.17 When you insert a Library Item into a page, it is highlighted—thereby denoting that it is locked.

Detaching Items from the Library

By this time, I'm sure you've caught on to the fact that if you change the parent Library Item, all the associated children scattered throughout your Local Site will update to reflect the change. This is an all or nothing kind of process. Unfortunately, it's quite impossible to be selective about which instances are updated. This can be rather frustrating if you find yourself in a situation where you want some but not all of the instances to be updated. Never fear; Dreamweaver features a manageable workaround for this problem. Essentially, individual instances of a Library Item can be detached from their parent, thereby making them fully editable. The drawback to this is that once they are detached, they are no longer included in the sweeping update that occurs when you make changes to their former parent.

Here's how to detach an instance from its parent in the Library:

1. With the document open, select the instance that you want to detach from its parent. (Remember, you can't select subitems within the instance, so the entire instance will be selected.)

2. Open the Property Inspector (Window > Properties).

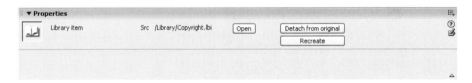

3. Click the Detach From Original button. Now, because the item has reverted back to being "normal," you are free to make any changes you want to the former Library Item.

Adding Multimedia

The Web has developed into a medium in which a veritable cornucopia of exciting media can be used to fashion your interactive creation. Whether you want to create a stunning visual experience with Flash, a serious (or fun) interactive application with Shockwave, a rich audio experience with any given sound format, or a marvelous digital video event with QuickTime, the options available for adding that extra oomph to your HTML creation are quite numerous.

In this chapter, you'll explore how to use Dreamweaver to integrate the myriad available multimedia formats into your HTML creation.

Chapter Contents

Adding Flash Movies

There is little doubt that Flash is one of the coolest things to come down the pipe in terms of web design in…well…ever. Essentially, Flash, the file format, started out life a few years back as a simple vector animation tool. Because vector-based images are described using mathematical equations (as opposed to bitmap images, which are composed of individual pixels whose color and position take up a fixed amount of computer memory), they are very small (in terms of file size) and appear incredibly crisp and clean. In addition, they can be resized without any image degradation (something that is impossible with bitmaps). All of these characteristics make vectors a wonderful medium to produce animations of all kinds, which is what Macromedia Flash was originally designed for.

Several years and several software versions later, Flash (which is the name of both the authoring program and the format it produces) has evolved enormously. No longer is Flash suited just for simple vector animations; it is now pretty much the de facto standard for producing highly interactive and visually stunning interactive experiences for delivery both on and off the Web.

Flash has opened up a new world (nay, a new universe) of possibilities for interactive designers. While it would be unfair (and inaccurate) to say that Flash is the future of the Web, it's pretty safe to say that it's *one* of the futures of the Web. Anyone interested in breaking free of the (many) creative constraints of HTML would be wise to roll up their sleeves and dive into Macromedia Flash as soon as possible.

 Note: For those excited about the possibilities of Macromedia Flash, check out *Flash MX 2004 Savvy* by Ethan Watrall and Norbert Herber (Sybex, 2003)…wink, wink.

Now that I've gotten you all worked up about the power and possibilities of Macromedia Flash, let's take a look at how to work with Flash files in Dreamweaver. I will first discuss how you go about inserting a Flash file and will go on to explore how you set that file's properties.

Flash is not natively supported by web browsers. To view a Flash movie (either on or off the Web), you must have Flash Player installed on your computer. It's a relatively small plug-in for both Mac and Windows that's available on the book's accompanying CD-ROM and is also downloadable from the Macromedia website (www.macromedia.com/downloads).

Demo copies of the two newest versions of Flash (yes, there are two of them), Flash MX 2004 and Flash MX Professional 2004, have also been included on this book's CD-ROM.

Flash Inspiration

For some great examples of what you can do with Flash, check out these websites:

www.becominghuman.org

www.djojostudios.com

www.digitalorganism.com

www.mnh.si.edu/africanvoices

www.rustboy.com

www.xl5designs.com

www.daringplanet.com

To insert a Flash file into your Dreamweaver document, follow these steps:

1. With the HTML file open in Dreamweaver, place your cursor where you wish the Flash movie to be inserted. (*Movie* is the term most commonly used to refer to something created in the Macromedia Flash authoring program.)

2. Open the Insert bar (Window > Insert), make sure you are working in the Common section, and click the down arrow to the right of the Media button. Select Flash from the subsequent drop-down menu.

Alternatively, you can choose Insert > Media > Flash.

3. When the Select File dialog box opens, navigate to the Flash movie you wish to insert, select it, and click OK.

Note: Flash comes in a couple of different file types. FLA is the native file type produced by the authoring program (just as Photoshop produces PSD files). SWF (sometimes pronounced "swif") is the file type created when you want to mount your Flash movie on the Web. When inserting a Flash movie, make absolutely sure that you insert the SWF file, not the FLA file. If you don't, the Flash Player won't be able to display it.

You'll notice that when inserted, Flash movies are represented by a gray place-holder (Figure 8.1). Don't worry—you'll soon learn how to preview the actual Flash file from within the Dreamweaver document.

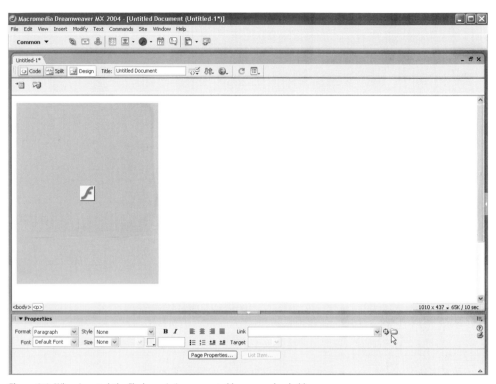

Figure 8.1 When inserted, the Flash movie is represented by a gray placeholder.

Now that you've learned how to insert a Flash movie into your Dreamweaver document, it's time to set that movie's specific properties with, you guessed it, the Property Inspector. For the most part, the properties you can manipulate are directly related to the way the movie itself is displayed and behaves from within the HTML document.

Changing Flash Movie Dimensions

When Flash movies are created, they have a set width and height. However, because they are vector based, they can be easily resized without any loss of image quality. To resize an image from within Dreamweaver, follow these steps:

1. Select the Flash movie whose dimensions you wish to change.

2. Open the Property Inspector (Window > Properties).

3. Enter a new value into the Width (W) field.

4. Enter a new value into the Height (H) field.

5. When you're finished changing the movie's dimensions, press Return (Mac)/ Enter (Win) or click anywhere off the Property Inspector for your changes to take effect.

Much as you can resize an image, you can also resize a Flash movie by using the resize handles:

1. Click the Flash movie you want to resize.

2. Click and hold one of the resize handles located on the movie's sides and corners (Figure 8.2).

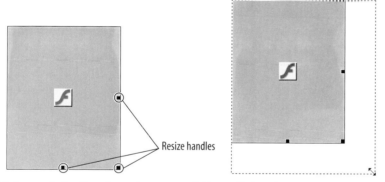

Resize handles

Figure 8.2 Drag a resize handle to change the space occupied by your Flash movie.

3. Drag the resize handles until your Flash movie is the desired size and release your mouse button. If you hold down the Shift key while dragging a corner resize handle, your Flash movie will maintain the same proportions.

Note: If you have the Property Inspector open while you are using the resize handles, you'll notice that the values in the W and H boxes change dynamically to reflect the increasing size of the image.

Setting a Flash Movie's Background Color

One of the things you do when you author a Flash movie is set its background color. Under normal circumstances, this color remains constant whenever the Flash movie is played. However, after inserting a movie into a Dreamweaver document, you can override the original background color of the movie and replace it with a color of your choice:

1. Select the Flash movie whose background color you wish to change.

2. Open the Property Inspector (Window > Properties).

3. Click the Bg swatch to open the Color palette and select the color to which you want to change the Flash movie's background.

 Note: The movie's background color also appears when the movie isn't playing—for example, while it's loading or after it's stopped playing.

Changing a Flash Movie's Quality

While Flash movies are relatively compact in terms of file size (compared to other multimedia), they can sometimes get large. When any movie is created, you have the option of setting the quality at which it plays. Higher quality means that the movie will play slower over a slower connection. Lower quality means that it will play faster over a slow connection. The level of quality you set determines whether speed is sacrificed for quality in your movie or vice versa. Ultimately, the choice you make is based on your audience.

One of the great things about Dreamweaver is that you can set the quality of any given Flash movie that you've inserted into your document:

1. Select the Flash movie whose quality you want to set.

2. Open the Property Inspector (Window > Properties).

3. Open the Quality drop-down menu and choose one of the following options:

Low sacrifices speed to visual quality by turning off any anti-aliasing.

Auto Low starts the movie playing without anti-aliasing but bumps the quality up to High if the user's computer can cope with the improved quality while still maintaining quick playback.

> **Note:** So, what exactly is anti-aliasing? It's the process by which the edges of text are smoothed out. The kicker is that anti-aliased text, because it is more visually complex, generally results in larger file sizes.

Auto High begins playback at High quality but shifts into Low mode if the user's computer can't cope with the increased visual quality and playback speed.

High forces your movie to be anti-aliased. If the movie contains bitmaps that aren't animated, they will be smoothed. On the other hand, if the bitmaps are animated in any way, they won't be smoothed.

> **Note:** When the Flash movie plays in a browser, the user can dynamically change its quality through the context menu (Option-click (Mac)/right-click (Win).)

Altering a Flash Movie's Scale

When you learned how to set the width and height of a Flash movie, you weren't really learning how to change the movie's dimension. Instead, you were setting the width and height of the area in which the movie displays. The manner in which the movie itself is displayed within that area is set by the Scale property. Follow these steps to set the movie's scale:

1. Select the movie whose scale you wish to set.

2. Open the Property Inspector (Window > Properties).

3. Open the Scale drop-down menu and choose one of the following options:

Default (Show All) displays the entire movie (with its correct aspect ratio) in the area defined by the movie's W and H values. This may leave some blank area if the Dreamweaver W/H ratio is not the same as the movie's.

No Border expands (without distortion) to fill the entire area defined by the Dimensions setting. As with the Show All option, the movie will maintain its aspect ratio. The difference, however, is that to maintain the movie's aspect ratio with No Border, your movie may expand to be larger than the area defined by the Dimensions settings. As a result, the edges of your movie might appear as if they've been cut off.

Exact Fit displays the entire movie in the specified area without reserving the original aspect ratio. Your movie might be slightly skewed.

Aligning Flash Movies to the Page or to Text

One of the most basic things you can do with a Flash movie after it's inserted is to align it to the page or to some text on the page. To align a movie to your web page, follow these steps:

1. Place your cursor anywhere along the line that contains the movie (do not select the movie itself).

2. Open the Property Inspector (Window > Properties).

3. Click one of the alignment buttons ▤ ▤ ▤ (in the top-right corner).

   Just as in the case of an image, a Flash movie (as well as the vast majority of the other multimedia elements that will be discussed in this chapter) can be aligned not only to the page but also to text: just select the movie, open the Property Inspector, and then select one of the options from the Align drop-down menu.

   For a full description of what each of the options do, refer to the section "Aligning Images" in Chapter 4.

Making Flash Movies Loop and Play Automatically

For the most part, the way a Flash movie plays is determined when the movie itself is initially authored. With Dreamweaver MX 2004, however, you have a small amount of control over how an inserted Flash movie plays. Follow these steps to manipulate the manner in which an inserted Flash movie plays:

1. Select the Flash movie you wish to manipulate.

2. Open the Property Inspector (Window > Properties).

3. Select from the Play options. Loop causes your movie to loop indefinitely. Auto-play causes the movie to automatically begin playing when the user loads the HTML file in which it is embedded.

Previewing Flash Movies from within the Document Window

As mentioned earlier (and as I'm sure you've noticed on your own), when a Flash movie is inserted into a Dreamweaver MX 2004 document, you don't see the movie itself, you see a gray placeholder. This is primarily memory related. If the Flash movie automatically played when it was inserted, it would consume a lot of precious system memory resources. But what happens when you want to see how the changes you've made will affect the way the movie behaves? Well, you could easily preview the entire document in a browser. However, this can get a little cumbersome if you constantly need to check a rather small change. Don't worry. Macromedia has provided a way to "turn on" the Flash movie so it can be previewed directly from within Dreamweaver:

1. Select the Flash movie that you want to preview.

2. Open the Property Inspector (Window > Properties).

3. Click the Play button ⊳ Play .

To stop the movie from playing (which is vital if you want to set any of the movie's properties), click the Stop button ■ Stop .

Note: To preview the Flash file, you *must* have Flash Player installed on your computer.

Adding Shockwave Files

Shockwave, which is often erroneously confused with Flash, is another web-based multimedia file format developed by Macromedia. The reason for the confusion is understandable: both have their origins at Macromedia, both are used to create stunning interactive experiences, and both are web based. The similarities, however, are less apparent if you drill a little deeper. First, Flash files are created by Macromedia Flash, while Shockwave files are created by Director, Macromedia's flagship portable media (CD-ROM, DVD-ROM, and so on) authoring program. With an astoundingly complex programming language called Lingo, the capability to deal much more efficiently with bitmaps, and the capability to cope far better with audio and video, Director is considerably more full featured than Flash. However, because Director is more of an extensive authoring program than Flash, it is far more difficult to learn. If one were to make a silly analogy, Flash is a spider monkey, graceful and lithe, while Director is a 700-pound gorilla.

For our purposes, the origins and capabilities of Director are neither here nor there. What is really important is that Shockwave files—which are essentially Director movies but exported to a format geared toward distribution over the Web (as opposed to on a CD or DVD)—are generally more complex multimedia applications than Flash files. As with Flash, for the user to view Shockwave files, they must have a special plug-in (called Shockwave Player, not to be confused with Flash Player) on their computer.

Thankfully, the way Dreamweaver copes with Shockwave files is almost identical to the way it copes with Flash files. In fact, both Shockwave and Flash files share almost all of the same properties.

The process of inserting a Shockwave file into your Dreamweaver document is quite simple:

1. Select the HTML file open in Dreamweaver, place your cursor where you wish the Shockwave movie to be inserted.

Note: As was the case with Flash, *movie* is the term most commonly used to refer to something created in the Macromedia Director authoring program (whether its exported to Shockwave format or some other format).

2. Open the Insert bar (Window > Insert), make sure you are working in the Common section, and click the Media button.

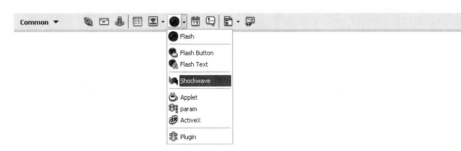

3. When the drop-down menu opens, select Shockwave. Alternatively, you can choose Insert > Media > Shockwave.

4. When the Select File dialog box opens up, navigate to the Shockwave movie you wish to insert, select it, and click OK.

Note: Shockwave files have a .dcr extension.

You'll notice that, like Flash files, Shockwave files are represented in the Document window by a gray placeholder. The process of previewing a Shockwave file within the Document window is exactly the same as with a Flash file.

In addition, many of the properties of a Shockwave file can be manipulated in the same way the properties of a Flash file can. So, to learn how to resize, align, and scale a Shockwave file, all you need to do is refer back to the earlier Flash sections of this chapter that discuss these procedures.

Adding Java Applets

Back in 1990, Sun Microsystems, a company best known for its Unix workstations and Solaris operating system, started a project called Green, whose primary thrust was to create software for consumer appliances—you know, toasters, ovens, microwaves, and the like. One of the results of the project was a programming language called Oak. It soon became obvious to the project participants that, while Oak wasn't particularly appropriate for its intended reason (mainly because it was *way* ahead of its time), it would make a great language for Internet programming.

In 1995, Oak was renamed Java and debuted at Sun Microsystems's annual tradeshow, SunWorld. Since then, it has risen tremendously in popularity and is used for the development of all sorts of self-contained lightweight Internet applications, called *applets*. Java applets can do all manner of groovy things, from online multimedia presentations to web-based public-access order-entry systems.

When it comes to using Java applets, a few general caveats should be observed. First, most (but not all) browsers natively support Java applets without the aid of a plug-in. Unfortunately, while the most recent version of Java (v2) is quite powerful and has a bucketload of interesting features, it has the least amount of browser support. Second, and perhaps most important, primarily for the sake of security all browsers give users the ability to disable Java. Last, there has been an overall trend to move toward executing programs on the web server and returning only HTML to the user's browser.

Because applets are self contained mini-applications (programs) that are launched from an HTML document into which they are embedded, they are added to a Dreamweaver document much in the same way you'd add a Flash or Shockwave file. In the following sections, you'll look at how to insert a Java applet into an HTML document. Then, you'll proceed to learn how to manipulate the properties of the inserted applet with the Property Inspector.

Note: Java is a fully featured programming language, and a thorough explanation of it would be well beyond the scope of this book. You can get a thorough treatment in *Mastering Java 2, JDK 1.4* by John Zukowski (Sybex, 2002). Alternatively, you can go straight to the source at Sun's Java applet page at http://java.sun.com/applets.

Here's how to insert a Java applet:

1. With the HTML file open in Dreamweaver, place your cursor where you wish the Java applet to be inserted.

2. Open the Insert bar (Window > Insert), make sure you are working within the Common section, and click the Media button.

3. When the drop-down menu opens, select Applet. (Alternatively, you can choose Insert > Media > Applet.)

4. When the Select File dialog box opens, navigate to the applet you wish to insert, select it, and click OK.

Note: The path to your Java applet cannot be expressed absolutely; it must be relative. It's important to note that if you have not yet saved the document in which the applet resides, the URL automatically defaults to an absolute file:// path. When the document is saved, the path will automatically turn relative.

You'll notice that, like Flash and Shockwave files, applets are represented in the Document window by a gray placeholder. Unfortunately, unlike with Flash and Shockwave files, there is no way to preview the applet short of previewing the entire HTML document in a browser.

Now that you know how to insert a Java applet, it's time to roll up your sleeves and learn how to set its properties. It's important to note that most properties of a Java applet are managed in exactly the same way other multimedia elements that we've already discussed are managed. For example, to change the size of the area a Java applet occupies on your web page, you can set the W and H fields in the Property Inspector just as you did earlier (in "Changing Flash Movie Dimensions") or you can click the applet and drag the resize handles. So, to learn about these properties, all you need to do is refer back to the section "Adding Flash Movies" earlier in this chapter.

Setting an Applet's Alt Image or Text

As was mentioned earlier, there are some cases in which a browser won't display your Java applet: either the browser doesn't natively support it or, due to security reasons, the user has Java disabled. In cases such as these, you'll want to add some alternate content, such as a static image or text, that will be displayed instead:

1. Select the Java applet to which you want to add some alternate content.

2. Open the Property Inspector (Window > Properties).

3. From here, you can continue two different ways:

- If you want the alternate content to be textual, type the text into the Alt field. Any text will be represented in the same manner an ALT tag for an image is displayed.

- If you want instead to display an image, click the Browse For File button 📁. When the Select File dialog box appears, navigate to where the image is saved and click OK.

4. To apply the change you made, press Return/Enter or click anywhere off the Property Inspector.

Adding Multimedia That Requires a Netscape Plug-In

So far in this chapter, we've talked about a heck of a lot of different media types (and we'll talk about more). We've talked about Flash movies, Shockwave files, and Java applets. When it comes to media on the Web, these are only the first molecules on the tip of the iceberg. Other media types include digital video, audio, screen-based VR, immersive imaging, and animation. If Dreamweaver were to include a way to insert each individual media type, the Insert bar would probably have to be as large as Finland to accommodate them all. The conundrum is that many of the media types that aren't directly covered by Dreamweaver (such as QuickTime) are as popular (or perhaps more popular) than those that are covered.

So, what's a visual web designer to do? Well, in an effort to resolve the problem, Dreamweaver MX 2004 lets you use one simple process to insert any kind of media that requires a plug-in (tiny little programs that extend the browser's features) to be displayed in Netscape.

Note: For the most part, Internet Explorer doesn't use plug-ins to add extra features but instead uses something called ActiveX Controls. These will be discussed a little later in the chapter.

It's important to note that, despite what Dreamweaver's menus and dialog boxes say, you are not actually inserting the plug-in itself; you're inserting a file that requires a plug-in. When the plug-in media is inserted, a reference to the file is included in its <embed> tag. When the HTML page is loaded by the browser, the reference indicates the type of file and which plug-in must be used to display it.

The process to insert Netscape plug-in media in your document is remarkably easy:

1. With the HTML file open in Dreamweaver, place your cursor where you wish to insert the Netscape plug-in media.

2. Open the Insert bar (Window > Insert), make sure you are working in the Common section, and click the Media button.

3. From there, select Plugin from the subsequent drop-down menu. Alternatively, you can choose Insert > Media > Plugin.

4. When the Select File dialog box opens up, navigate to where the Netscape plug-in media file is located, select it, and click OK.

You'll notice that, like Flash and Shockwave files, the Netscape plug-in media file is represented in the Document window by a gray placeholder.

Now that you've inserted the Netscape plug-in media (not that it was particularly hard), you can learn how to set the media's properties. It's important to remember that because the inserted media can be any number of things, the Property Inspector lets you set only the most general of properties. Also, there are some properties, like dimensions and alignment, that are identical to the properties for all the other types of media already explained and therefore don't bear discussion in this section.

Adding a Plug-In URL

Because Netscape plug-in media requires an actual plug-in to be displayed, it's a good idea to provide a link to the location where the user can download it. To add the necessary link, follow these steps:

1. Select the Netscape plug-in media to which you wish to add the plug-in link.

2. Open the Property Inspector (Window > Properties).

3. Enter a URL (such as www.quicktime.com) into the Plg URL field.

4. Press Return/Enter or click anywhere off the Property Inspector for your changes to take effect.

Adding a Border

You might find yourself in a situation where you'd like to set the Netscape Media plug-in farther apart from the rest of your page's content. This can be accomplished by giving the media a border.

Here's how to add a border:

1. Select the media to which you wish to add a border.

2. Open the Property Inspector (Window > Properties).

3. Enter a value (in pixels) into the Border field; the value you enter represents the thickness of the border.

4. Press Return/Enter or click anywhere off the Property Inspector for your changes to take effect.

Previewing Netscape Plug-In Media from within the Document Window

Thankfully, Dreamweaver lets you preview the media directly from within the Document window. This means you don't have to preview the document in a browser every time you want to see how the media looks/plays.

Note: Just as with both Flash and Shockwave, Dreamweaver can't play the media unless you have the plug-in installed on your computer.

To preview a media file, just follow these steps:

1. Select the Netscape plug-in media that you want to preview.

2. Open the Property Inspector (Window > Properties).

3. Click the Play button ▶ Play .

4. When you want to stop the media file from playing, click the Stop button ■ Stop .

Adding Multimedia That Requires an Internet Explorer ActiveX Control

ActiveX Controls are to Internet Explorer what plug-ins are to Netscape. They function by allowing Internet Explorer to play multimedia content that isn't natively supported.

 Note: Unfortunately, due to the specific software architecture of ActiveX Controls, they can only be used with Internet Explorer 3.0 or above. In addition, Mac users are out of luck because ActiveX Controls only work on Windows—bummer.

As with Netscape plug-in media, Dreamweaver provides you with a relatively easy way to include ActiveX Controls in your document. However, unlike with Netscape plug-in media (where you insert the media, not the actual plug-in, directly into the document), you do insert the ActiveX Control directly into your Dreamweaver document. From there, with the Property Inspector, you configure the ActiveX Control to load the specific type of media and file you wish to display.

 Note: If you are interested in leaning more about ActiveX Controls, go to www.activex.com or www.active-x.com.

The process by which you insert an ActiveX Control into your Dreamweaver Document is quite easy:

1. With the HTML file open in Dreamweaver, place your cursor where you wish to insert the ActiveX Control.

2. Open the Insert bar (Window > Insert), make sure you are working in the Common section, and click the Media button.

3. Select ActiveX from the subsequent drop-down menu. Alternatively, you can choose Insert > Media > ActiveX.

You'll notice that, instead of opening up a Select File dialog box, Dreamweaver inserts a small placeholder . This is as it should be. Later, you'll learn how to tell Dreamweaver which file will be accessed and played by the ActiveX Control.

If you were to line up all the different media types that are discussed in this chapter and decide which is the most Property Inspector intensive (that is, which requires the most work with the Property Inspector), it would definitely be ActiveX Controls. As you've already learned, the process of inserting the ActiveX Control results only in a placeholder being inserted into the document. You must use the Property Inspector to set the location of the file, the media type, and myriad other properties.

> **Note:** Because we've already explored how to align media (both to text and to the page itself), I'll skip that process for an ActiveX Control—the process is exactly the same as with the other media types.

Setting an ActiveX Control's Class ID

The Class ID is a unique code that identifies the specific ActiveX Control needed to play/display the media file. Without it, the ActiveX Control you inserted into your Dreamweaver document is totally useless and will not display the file properly. A Class ID is a complex string of numbers and letters; it is best to copy and paste it into the appropriate place in the Property Inspector so that you can avoid mistyping it.

When attempting to integrate the Class ID, you'll find yourself running into a rather large wall. Unfortunately, there isn't a central location where the most commonly used Class IDs are listed. They need to be painstakingly gleaned from the documentation when the ActiveX Control is acquired.

To set the ActiveX Control's Class ID, just follow these steps:

1. Select the placeholder of the ActiveX Control whose Class ID you need to set.

2. Open the Property Inspector (Window > Properties).

3. Enter the Class ID into the ClassID field.

 Note: If you've already entered a Class ID for another ActiveX Control, it will appear in the Class ID drop-down menu.

4. To apply your changes, press Return/Enter or click anywhere off the Property Inspector.

Setting an ActiveX Control's CodeBase

The CodeBase is a URL that provides a location where the ActiveX Control can be downloaded if it isn't installed on the user's computer.

 Note: If the user doesn't have the necessary ActiveX control to display a certain type of media, the browser will automatically go to the CodeBase URL.

For example, the CodeBase for the QuickTime ActiveX Control is
www.apple.com/quicktime/download/qtcheck/

As with the Class ID, there is no real central location where you can find the various CodeBase URLs for all the most commonly used ActiveX Controls. You'll either have to glean the information from the ActiveX Control's documentation or visit the manufacturer's website.

To set an ActiveX Control's CodeBase, follow these steps:

1. Select the placeholder of the ActiveX Control whose CodeBase you need to set.

2. Open the Property Inspector (Window > Properties).

3. Enter the necessary URL into the Base field.

4. To apply your changes, press Return/Enter or click anywhere off the Property Inspector.

Setting a File's Path

As you probably remember, when you insert an ActiveX Control into your Dreamweaver document, you aren't actually inserting the media file itself. One of the steps you need to go through after you insert the ActiveX Control is to point it in the direction of the media file it needs to play (an MPEG file, for example). Unfortunately, the process itself, which is absolutely necessary if you want the ActiveX Control to work properly, is a little counterintuitive and not particularly user friendly.

To set the path of file you want the ActiveX Control to play/display:

1. Select the placeholder of the ActiveX Control with which you are currently working.

2. Open the Property Inspector (Window > Properties).

3. Click the Parameters button [Parameters...] to open the Parameters dialog box (Figure 8.3)

Figure 8.3 The Parameters dialog box

4. Type **Filename** into the first position of the Parameter columns, which is automatically an editable field.

5. Press Tab to move to the first position in the Value column, which automatically becomes an editable field. Alternatively, instead of pressing Tab, you can click the first position in the Value column.

6. Type the path (either relative or absolute).

7. When you finish, click OK.

Making ActiveX Control Media Accessible by Netscape

When you insert the ActiveX Control, the <object> tag is used, as opposed to the <embed> tag, which is used by Netscape to integrate plug-in media. This causes a bit of a problem because Netscape doesn't recognize the <object> tag 100 percent of the time, nor does Internet Explorer recognize the <embed> tag 100 percent of the time. Fortunately, Dreamweaver lets you combine both tags (as if you were sticking the Netscape plug-in media and the ActiveX Control in the same space) so that both browsers are covered:

1. Select the ActiveX Control that you wish to work with.

2. Open the Property Inspector (Window > Properties).

3. Check the Embed check box. This combines the <embed> tag with the <object> tag, which is needed if you want to add Netscape accessibility. When you do this, the Src field becomes available.

4. Because the <embed> tag requires that you directly reference the file you are including, a path must be entered into the Src field. To do this, just click the Browse For File button (to the right of the Src field). When the Select File dialog box appears, navigate to where the file is located, select it, and click OK.

Adding an Alt Image

Usually, if you opt not to combine both the <embed> and <object> tags so that both Internet Explorer and Netscape will be covered, you run the risk of your ActiveX Control–enhanced HTML document being loaded by a browser that cannot cope with ActiveX. Fortunately, Dreamweaver provides a way to avoid this kind of painful situation. As with Java applets, you can add an alternate image that will display in the event that your audience is using a browser that is not enabled for ActiveX Controls:

1. Select the ActiveX Control to which you wish to add an alternate image.

2. Open the Property Inspector (Window > Properties).

3. Click the Browse For File button .

4. When the Select File dialog box opens, navigate to where the image is located, select it, and then click OK.

Adding Interactivity to Your Site with JavaScript Behaviors

One of the most important features of Dynamic HTML (DHTML) is that it gives you the ability to tightly integrate a scripting language (most commonly JavaScript or VBScript) with HTML. Granted, people were using JavaScript in web pages before DHTML hit the scene. However, this new relationship between HTML and JavaScript lets you create some cool eye candy as well as some genuinely useful widgets that were previously impossible to create.

9

Chapter Contents

In Dreamweaver, a behavior is a little JavaScript program that, through the help of some pretty snazzy tools, can be easily integrated into your document and used to extend the interactivity and usability of your HTML creation. The great thing about behaviors is that, with a relative minimum of effort, they can immediately be put to work without you having to learn how to hand-code JavaScript. This alone makes them one of the most exciting features in Dreamweaver MX 2004.

The Tao of Behaviors: Adding, Deleting, and Changing

Interactivity is a buzzword that is often used in conjunction with the Web. Well, truth be told, until recently, straight HTML design (as opposed to Flash or Shockwave) wasn't particularly interactive. Generally speaking, one clicked a hyperlink, a new HTML document was loaded into the browser, and that was it. However, this changed a fair amount when DHTML hit the scene.

One of the most important features of DHTML is that it gives you the ability to tightly combine JavaScript (and sometimes VBScript) with standard HTML to create truly interactive features in a website (relative to what was available before DHTML). While this feature was great, it was still well out of reach of most casual (or even experienced) designers. JavaScript, although certainly easier to write than other computer languages such as C, C++, or Pascal, was hardly a walk in the park. JavaScript is an object-oriented scripting language that definitely takes a good deal of dedication and brain sweat to learn.

Never one to follow, Dreamweaver was the first visual web design software to integrate a highly user-friendly way to insert tiny JavaScript programs, which Macromedia calls *behaviors,* into HTML documents. The program takes care of all the back-end JavaScript structure, leaving the designer free to focus on the best way to integrate a given behavior's interactive features into their document.

Structurally speaking, when you insert a behavior into your document (which is done with the use of Dreamweaver MX 2004's Behaviors panel), the bulk of its JavaScript is inserted into the <head> portion of the HTML document. However, if the behavior is associated with an object (an image, for example), you'll see some JavaScript in the <body> portion of the HTML source code.

 Note: Although this chapter covers Dreamweaver's built-in behaviors, you'll get time to explore how to acquire *new* behaviors in Chapter 13.

Although not often referred to in this manner, there are really only two types of behaviors: those that function in concert with the page itself (page behaviors) and those that are associated with a specific object (object behaviors). This doesn't mean that there are specific page behaviors and specific object behaviors—quite the contrary. Whether a behavior is a page behavior or an object behavior depends solely on the HTML tag to which it is attached. For instance, if a behavior is attached to a page's <body> tag, it becomes a page behavior. However, if the same behavior is associated with the <img> tag of one of the page's images, for example, it becomes an object behavior.

Adding Behaviors to Your Page

In all honesty, the process by which you add a behavior to your page is really quite easy.

Note: This section doesn't focus on behavior-specific settings. Instead, it covers the general, step-by-step process you need to go through to insert a behavior (any behavior) into your document. To learn more about the specifics of Dreamweaver's built-in behaviors, check out the section "Creating Interactivity with the Built-In Behaviors" later in this chapter.

To insert a behavior into your document, just follow these steps:

1. Depending on what you wish to attach the behavior to (the page or an object), choose from the following options:

    •   If you wish to attach the behavior to an object, select the specific object.

    •   If you wish to attach the behavior to the page itself, click your cursor anywhere in the document window, making sure you don't select anything or click within a table. Alternatively, you can select the <body> tag in the Tag Selector.

2. Open the Behaviors panel by choosing Window > Behaviors. Notice that the tag associated with the element you selected is displayed in the panel's title bar. In Figure 9.1, the <body> tag is displayed.

Figure 9.1 The Behaviors panel with the <body> tag displayed in the title bar

3. Click the Add Behavior button , and choose the specific behavior you'd like attached to the selected object from the subsequent pop-up menu.

 Note: Which behaviors are available depends on the content of your page as well as the object to which you attached the action. For example, if you don't have any Flash or Shockwave movies in your page, the Control Shockwave or Flash behavior will not be accessible.

4. When the dialog box for that specific action pops up, set the necessary properties and click OK.

5. If it isn't already selected, make sure you click the Show Set Events button ▤▤ .

6. Click the down arrow next to the behavior's event to open the Event drop-down menu and choose a specific event to trigger the behavior.

 Note: You can easily add more than one behavior to a single object. Just select the object again and repeat steps 2–7.

The Action/Event Equation

A behavior is made up of two discrete parts, an *event* and an *action*. On the whole, the event/action equation is a fairly simple concept to understand. For a behavior to work, the user must first do something (this is the event): load a page, move their cursor over a certain object, press a key on their keyboard, or click a certain object. When that event has happened, the JavaScript behavior (the action) executes. It's a basic cause-and-effect relationship. The event (which is user driven) must happen for the action to occur.

When you insert a behavior into your document, you must set the event, which is represented in the Behaviors panel by something called an *event handler*. Basically, an event handler is JavaScript code for a specific user action. But don't worry too much; event handlers, even though they are syntactically JavaScript, are pretty self-explanatory and easy to work with.

There are, however, a few other details you should know when it comes to understanding event handlers. First, some events are browser specific. Don't worry about having to know which ones work with which browsers: Dreamweaver will provide a list of all the appropriate events based on the behavior's target browser (which you can set in the Behaviors panel). Second, because behaviors are associated with specific HTML elements (something we'll discuss in a bit), different event handlers will be made available depending on the way the behavior is being used.

Changing Behavior Properties

Certain behaviors have detailed properties that are set when they're initially inserted into a document. During the course of your design, you'll probably find yourself in a situation where you need to go back and change the properties of a behavior you used previously. We'll explore the properties of *specific* Dreamweaver behaviors later in this chapter, but here's the general process for changing a behavior's properties:

1. Select the object to which the behavior you wish to edit is attached. If you attached the behavior to the <body> tag, place your cursor anywhere in the document (don't select anything or place the cursor in a table). Alternately, you can select the <body> tag in the Document window's Tag Inspector.

2. If it isn't already, open the Behaviors panel (Window > Behaviors).

3. Double-click the behavior (which, as you'll remember, is listed in the Behaviors panel's right column) you wish to edit.

4. When the behavior's dialog box appears, make your changes and click OK.

Deleting Behaviors

When you insert a behavior into your document, you certainly aren't stuck with it—you can quite easily delete it. To delete a behavior, just follow these steps:

1. Select the object to which the behavior you wish to delete is attached. If you are deleting a behavior that's been attached to the <body> tag, place your cursor anywhere in the document (don't select anything or place the cursor in a table). Alternately, you can select the <body> tag in the Document window's Tag Inspector.

2. If it isn't already open, open the Behaviors panel (Window > Behaviors).

3. Select the behavior to delete.

4. Click the Remove Event button — . Alternatively, you can press Backspace/Delete.

Changing the Order in Which Behaviors Execute

The cool thing about working with behaviors is that you can have multiple events attached to a single object or multiple actions attached to a single event. In cases like these, the behaviors and even the actions themselves will execute from top to bottom in the Behaviors panel. Although the default sequence is established by the order in which you attach the individual actions, you can easily change it to suit your needs.

When would you need to reorder the behaviors attached to a specific object? Say, for instance, you have a splash page in which you placed an Enter My Site button. When the user clicks the button, your site opens in a browser window with fixed dimensions (created and controlled by Dreamweaver's Open Browser Window behavior). Now, because your site also has DHTML elements, you use the Check Browser behavior to make sure the user's browser is 4.0 or above. This behavior also executes when the user clicks the Enter My Site button. However, for this system to work properly, you need to check the user's browser before you launch your site. As a result, you would have to be absolutely sure the Check Browser action is placed above the Open Browser Window behavior in the Behaviors panel.

Here's how to change the order of a behavior in the Behaviors panel:

1. Select the object to which the behavior you wish to reorder is attached. If you are reordering behaviors that have been attached to the page's <body> tag, place your cursor anywhere in the document (but don't select anything or place the cursor in a table). Alternately, you can select the <body> tag in the Document window's Tag Inspector.

2. If it isn't already, open the Behaviors panel (Window > Behaviors).

3. Select the action (behavior) you would like to reorder and click either the Move Event Value Up ▲ or Move Event Value Down arrow ▼ to move the action in the stack. Each time you click a button, the action will be moved one position upward or downward.

Creating Interactivity with the Built-In Behaviors

Dreamweaver comes with 24 built-in behaviors that let you do a whole range of interesting things. Want to check the user's browser for a certain plug-in or make sure they are using a specific version or browser? How about creating a pop-up message or a rollover? All of these things and many more are possible with standard Dreamweaver behaviors.

In the following sections, you'll learn how to work with the most common standard Dreamweaver behaviors. For the sake of economy, it's assumed that you're already familiar with how to insert a behavior and set its event, as described earlier in this chapter. The following discussion will pick up where you choose the action from the Behaviors panel's Add Action drop-down menu. The discussion will not rehash how you set the action's event.

Note: Chapter 13 explores how you go about acquiring new behaviors.

Calling JavaScript Code

JavaScript is a very versatile scripting language that lets you do far more than is available with Dreamweaver's prepackaged JavaScript behaviors. You can just as easily open up Code View and write your own JavaScript directly into the HTML source code. However, for those who might be just starting to learn JavaScript, the prospect of hand-coding might seem a little daunting. This is where the Call JavaScript action comes in. It lets you enter some JavaScript into a dialog box (which Dreamweaver automatically sticks in the appropriate place within the HTML) that will be executed when a given event occurs.

To use the Call JavaScript action, follow these steps:

1. Select the item to which you want to attach the behavior, and with the Behaviors panel open (Window > Behaviors), click the Add Behavior button ➕▾ and choose Call JavaScript.

2. When the Call JavaScript dialog box (Figure 9.2) pops up, type the code into the JavaScript field.

 Note: Although the Call JavaScript dialog box allows you to enter only a single line of code, the line itself can be long.

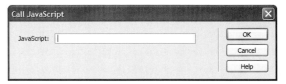

Figure 9.2 The Call JavaScript dialog box

3. When you finish entering the JavaScript into the field, click OK.
4. Click the down arrow to the right of the behavior's event to open the Event drop-down menu and choose the specific event you'd like to have trigger the Call JavaScript action.

Checking the User's Browser for a Plug-in

As you learned back in Chapter 8, there are many types of media you can use that aren't natively supported by most browsers and that therefore require a plug-in to display properly.

Plug-ins arc a double-edged sword. With them, you are free to incorporate incredibly cool stuff like Flash, Shockwave, or digital video into your page. However, because they aren't part of the browser itself, you can never be absolutely sure whether the user has the necessary plug-in to view your content. If they don't, they'll need to download it, a prospect that can often be particularly frustrating.

What if you could get your website to check the user's browser for necessary plug-ins and then automatically direct them to your main site (if they've got the plug-in necessary) or an alternate page (if they don't)? Well, if you hadn't figured it out by the title of this section, Dreamweaver MX 2004 has a behavior to do just that!

To use the Check Plug-in action, just follow these steps:

1. With the item selected to which you wish to attach the behavior, and with the Behaviors panel open (Window > Behaviors), click the Add Behavior button **+,** and choose Check Plugin. The Check Plugin dialog box (Figure 9.3) will open.
2. At this point, you've got a couple of options:
   - Click the Select radio button and then choose the specific plug-in from the Plugin drop-down menu.

- If the plug-in that you'd like to check for is not available in the Plugin drop-down menu, choose the Enter radio button and type in the name of the plug-in *exactly* as it appears in Netscape's About Plug-Ins page. (To open that page, choose Navigator's Help > About Plug-Ins command on a Windows machine, or choose About Plug-Ins from the Apple menu on a Mac.)

3. Click the Browse button to the right of the If Found, Go To URL field. When the Select File dialog box appears, navigate to the page you wish to load if the browser confirms the presence of the desired plug-in, select it, and click Select.

4. Click the Browse button to the right of the Otherwise, Go To URL field. When the Select File dialog box appears, navigate to the page you wish to load if the user's browser doesn't have the necessary plug-in, select it, and click Select.

5. Select the Always Go To First URL If Detection Is Not Possible option.

6. When you finish setting all of the Check Plugin behavior's properties, click OK.

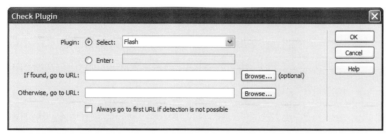

Figure 9.3 The Check Plugin dialog box

Checking the Version of the User's Browser

Unfortunately for you, many different browsers out there have varying levels of support for different web technologies. Given the fact that at some point during the design process, you are going to want to take advantage of some of the groovier web technologies—such as Cascading Style Sheets, behaviors, or absolute positioning—how do you cope with users who don't have the most up-to-date browsers? It's an incredibly bad move to create a website that isn't accessible or doesn't offer a lower-tech alternative. What's the solution? Well, as was the case with the Check Plugin behavior, Dreamweaver offers you the Check Browser behavior, which will check the version of the browser and send the user to an appropriate page.

Note: Logistically speaking, it's a good idea to attach the Check Browser behavior to the link that leads to your site proper. This way, you can check the version/make of the user's browser *before* they get to the place where they actually need specific software. Alternatively, you could also attach the Check Browser behavior to the page (the <body> tag) itself.

Here's how to use the Check Browser behavior:

1. With the item selected to which you wish to attach the behavior, and with the Behaviors panel open (Window > Behaviors), click the Add Behavior button **+,** and choose Check Browser. The Check Browser dialog box (Figure 9.4) will open.

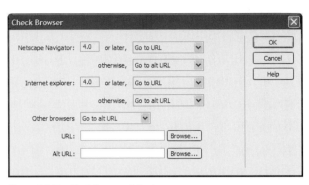

Figure 9.4 The Check Browser dialog box

2. Enter the earliest version of each browser that supports the features you are employing in your web page into the Netscape Navigator and Internet Explorer version fields.

3. From each of the various drop-down menus (Or Later, Otherwise, and Other Browsers), choose the location where you'd like to send users with that particular browser and version. Your choices for each are as follows:

   - Stay On This Page
   - Go To URL
   - Go To Alt URL

   For example, from the Netscape Navigator: Or Later drop-down menu, choose the location to which you'd like to send users who are using the version of Netscape Navigator you indicated or a later version. From the Netscape Navigator: Otherwise drop-down, choose the outcome for viewers with older versions of Netscape Navigator. Do the same for recent and older IE browsers and for those with browsers other than Netscape and IE.

4. Now you need to establish which files will act as the primary URL and Alt URL. You can type absolute URLs into these fields, or you can browse to the pages you want.

   To browse for the files, click the Browse button to the right of the URL field. When the Select File dialog box opens, navigate to the page that will act as the primary URL, select it, and click the Select button. Then click the Browse button to the right of the Alt URL field, navigate to the page that will act as the alternative URL, select it, and click OK.

5.   When you finish, click OK.

Dynamically Controlling Flash or Shockwave Files in Your Page

With the help of the Control Shockwave Or Flash behavior, you can play, stop, rewind, or jump to a specific frame of a Flash or Shockwave movie.

To use the Control Shockwave Or Flash behavior, follow these steps:

1.   With the item selected to which you wish to attach the behavior, and with the Behaviors panel open (Window > Behaviors), click the Add Behavior button ◆▾ and choose Control Shockwave Or Flash. A dialog box (Figure 9.5) will open.

Figure 9.5 The Control Shockwave Or Flash dialog box

2.   Select the Flash or Shockwave movie you wish to manipulate from the Movie drop-down menu.

3. Depending on what exactly you want to do, select one of the options (Play, Stop, or Rewind). If you wish the movie to jump to a specific frame, select the Go To Frame option and enter a specific frame number into the field.

4. Click OK.

Making Layers Draggable

One of the coolest things about Layers (which will be discussed in Chapter 10) is that they don't have to be static, fixed elements on your page. With the help of the Drag Layer behavior, you can create a layer that your user can interactively move around their browser. For example, you might want to add a touch of interactive whimsy to your page by creating a Mr. Potato Head game. You could place each of Mr. Potato Head's facial elements on individual layers and make those layers draggable?thereby allowing them to be stuck on a blank image of his body. If you aren't sure how to either create or name a layer, see Chapter 10.

 Note: Unfortunately, the Drag Layer behavior is not compatible with Netscape 6.0.

Follow these steps to use the Drag Layer behavior:

1. Make sure you have a named layer inserted in your document.

 Note: The Drag Layer behavior *will not work* unless the layer you want to make draggable is named. Don't worry too much, though, because Dreamweaver automatically assigns default names (Layer1, Layer2, etc.) to all newly created layers. However, if you are working with a document that has many layers, you might want to assign your own names.

2. Because the Drag Layer behavior will work only if it's attached to the page, you need to select the page's <body> tag with the Tag Inspector or click your cursor anywhere within the page itself (but be careful not to select anything or place your cursor in a tab).

3. With the Behaviors panel open (Window > Behaviors), click the Add Behavior button ➕▾ and choose Drag Layer. The Drag Layer dialog box (Figure 9.6) will open.

4. Make sure the Basic tab is selected and then choose the layer you wish to make draggable from the Layer drop-down menu.

Figure 9.6 The Drag Layer dialog box

5. Decide whether users will be able to drag the layer anywhere or only within a limited area:

   • If you want the user to be able to drag the layer anywhere within the browser window, choose Unconstrained from the Movement drop-down menu.

   • If you wish to restrict the movement of a layer, choose Constrained from the Movement drop-down menu. As illustrated in Figure 9.7, when you do this, four additional fields appear (Up, Down, Left, Right). The values you enter into these fields represent (in pixels) the edges of the constrained area and are relative to the original position of the layer's top-left corner.

6. Set a drop target by entering values in the Left and Top fields. Essentially, a drop target is a specific location (in the page) to which you want the user to drag the layer. A layer is considered to have reached the drop target when its left and top coordinates match the coordinates you enter. These fields represent the distance in pixels of the drop target from the left side and top edge of the Document window, respectively.

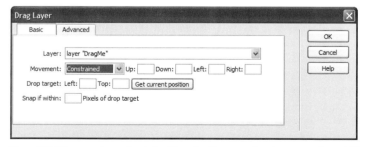

Figure 9.7 When you choose Constrained from the Movement drop down menu, four additional fields appear.

Note: To use the current coordinates of the layer's top-left corner as the drop target, click the Get Current Position button and the Top and Left fields will be automatically filled in.

7. If you want the layer to automatically snap to its drop target within a certain area (as opposed to just the coordinates themselves), enter a value (in pixels) for the distance into the Snap If Within field.

8. If you are interested in creating a simple puzzle or manipulatable scene, you don't have to delve into the Advanced properties. However, if you wish to, click the Advanced tab in the Drag Layer dialog box (Figure 9.8).

Figure 9.8 The Advanced section of the Drag Layer dialog box

9. You have two choices for the location of the layer's drag handle (a drag handle is the specific area that can be used to click and drag the layer itself):

   • To make the entire layer act as the handle (that is, to allow the user to click and drag anywhere in the layer), choose Entire Layer from the Drag Handle drop-down menu.

   • To define a specific area where the user needs to click in order to drag the layer, choose Area Within Layer from the Drag Handle drop-down menu. When you do this, you'll notice that four additional fields appear (L, T, W, and H). The values you enter into these fields represent (in pixels) the left (L), top (T), width (W), and height (H) of the drag handle area. The values themselves are measured from the top and left of the layer.

   Remember, even if you define a specific drag handle within the layer, it won't be visible. You might want to include some sort of visual indicator (for example, a button) that is placed exactly in the same location at the defined drag handle area so the user will know where to click and drag.

10. If you want the layer's Z Index to change when the user drags it, select the When Dragging, Bring Layer To Front option.

Z Index

When two or more layers overlap, a spatial relationship is instantly established determining the position of all the layers in an imaginary three-dimensional stack. You can think of overlapping layers as a stack of papers. If one of the sheets of paper is at the bottom of the pile, its content might only be partially visible, depending on how the remaining sheets are positioned. On the other hand, the sheet on the top of the stack will have all of its content visible. Each layer's position in the stack is called its *Z Index* and is represented by a numerical value.

11. Decide what happens to the layer (in terms of its Z Index) once it's released:
    - If you want it to be placed on the top of the layer "stack" (and therefore overlay all other layers), choose Leave On Top from the Then drop-down menu.
    - If you want the layer to be stuck back in its original place in the Z Index, choose Restore ZIndex from the drop-down menu.

12. If you want some JavaScript to be executed while the layer is being dragged, enter the code or function name into the Call JavaScript field.

13. If you want some JavaScript to be executed when the layer is released, enter the code or function name into the When Dropped: Call JavaScript field. The JavaScript entered into this field will execute regardless of where the layer is released by the user unless you check the Only If Snapped option, which limits the code to being executed when the layer is released in the drop target area.

14. When you finish setting the Drag Layer behavior's properties, click OK.

Opening Multiple URLs with a Single Click

One of the biggest drawbacks of using standard hyperlinks (either with text or an image) is that it's impossible to load multiple documents into multiple frames or windows with a single click of the mouse. Granted, the one click/one load document equation isn't usually that limiting. However, if you are doing anything moderately complex with frames, it's vital that you be able to load different files into different frames with a single click. This is where the Go To URL behavior enters the picture. With it, you can load up any number of documents in any number of frames with a single click of the mouse. To use this behavior, follow these steps:

1. With the item selected to which you wish to attach the Go To URL behavior, and with the Behaviors panel open (Window > Behaviors), click the Add Behavior button **+** and choose Go To URL.

2. When the Go To URL dialog box pops up (Figure 9.9), select the frame into which you'd like to load the URL from the Open In list box. (If you don't have any frames in your document, the only option in the Open In field will be Main Window.)

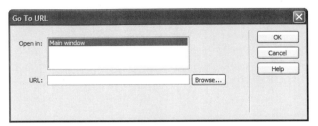

Figure 9.9 The Go To URL dialog box

3. Identify the file that should be loaded into the selected frame. To do this, either enter the URL in the URL field or click the Browse button to the right of the field. When the Select File dialog box opens, navigate to where the desired file is located, select it, and click the OK button.

4. Repeat steps 2 and 3 to load additional files into additional frames.

5. When you finish, click OK.

Opening Custom Browser Windows

I'm sure in your travels on the Web you've noticed sites (there are quite a few) that will load up a page into a browser window that has a fixed size. In addition, these fixed-size windows often aren't adorned with the usual browser window accoutrements (such as a scroll bar, navigational toolbar, or menu bar). When used properly, this is definitely a cool design technique. Well, with the help of Dreamweaver's Open Browser Window behavior, you can do it also:

1. With the item selected to which you wish to attach the behavior, and with the Behaviors panel open (Window > Behaviors), click the Add Behavior button ＋, and choose Open Browser Window. This will open the Open Browser Window dialog box (Figure 9.10).

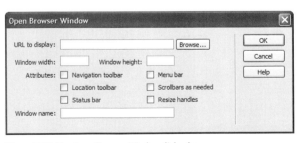

Figure 9.10 The Open Browser Window dialog box

2. Identify the file that will be loaded up into the opened browser window. You can type the URL (either absolute or relative) into the URL To Display field. Alternatively, click the Browse button to the right of the field, navigate to the intended file, select it, and click OK.

3. Enter values (in pixels) for the width and height of the browser window into the Window Width and Window Height fields. If you leave these blank, the behavior just won't work.

4. Select the attributes you would like *included* (as opposed to those you would like to exclude) in your opened browser window.

5. Enter a unique name for your window into the Window Name field. For the behavior to work properly, it must have unique name that contains no spaces or special characters.

6. When you finish, click OK.

Playing Sound Files

What if you wanted to create a interactive audio experience, such as a sound playing when someone moved their mouse over a particular object? This is where the Play Sound behavior comes in. As its name suggests, it can be used to play an audio file.

Note: It's important to remember that the only types of audio that are natively supported by *most* browsers are WAV, AIFF, and AU. If you want to use the behavior to play another type of audio file, your user will require a plug-in of one type or another.

To use the Play Sound behavior, first have the item selected to which you wish to attach the behavior. In the Behaviors panel, click the Add Behavior button +, and choose Play Sound. The Play Sound dialog box (Figure 9.11) will appear.

Figure 9.11 The Play Sound dialog box

Enter the sound file's URL in the Play Sound field (as an alternative, you can click the Browse button to the right of the field, navigate to the audio file, select it, and click OK). When you finish, click OK.

Creating Pop-Up Messages

A JavaScript pop-up message (Figure 9.12) is a cool way to provide your users with a little extra information.

Figure 9.12 A JavaScript pop-up message

To use the Pop-up Message behavior, first select the item to which you wish to attach the behavior In the Behaviors panel, click the Add Behavior button **+** and choose Popup Message. The Popup Message dialog box (Figure 9.13) will appear.

Figure 9.13 The Popup Message dialog box

Type the text of the pop-up message into the Message field. When you finish, click OK.

Preloading Images

A great way to streamline your users' experience is to preload your site's images so that they'll load quickly (as opposed to loading slowly). To preload an image, follow these steps:

1. Select the item to which you wish to attach the Preload Images behavior and open the Behaviors panel (Window > Behaviors).

 Note: A good strategy is to attach the Preload Images action to the page itself (the <body> tag). This way, the user doesn't have to do anything for the behavior to be executed.

2. Click the Add Behavior button **+** and choose Preload Images.This will open the Preload Image dialog box (Figure 9.14).

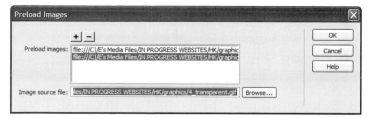

Figure 9.14 The Preload Images dialog box

3.   To add the first image to be preloaded, click the Browse button to the right of the Image Source File field.

4.   When the Select Image Source dialog box opens, navigate to where the image you want to preload is located, select it, and click OK.

5.   To add additional images, click the Add Item button **+** in the Preload Images dialog box, and then repeat the browse and select actions in steps 3 and 4.

6.   When you finish adding all the images to be preloaded, click OK.

Preloading Precautions

Given the fact that images load at the same rate whether or not you are using the Preload Images behavior, you need to be wise about where in your site you preload them. For instance, you don't want to be preloading a bunch of images that are used in lower areas of your site when the user is trying to load your main page. The best place to preload a batch of images is when the user reaches a page at which they'll be spending more time. Instead of preloading all the images from your site in one fell swoop, another good strategy is to load all the images for a given subsection of your site at that subsection's top page.

Changing the Text of the Browser Status Bar

Like a JavaScript pop-up message, integrating status bar text into your page is a great way to provide the user with some extra information.

To use the Set Text Of Status Bar behavior, first select the item to which you wish to attach the behavior and open the Behaviors panel (Window > Behaviors). Click the Add Behavior button ➕ and choose Set Text > Set Text Of Status Bar. This will open the Set Text Of Status Bar dialog box (Figure 9.15).

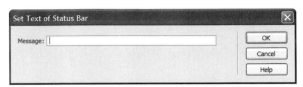

Figure 9.15 The Set Text of Status Bar dialog box

Type the text you'd like to have appear in the status bar into the Message field. When you finish, click OK.

Dynamically Changing Frame or Layer Contents

Under normal circumstances, if you want to change the content of a frame or a layer, you need to load a new document. However, through the use of the Set Text Of Frame and Set Text Of Layer behaviors, you can dynamically change the content of a frame or layer.

To change the content of a frame, just follow these steps:

1. Select the item you want to use to activate the behavior, and with the Behaviors panel open (Window > Behaviors), click the Add Behavior button ➕ and choose Set Text > Set Text Of Frame. This will open the Set Text Of Frame dialog box (Figure 9.16).

 Note: If you don't have any frames in your document, you won't be able to access the Set Text Of Frame behavior.

Figure 9.16 The Set Text of Frame dialog box

2. From the Frame drop-down, select the frame whose contents you wish to manipulate.

3. Enter new content into the New HTML field. If you want to populate this field with the page's existing content (which you can then change), click the Get Current HTML button.

> **Note:** The content of the New HTML field will automatically overwrite the frame's code.

4. If you wish to preserve the background color of the frame, click the Preserve Background Color option.

5. When you finish, click OK.

If you aren't using frames in your document but you still want to be able to dynamically change the text in your page, a good alternative is to use the Set Text Of Layer behavior. With it you can dynamically change a layer's content and formatting while retaining layer attributes.

> **Note:** See chapter 10 for more information on layers.

Follow these steps to use the Set Text Of Layer behavior:

1. Select the item you want to use to activate the behavior, and with the Behaviors panel open (Window > Behaviors), click the Add Behavior button **+** and choose Set Text > Set Text Of Layer. This will open the Set Text Of Layer dialog box (Figure 9.17).

> **Note:** This may seem obvious, but if you don't have any layers in your document, you won't be able to access the Set Text Of Layer behavior.

Figure 9.17 The Set Text of Layer dialog box

2. From the Layer drop-down, select the layer whose contents you wish to manipulate. If you haven't named your layer, it will show up in the Layer drop-down menu with its default name (Layer1, Layer2, and so on).

3. Enter new content into the New HTML field. If you want any HTML formatting, you'll need to add the proper tags yourself.

Note: The content you place in the New HTML field can be any valid HTML source code, including images.

4. When you finish, click OK.

Changing the Text of Text Fields

With the help of the Set Text Of Text Field behavior (whoa, that's a mouthful), you can dynamically change the text within a text field (either single or multiline).

Note: Most people associate text fields with forms; for more information about forms, see Chapter 14. However, you can add a text field without a form. This behavior works just fine on a form-less text field.

Here's how to use Set the Text Of Text Field behavior:

1. With the item selected that you want to activate the behavior, and with the Behaviors panel open (Window > Behaviors), click the Add Behavior button and choose Set Text > Set Text Of Text Field. This will open the Set Text Of Text Field dialog box (Figure 9.18).

Note: If you don't have any text fields in your document, you won't be able to access the Set Text Of Text Field behavior.

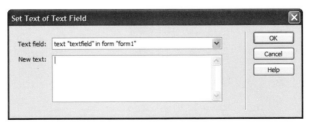

Figure 9.18 The Set Text of Text Field dialog box

2. From the Text Field drop-down, select the text field that you wish to manipulate. Individual text fields are listed in association with their particular form. So if you have multiple forms on a single page, you'll be able to easily select the specific text field you want to work with.

3. Enter the desired text into the New Text field. Remember, if you have multiple lines in the New Text field, a single-line text field won't be able to display them in the same way a multiple-line text field will. It will simply compress the multi-line text into a single line.

4. When you finish, click OK.

Dynamically Controlling Layer Visibility

With the help of the Show-Hide Layers behavior, you can dynamically control whether or not a layer is visible or invisible (a property you'll explore in Chapter 10).

Select the item to which you wish to attach the Show-Hide Layers behavior and open the Behaviors panel (Window > Behaviors). Then click the Add Behavior button **+.** and choose Show-Hide Layers; this will open the Show-Hide Layers dialog box (Figure 9.19).

Figure 9.19 The Show-Hide Layers dialog box

From the Named Layers list box, select the layer whose visibility you want to manipulate. Remember that if you haven't named your layer, it will show up with its default name (Layer1, Layer2, and so on). Then click a visibility option:

- To show a layer whose visibility was previously set to Hide, click the Show button Show .

- To hide a layer who visibility had previously been set to Show, click the Hide button Hide .

- To return the layer to its default visibility, click the Default button Default .
  When you finish, click OK.

Validating Forms

When you create a form, you assume that the user will fill out all of the form and, if need be, constrain their data entry to a certain format, such as a two-character province/state code or a complete e-mail address.

Note: For more information on forms, check out Chapter 14.

Under normal circumstances, a user can fill a form out any way they please (either intentionally or by accident) and then submit it to you. This can be pretty frustrating if the point of the form is to collect some very specific data. So, aside from standing over the user with a big stick and whacking them whenever they make an error, how can you prevent this type of thing from happening? By using the Validate Form behavior. Essentially, this behavior works by checking the data entered into any text field against a standard you've already set. If the data doesn't conform, the form will simply not submit.

Note: If you don't have a completed form on your page (in which all the text fields have been properly labeled), you won't be able to access the Validate Form behavior.

To use the Validate Form behavior, follow these steps:

1. Select the item to which you wish to attach the Validate Form behavior, and with the Behaviors panel open (Window > Behaviors), click the Add Behavior button **+.** and choose Validate Form. This will open the Validate Form dialog box (Figure 9.20).

Note: There are a couple of different elements to which you can attach the Validate Form behavior. You can attach it to the Submit button using an onClick event. Alternatively, you can attach the behavior to each individual field you'd like to validate and then execute it with an onBlur event. Finally, you can attach it to the form (<form> tag) itself and then execute it with an onSubmit event.

2. Select a field to which you'd like to add a validation from the Named Fields list.
3. If you wish the field to be required (that is, the user must fill it out in order to submit the form), select the Value: Required option.

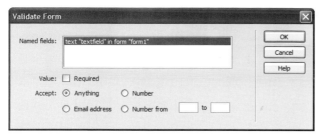

Figure 9.20 The Validate Form dialog box

4. For validating the contents of the field, you have the following options:

   - If you aren't concerned with exactly what kind of data is entered into the field but you want to make sure *something* has been added to the text field, select the Anything radio button.

   - To make sure that the field is filled with only numbers, select the Number radio button.

   - To make sure that the data entered into the field is a syntactically correct e-mail address (something@something.something), select the Email Address radio button.

Note: The Validate Form behavior will not check whether the e-mail address entered is real, only whether it conforms to the expected e-mail address syntax.

   - If you want the data entered to be a number that falls within a certain range, select the Number From radio button. Then enter the beginning number in the range into the first field and the ending number in the range into the second field.

5. When you finish, click OK.

Creating Rollovers

A rollover (an image that changes when it's moused over and then reverts back to the original when it's moused out) is arguably one of the most popular effects in web pages these days. In Dreamweaver MX 2004, the most popular way to make a rollover is with the Swap Image behavior:

1. With the item to which you wish to attach the Set Text Of Layer behavior selected and with the Behaviors panel open (Window > Behaviors), click the Add Behavior button and choose Swap Image. This will open the Swap Image dialog box (Figure 9.21).

Figure 9.21 The Swap Image dialog box

2. From the Images list box, identify the image you wish to turn into a rollover. If you selected the image before opening the Swap Image dialog box, it will be automatically highlighted. If you haven't named any of your images, they will all show up with the same default name (unnamed <img>). To avoid confusion, if you are creating a number of different rollovers on the same page, you should name all of your images.

Note: The name of an image is entered into the unlabeled field to the left of the H field in the Property Inspector when the image is selected.

3. Identify the image that will replace the selected image. To do this, either enter its URL in the Set Source To field or click the Browse button to the right of the field, navigate to the image, select it, and click OK.

4. If you want the second image to be preloaded when the page itself loads (which is definitely a good idea if you want the rollover to be smooth), click the Preload Images option. This will automatically attach a Preload Images behavior to the <body> tag of the page itself.

5. If you want the image to switch back to the original when the user moves their mouse off it, click the Restore Images onMouseOut option. This will add a Swap Image Restore behavior to the image (which doesn't have much use beyond this situation).

6. When you've finished, click OK.

Note: You can also create a rollover by choosing Insert > Image Objects > Rollover Image and then entering the necessary properties in the Insert Rollover Image dialog box.

Creating Pop-Up Menus

Arguably one of the coolest behaviors lets you create graphical JavaScript pop-up menus—a feature that was previously available only if you were working with Macromedia Fireworks. With the help of the Show Pop-Up Menu behavior, you can easily create a complex (and terribly cool) navigational element, the creation of which otherwise might prove somewhat complicated and beyond the reach for someone starting out in the world of web design (Figure 9.22).

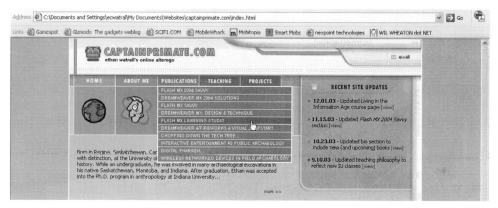

Figure 9.22 A pop-up menu in action

Note: Because of its very nature, the process by which you add a pop-up menu is more involved than any of the other behaviors covered in this chapter.

Before you begin, know that the Show Pop-Up Menu behavior can only be attached to a named image. Also, if the document in which you are working has yet to be saved, you will be unable to use the Show Pop-Up Menu behavior.

Note: Pop-Up Menus created in Macromedia Fireworks MX or Fireworks MX 2004 can be edited in Dreamweaver MX 2004.

To create a pop-up menu using the Show Pop-Up Menu behavior, follow these steps:

1. Select the item you want to use to activate the behavior , and with the Behaviors panel open (Window > Behaviors), click the Add Behavior button **+,** and choose Show Pop-up Menu.

2. When the Show Pop-Up Menu dialog box (Figure 9.23) appears, first make sure the Contents tab is open.

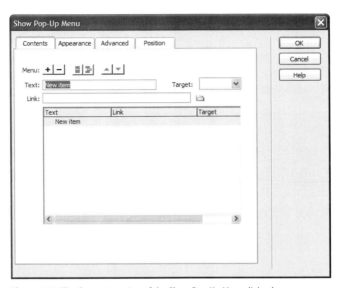

Figure 9.23 The Contents section of the Show Pop-Up Menu dialog box

3. In the Text field, enter the text that will appear as the first item in the drop-down menu

4. Enter the menu item's corresponding URL into the Link field. If you want to link to another page in your site, click the Browse For Folder button . When the Select File dialog box appears, navigate to the file, select it, and click OK to return to the Show Pop-Up Menu dialog.

5. From the Target drop-down, select the location where you want the link to load.

6. To add additional menu items, click the Add Item button ➕ and repeats steps 3–5. To remove an item from the menu, highlight it and click the Remove Item button.

7. If you want one of the items in your menu to be nested below the primary menu (see Figure 9.24), highlight the item in the list and click the Indent Item button . To un-nest the menu item, click the Outdent Item button .

8. To change the position of an item in the menu, highlight it and click either the Move Item Up ▲ or Move Item Down ▼ button.

Figure 9.24 A menu item can be nested below the primary pop-up menu.

9. When you finish adding all the items to your pop-up menu, click the Appearance tab. From here, you will configure the way your menu looks. As you change the properties in the Appearance tab, the preview at the bottom of the dialog box will change accordingly (Figure 9.25).

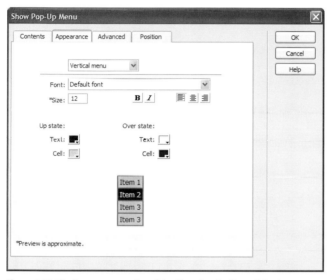

Figure 9.25 The Appearance section of the Show Pop-Up Menu dialog box

Select the direction in which the menu will flow (either Horizontal or Vertical) from the Orientation drop-down menu.

Select the font for the menu's items from the Font drop-down menu.

To change the style of your menu's text, click the Bold **B** or Italic *I* button.

To align the items within the menu, click one of the Align buttons.

To set the color of the text when the user's mouse is *not* over the menu item, click the Up State Text Color swatch and choose a color from the color palette. To set a color for the *cell* in which the text of each individual menu item resides, click the Up State Cell Color swatch and choose a color from the Color Palette.

To set a color of the text or cell when the user's mouse *is* over the menu item, click the Over State Text or Up State Cell Color swatch and choose a color from the color palette.

10. When you've finished setting the appearance of the pop-up menu, click the Advanced tab (Figure 9.26)—this is where you'll fine-tune how your pop-up menu looks.

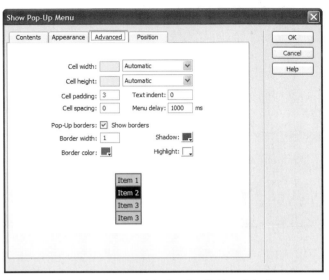

Figure 9.26 The Advanced section of the Show Pop-Up Menu dialog box

To set the width and height of the cells in your menu, either select Automatic or Pixels from the Cell Width and Cell Height drop-down menus. If you choose Automatic, the cell width or cell height is automatically set by the widest or tallest item in the menu, respectively. If, however, you choose Pixels, you can set the width or height manually by inputting a value into the field.

Enter values for the cell padding and cell spacing of each of your menu items into the Cell Padding and Cell Spacing fields. (If you are having trouble remembering how cell padding and cell spacing affects how content in a cell is displayed, see Chapter 6, "Laying Out Tables and Frames.")

To change the distance between the menu item and the left side of the cell, enter a value (in pixels) into the Text Indent field.

To set the delay between the user moving their mouse over the object to which the pop-up menu behavior has been attached and the menu actually appearing , enter a value into the Menu Delay field. The value you enter is in milliseconds; for example, 1000 is 1 second, 2000 is 2 seconds, and so on.

If you want your pop-up menu to have a solid border, click the Show Borders option. Then enter the value for the border width and set the color for the border by clicking the Border Color swatch and making your choice from the color palette.

To set the menu's shadow or highlight color, click the Shadow Color or Highlight Color swatch and make a choice from the color palette. Neither the highlight color nor the shadow color are displayed in the preview section of the Show Pop-Up Menu dialog box.

11. When you finish setting the pop-up menu's advanced properties, click the Position tab (Figure 9.27)—this is where you'll manipulate the position of the pop-up menu when it's opened.

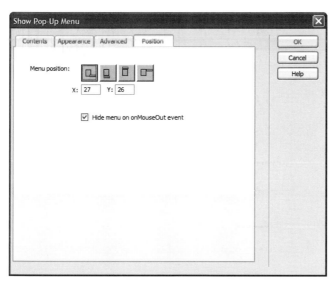

Figure 9.27 The Position section of the Show Pop-Up Menu dialog box.

- Click one of the preset Menu Position option buttons to set the location where the menu will appear when the user triggers the event.

- To manually set the location of the menu, enter a value (in pixels) into the X (x-coordinate) and Y (y-coordinate) fields—the position is relative to the top left-hand corner of the menu itself.

- If you want the menu to disappear when the user moves their mouse off it, click the Hide Menu on onMouseOut Event. When you do this, Dreamweaver adds an additional behavior (Hide Pop-Up Menu).

12. When you are done setting the properties of the pop-up menu, click OK.

Formatting with CSS and Layers

10

One of the chief frustrations of HTML is that it has been limiting in terms of content layout and design. There was almost no typographic control, and it was impossible to place content exactly where you wanted it. Although layout and design in previous versions of Dreamweaver were primarily based on an HTML paradigm, Dreamweaver MX 2004 completely integrates Cascading Style Sheets (CSS) to format and manipulate the appearance of your content—thereby allowing you an incredibly high degree of control over your page's layout.

Chapter Contents

In this chapter, you are going to learn how to use Cascading Style Sheets and layers (Dreamweaver's name for the Absolute Positioning feature of CSS) to do all sorts of groovy things.

Understanding Cascading Style Sheets

For those designers who grew up in the print world, Cascading Style Sheets (CSS) is one of the exciting new developments to come to HTML in recent years. As has been mentioned numerous times, HTML is not a designer's medium. The inherent limitations of the markup language make it very difficult to get a document looking exactly as you want. However, with CSS, you have a level of control over an HTML document that is far more like the control you have over a print document.

 Note: Generally speaking, a *style* is a group of characteristics (like font, position, color, and so on) that are referred to by a single name. A *style sheet* is a group of these styles.

Basically, a CSS is a list of rules governing the way the elements of an HTML document are displayed. While HTML already is filled with rules that are designed to dictate how things are displayed (that is what tags are for), Cascading Style Sheets is cool for two basic reasons. First, with the help of DHTML's ability to access a document's DOM (Document Object Model), CSS lets you manipulate a greater range of the document's features than ever before.

Second, with the help of CSS, you can actually redefine the way the browser displays a whole range of HTML tags.

Strictly speaking, there are two different kinds of styles in CSS: a style class and a redefined tag. A redefined tag style involves an HTML tag whose properties have been changed. For instance, you can create a redefined tag style in which the <b> (bold) tag is altered so that when it is applied, the text is not only bolded, it also changes to green. The second type of style, called a style class, involves a style that has many different attributes. This style is then applied to a block of selected text to change the text's appearance. The great thing about both types of styles is that they can be changed well after they are created and all of the elements to which they were applied will update.

After you create a style (something we'll talk about shortly), there are three different ways the information is stored:

An external style sheet, as illustrated in Figure 10.1, is where you define all of your styles in a stand-alone style sheet file with a **.css** extension. The strength of external style sheets is that you can use the styles across *multiple documents* using the <link rel> tag.

An embedded style sheet is where you define all of the styles in the <head> section of your HTML document (Figure 10.2) between the <style> and </style> tags. This is a good way to assign attributes to all instances of a specific tag on a page. For example, you can make all of your <p> text dark red or space all of your list items <li> closer together. The thing about embedded styles is that they are specific to the *single document in which the style definitions appear.*

In the CSS panel, Dreamweaver displays an embedded style sheet as having the heading <style> and lists all of the style definitions beneath it.

An inline style can be applied to *selected elements* in an HTML document (such as a string of selected text) using the style attribute, as in the following:

```
<p style="text-indent: 10pt">This text indents 10 points</p>
```

```
 1  body {
 2      font-family: Arial, Helvetica, sans-serif;
 3      font-size: 12px;
 4  }
 5
 6  td {
 7      font-family: Arial, Helvetica, sans-serif;
 8      font-size: 12px;
 9  }
10
11  th {
12      font-family: Arial, Helvetica, sans-serif;
13      font-size: 12px;
14  }
15
16  form {
17      font-family: Arial, Helvetica, sans-serif;
18      font-size: 12px;
19      }
20
21  input {
22      font-family: Arial, Helvetica, sans-serif;
23      font-size: 12px;
24  }
25
26  textarea {
27      font-family: Arial, Helvetica, sans-serif;
```

Figure 10.1 An external style sheet is a document that contains only the style information.

```
38    <td width="50%" rowspan="100" background="bg.jpg"></td>
39    <td rowspan="100" bgcolor="#000000"><img src="spacer.gif"></td>
40
41    <TD WIDTH=125 HEIGHT=160 background="logo.gif"> </TD>
42
43    <TD WIDTH=83 HEIGHT=160 COLSPAN=2> <a href="course_info.htm"><IMG SRC="course_info.gif" A
44
45    <TD WIDTH=85 HEIGHT=160 COLSPAN=2> <a href="schedule.htm"><IMG SRC="schedule.gif" ALT="T1
46
47    <TD WIDTH=91 HEIGHT=160> <a href="grading.htm"><IMG SRC="grading.gif" ALT="T101 Grading"
48
```

Figure 10.2 An embedded style is stored in the <head> section of an HTML document.

The class attribute can be used if you have already defined a style class in the document head:

<p class="style1">This text is style 1</p>.

 If the document has external or embedded styles attached to it, inline styles can override their values.

Now, don't get me wrong, CSS is pretty darned groovy, but it isn't all sunshine and roses. First, at the very minimum, the feature is only supported by 4.0 browsers and above. In addition, many aspects of CSS are supported by only one browser, and some don't even work with any browsers. Wait, it gets even worse than this: some CSS attributes that, theoretically, are supposed to be supported by both Netscape and Internet Explorer are often unpredictable. So, what is one supposed to do? Well, when you're using Dreamweaver MX 2004 to leverage the power of CSS, always preview your document to see if it works properly in your target browser.

Understanding Styles and Their Attributes

There are more than 70 different style attributes that you can manipulate, and it's well worth your while to become at least passingly familiar with each so that you can truly leverage the power of CSS.

The information in the following section will become useful only after you learn how to create and manipulate a style sheet, something that will be covered a little later in the chapter. Because of this, there will be no real indication of how to get to the dialog boxes that are displayed—that will be looked at later. For now, it's important to become familiar with each of the styles, where they reside in the CSS Style Definition dialog box, and how they can be used. When you get to the point where you are working with style sheets, you can refer back to this section. Also, you could always flip past this particular section, to the "Creating Styles" section later in the chapter, and refer back to this section when necessary.

 Note: In many cases, Dreamweaver can't display a given attribute. These cases will be noted in the following sections; they are also marked in the CSS Style Definition dialog box with an asterisk (*).

Type

As you'd expect, the Type attributes primarily affect how type appears in your document.

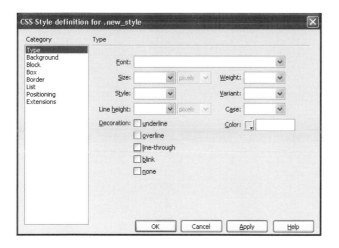

Font The Font drop-down menu lets you set the specific font of the style you are creating. With it, you can choose from the run-of-the mill HTML fonts as well as additional fonts. To do so, just click the Edit Font List option and add the desired font(s) in the resulting dialog box.

Size With the Size drop-down menu, you can choose the size of your text: a numerical value or one of a series of preset size options. When you choose a numerical value, the units drop-down menu becomes accessible, and from it you can choose the specific unit (the default is points) of the numerical size value.

Style The Style drop-down menu lets you choose from three options: normal, italic, or oblique.

Line Height The Line Height drop-down menu lets you set the distance between individual lines in a block of text. The line height, traditionally referred to as leading, can be set by choosing [value] from the drop-down menu (which is a placeholder for a value you enter), typing a value into the drop-down menu (which replaces [value]), and choosing the units in which the value will be expressed from the units drop-down menu.

Blink: The Bane of Web Design

Although using blinking text might be attractive to those who want to create a movement-filled website, using the Blink decoration option is a surefire way to annoy your audience. The <blink> tag, in addition to no longer being supported by any modern standard, is probably one of the most universally hated features of HTML.

Weight The Weight drop-down menu, which lets you choose from a series of numerical values (100 to 900) or relative settings (normal, bold, bolder, or lighter), affects the "boldness" of text.

Variant The Small-Caps Variant option switches the style's text from the way it would normally look to a style in which all the characters are uppercase with the capital letters being slightly larger. Be wary, however: the Variant option is neither previewable in Dreamweaver nor supported by the vast majority of browsers.

Decorations The various text decoration options (Underline, Overline, Line-Through, Blink, or None) let you add extra style to the way text appears. Choosing Underline will underline the style's text. Overline will insert a line along the top of the text. Line-Through strikes the text with a line running straight through its middle. Blink would make your text appear and then disappear repeatedly, but don't choose that.

Case The options in the Case drop-down menu let you set whether the text is displayed in lowercase or uppercase characters. Be advised, if you manipulate the style's case, it won't be displayed in Dreamweaver.

Color You can choose a text color for the style by clicking the Color swatch to open the Color palette.

Background

As you've probably noticed, when you are working in HTML you can only apply a background color or image to an entire page, table, or cell. This is rather frustrating if you want to exercise a little more control over how background colors or images are used in your design. With the CSS background attributes, however, you *can* exert more power background colors and images.

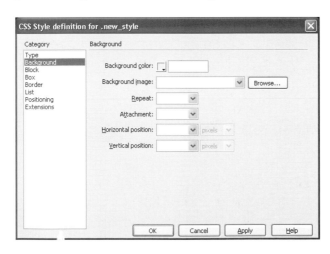

Background Color Click the Color swatch to open the Color palette. From here, you can choose the color of the style's background.

Background Image You can set the style's background image by clicking the Browse button to open the Select Image Source dialog box. Navigate to where the image is located, select it, and click Select.

Repeat The options in the Repeat drop-down menu (No-Repeat, Repeat, Repeat-X, Repeat-Y) determine the way the style's background image tiles. Choosing No-Repeat displays the selected image only once. If you select Repeat, the image will tile both vertically and horizontally to fill the style's entire area. Choosing Repeat-X causes the image to tile only horizontally (as a single line), while choosing Repeat-Y causes the image to tile vertically (as a single line).

Attachment The Attachment attribute really comes into play when you apply a style to the <body> tag of an HTML document (which effectively applies it to the entire visible portion of the page). Choosing Scroll from the Attachment drop-down menu will make the background image behave as it would under normal circumstances: it will move in or out of view when the page is scrolled. If you choose Fixed, the background image remains and will move when the page is scrolled, thereby remaining in the position where it was originally placed. Unfortunately, only Internet Explorer 4.0 and above support the Fixed attribute. Netscape will treat it as scroll.

Horizontal Position The Horizontal Position attribute lets you set the location of the background image relative to the element to which you are applying the style. You can choose Left, Center, or Right, and they work the same as any alignment options. Alternatively, you can set a value by selecting [value] from the drop-down menu (which is a placeholder for a value you enter), typing a number into the drop-down menu (which replaces [value]), and then choosing the units in which the value will be expressed from the units drop-down menu.

Vertical Position The Vertical Position attribute works exactly the same as the Horizontal Position attribute, except it affects the vertical position of the background image relative to the element to which you applied the style.

Block

The various Block attributes affect the typographic characteristics of all text within a selected element.

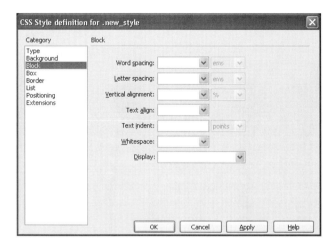

Word Spacing The Word Spacing attribute lets you set the amount of space between words in a selected block. To alter the spacing, just select [value] from the drop-down menu (which is a placeholder for a value you enter), type a number into the drop-down menu (replacing [value]), and choose the units in which the value will be expressed from the units drop-down menu. Word Spacing isn't displayed in the Dreamweaver environment, and the only browser that currently supports word spacing is Netscape 6.

Letter Spacing While Word Spacing affects the distance between individual words, Letter Spacing affects the distance between individual characters within a block. To set Letter Spacing, select [value] from the drop-down menu (which is a placeholder for a value you enter), type a number into the drop-down menu (which replaces [value], and choose the units in which the value will be expressed from the units drop-down menu to the right. Letter Spacing isn't displayed in the Dreamweaver environment, and it is currently only supported by version 6 browsers.

Vertical Alignment The Vertical Alignment attribute sets the vertical position of an image within a selected block.

Text Align The Text Align attribute lets you set the alignment of the text within the selected block. Your alignment options include left, center, right, and justify (which stretches the lines so that they are both right and left justified).

Text Indent With the Text Indent attribute, you can set a tablike space in the first line of any block of text. To do this, type a value into the Text Indent field, and when the units drop-down menu goes live, select a unit in which you want the indent expressed.

Whitespace The Whitespace attribute, which isn't displayed in Dreamweaver, controls the way the tabs and spaces appear in a block of text. Selecting the Normal option causes any *additional* white space to collapse. Choosing the Pre option will preserve all white space. If you select the Nowrap option, the line will break only if a line break (
 tag) is used.

Display The Display attribute lets you set whether and how an element is displayed.

Box

When working with CSS, think of the selection to which attributes are applied as an invisible box. The Box attributes let you control the way in which the elements within the selection (box) act in relation to the box itself.

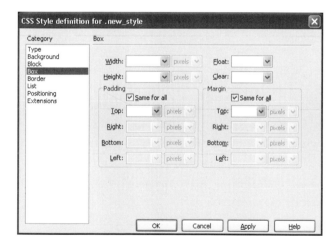

Width The Width attribute sets the width of the selected element's box. To leave the box as is, leave the field blank (don't choose anything from the drop-down menu) or choose Auto. To alter the width of the box, select [value] from the drop-down menu, type a number into the drop-down menu (which replaces [value]), and choose the units in which the value will be expressed from the units drop-down menu.

Note: If the selection is wider than the value of the box itself, it will wrap to fit within the box.

Height The Height attribute sets the height of the selected element's box. To leave the height as is, leave the field blank or choose Auto. To change the height of the box, select [value] from the drop-down menu, type a number into the drop-down menu (which replaces [value]), and choose the units in which the value will be expressed from the units drop-down menu.

Float By setting the Float attribute, you can take the element to which you are applying the style and stick it on either the left or right side of the page. If any other text encounters the floating object, it wraps itself around the element's box.

Note: Unfortunately, Dreamweaver will properly display only floating images and not other elements such as text.

Clear The Clear attribute determines the way floating objects interact with the element to which you're applying the style. If you choose Left, floating objects won't be able to occupy the margin to the left of the selected object. Choosing Right prohibits floating objects from occupying the right margin of the selected object. If you want floating objects to be able to occupy both left and right margins of a selected object, choose Both. To prohibit floating objects from occupying both the left and right margins of the element to which you are applying the style, select None.

Padding The Padding attributes work almost the same as they do with tables. Essentially, each value (Top, Right, Bottom, Left) determines the distance between the element to which the style was applied and the inside edge of its box. To change any of the padding values, select [value] from the specific drop-down menu, type a number into the drop-down menu itself (which replaces [value]), and choose the units in which the value will be expressed from the units drop-down menu. If you want the same value to apply to all of the Padding attributes, click the Same For All check box. The Padding attribute only works if the box's border is set to Visible.

Margin The Margin attributes let you set the margin (Top, Right, Bottom, or Left) between the element to which you applied the style and all other elements in a page. To leave the margin unchanged, select Auto from any of the four drop-down menus. If you want to set a specific margin on any of the four sides of the object, select [value] from the drop-down menu, type a number into the drop-down menu (which replaces [value]), and choose the units in which the value will be expressed from the units drop-down menu. As with the Padding attributes, if you want all the Margin attributes to be the same, check the Same For All check box.

Border

The various Border attributes are closely related to the Box attributes. By default, the box of an element to which you've applied a style is invisible. However, with the Border attributes, you can control the way the edge (border) of the box looks.

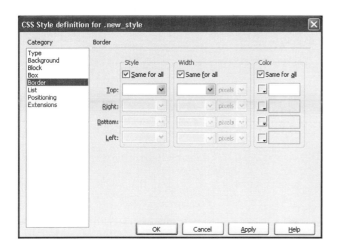

Width The four independent Width attributes (Top, Bottom, Right, Left), which do not display in Dreamweaver, determine the *thickness* of the element's border. To set a specific value for any of the edges, select [value] from the drop-down menu, type a number into the drop-down menu itself (which replaces [value]), and choose the units in which the value will be expressed from the units drop-down menu. In addition, you've got several preset options (Thin, Medium, Thick) from which you can choose.

Note: Remember, you can set the width value for any edge independently of any other.

If you want all of the Width values to be the same, click the Same For All check box.

Color The four independent Color attributes (Top, Bottom, Right, Left) let you set the color of the element's border. Just click the Color swatch to open the Color palette and choose a border color for the style. As with all of the Border attributes, you can set the color of all the borders to be the same by clicking the Same For All check box.

Style The various Style attributes let you change the look of the element's border. As with all of the Border attributes, you can set the style of all the borders to be the same by clicking the Same For All check box.

List

The way default lists (either ordered or unordered) look is pretty limiting and thereby frustrating. (If you are having trouble remembering how lists work, see Chapter 3.) However, with the CSS List attributes, you can exert a more control over how an ordered or unordered list appears.

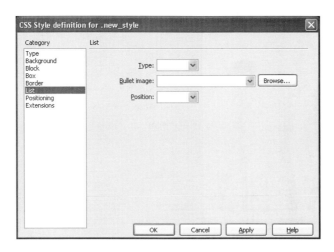

Type The Type drop-down menu lets you select from a preset list of bullets or numbers that are used in a list. The Type attribute doesn't display in Dreamweaver.

Bullet Image Even with the additional types available, bullets can be pretty humdrum and boring. You can add a little extra "oomph" with the Bullet Image attribute, which lets you choose an image that will be used in place of the regular bullet. Click the Browse button. In the Select Image Source dialog box, navigate to the place where the image is located, select it, and click Select.

 Note: The Bullet Image attribute doesn't show up in Dreamweaver.

Position The Position attribute lets you determine how the text wraps in relation to the bullet. Choosing Inside will line up all the text with the bullet point; choosing Outside will line the text up with the page's margin.

 Note: The Position attribute doesn't display in Dreamweaver.

Positioning

One of the coolest things about CSS is that you can use it to position elements on your page using an absolute coordinate system.

In Dreamweaver, there are two ways that this can be accomplished: with the Positioning attributes in the CSS Style Definition dialog box or with layers. Because the latter half of this chapter is devoted to layers, I'm skipping over the Positioning attributes in the section.

Extensions

The Extensions attributes section of the CSS Style Definition dialog box is where Macromedia has placed the most advanced CSS features. The kicker is that currently, the Extensions attributes have extremely spotty browser coverage.

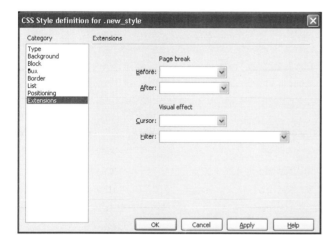

Page Break While all of the attributes we've discussed thus far have been supported by either Netscape or Internet Explorer, the Page Break attribute isn't currently supported by either—it's still in the "recommendation" phase. When (and if) it is adopted, it would let you set a page break either before or after a block of text for the purposes of printing.

Cursor The Cursor attribute (which is supported by only Internet Explorer 4, Netscape 6, and above) lets you change the user's cursor. Simply choose an option from the drop-down menu.

Filter The Filter attribute is a proprietary (Microsoft owns it lock, stock, and barrel) widget, which functions only with Internet Explorer 4 and above, that lets you apply a special effect to a selected object. However, don't be too surprised that some Filter attributes won't even work in Internet Explorer—they are pretty unreliable.

Creating Styles

Now that you've spent some time exploring the various attributes you can set for a given style, it's time to put that knowledge to work and learn how you use Dreamweaver MX 2004 to actually create Cascading Style Sheets.

As mentioned earlier, there are two different kinds of styles (redefined tags and style classes) and three kinds of style sheets (inline, embedded, and external) you can create. While not exactly accurate, for the purposes of this section, I'll refer to all of these as style sheets, but they are sometimes called CSS or simply styles.

Now, before we forge ever forward, there is something you need to know about the way in which Dreamweaver MX 2004 creates styles and style sheets. Unlike previous versions of Dreamweaver, where you had to manually create classes and style sheets, Dreamweaver MX 2004 automatically generates CSS markup based on the formatting you apply to text. So, for instance, if you change the font, color, and size of a block of text, Dreamweaver automatically creates a new style with those attributes. The newly created style is stored in an embedded style sheet and appears in the Property Inspector's Style drop-down menu (Figure 10.3) so that it can be used again. Don't get me wrong; you can manually create style sheets and classes using the CSS Styles panel (something we'll talk about a little later) just as you did in previous versions of Dreamweaver. However, in order to leverage the full power of CSS in Dreamweaver MX 2004, you should be aware of the Property Inspector's new functionality.

Figure 10.3 Styles that are automatically generated by Dreamweaver MX 2004 based on your text formatting appear in the Property Inspector's Style drop-down menu.

In the following sections, you'll learn how to manually create a style class, redefine an HTML tag, and redefine hyperlink properties with selectors—all with the CSS Styles panel. For the purposes of these sections, however, you're going to focus exclusively on how to create an embedded Cascading Style Sheet. A little later on in the chapter, you'll take what you learned here and apply it to creating an external Cascading Style Sheet.

Defining Style Classes

A style *class* is basically a style with many different attributes that can be applied to any tag. In this section, you'll explore how to create a style class:

1. Make sure the document in which you want to create the style class is open.

2. Open the CSS Styles panel by choosing Window > CSS Styles.

3. Click the New CSS Style button to open the New CSS Style dialog box (Figure 10.4).

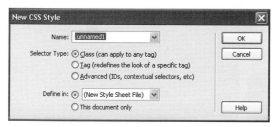

Figure 10.4 The New CSS Style dialog box

4. If it isn't already selected, select the Class radio button in the Selector Type section.

5. You'll notice that the text .unnamed1 appears in the Name field. This is the name of the style that will appear in the CSS Styles panel (and the Property Inspector's Style drop-down menu). Since you probably don't want to use this default name, click anywhere in the Name field and type a new name. The name that you give shouldn't have any spaces and it must begin with a period; if you don't add a period yourself, Dreamweaver will automatically do it for you.

6. From the Define In options, choose This Document Only.

Note: Remember that the style created using the process outlined in this section applies only to the document from which it is being created. If you want to create a style that can be applied to many different documents, you'll need to create an external CSS—something we'll talk about later in this chapter.

7. Click OK. The CSS Style Definition dialog box appears. Note that the name of the style sheet appears in the title bar of the Style Definition dialog box.

8. Set all the attributes of your style.

Note: If you are having trouble remembering what each attribute does, see the previous section, "Understanding Styles and Their Attributes."

9. Click OK. The style class will appear in the CSS Styles panel (Figure 10.5).

Note: After having gone though the preceding steps, you'll be faced with a totally blank page because you need to actually apply it to something (as an inline style) for it to affect that way your page looks. If you want to put that newly created style to work, see the section "Applying Styles" later in this chapter.

Figure 10.5 Once created, the new style appears in the CSS Styles panel. Note that to the right of the actual style name, the panel lists the style's attributes.

Changing HTML Tags

The process by which you redefine an HTML tag is just as easy as creating a style class:

Note: t's important to remember that even though you change the properties of an HTML tag, it will always retain its original characteristic: the new one(s) will just be added on.

1. In the document for which you want to change an HTML tag, open the CSS Styles panel (Window > CSS Styles).
2. Click the New CSS Style button ⬛ to open the New CSS Style dialog box.
3. From the Selector Type list, choose the Tag option.
4. From the Tag drop-down menu (which replaces the Name dropdown menu at the top of the New CSS Style dialog box), choose the tag that you wish to redefine. The items that populate the Tag drop-down menu depend on the type of CSS being used.
5. Choose the This Document Only from the Define In options.

Note: Remember, we'll discuss creating external CSS later in this chapter.

6. Click OK.

7. In the Style Definitions dialog box, select the attributes you'd like to add to the tag and click OK.

Just as a style class does, the redefined tag will appear in the CSS Styles panel under the <style> heading that defines the embedded style sheet. (Figure 10.6).

Redefined HTML Tag

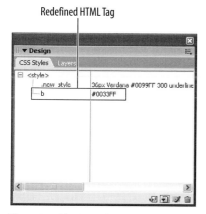

Figure 10.6 The CSS Styles panel with a redefined HTML tag

Redefining Hyperlink Properties with Contextual Selectors

CSS contextual selectors let you create a *pseudoclass* (not really a class, but close enough) that combines a style class with a redefined HTML tag. Affecting only the <a> tag, CSS selectors are most commonly used to change the way a hyperlink looks when a user moves their mouse over it. Say, for instance, you don't want a hyperlink to have its typical underline but you want it to change to a different color or to appear with a strikeover line through it when the user moves their cursor over it: this would be done with a CSS selector.

Follow these steps to redefine hyperlink properties with a CSS selector:

1. In the document for which you want to change hyperlink properties, open the CSS Styles panel (Window > CSS Styles).

2. Click the New CSS Style button.

3. Choose the Advanced option from the Selector Type list.

4. From the Selector drop-down menu, choose the hyperlink state whose properties you want to change:

- Choosing a:active will let you change the look of an active hyperlink (that is, when it's clicked by the user).

- By selecting a:hover, you'll be able to manipulate the properties that the hyperlink displays when the user's mouse is over the link itself.
- By choosing a:link, you can change the properties of the hyperlink as it would appear normally (just hanging out on the page doing its thing).
- Selecting a:visited lets you manipulate the way the hyperlink looks after it has been clicked by the user.

5. From the Define In options, choose This Document Only.

6. Click OK.

7. In the Styles Definitions dialog box, select the attributes you want applied to the hyperlink.

8. Click OK.

As with a redefined tag, the CSS contextual selector will appear in the CSS Styles panel (Figure 10.7).

CSS contextual selector

Figure 10.7 The CSS Styles panel with a contextual selector

 Note: The CSS contextual selector will apply to all the hyperlinks on the page.

Working with External Style Sheets

Now that you've got a handle on how CSS (and specifically embedded styles) works, it's time to explore the second type of style sheet: external. An external style sheet is a discrete file with a .css filename extension that is composed of nothing more than the actual style information (see Figure 10.1).

The primary benefit of an external style sheet is that it only needs to be created once. It can be reapplied *ad infinitum* to page after page without having to re-create the same styles for each page—which is what you must do if you use embedded styles.

In the following sections, you are going to explore two separate topics: how to create external style sheets and how to link an existing external style sheet to an HTML document.

Creating External Style Sheets

The process of creating an external style sheet is almost identical to creating an embedded one—*almost*. There are a few differences that warrant a full exploration of the process.

If you remember, a style class is a style with many different attributes that can be applied to any block of text as an inline style. Here's how to create a style class:

1. In the document for which you want to create the external style sheet, open the CSS Styles panel (Window > CSS Styles).

2. Click the New CSS Style button ⊞.

3. From the type options, choose either Class, Tag, or Advanced. Make sure that that if you select Class, you enter a name into the Name field. If you select Tag, select the tag you want to redefine from the Tag drop-down menu. If you selected Advanced, select the specific contextual selector from the Selector drop-down menu.

4. Select the Define In: (New Style Sheet File) option.

5. Click OK.

6. In the Save Style Sheet File As dialog box, navigate to the location where you want to save the CSS file (remember, an external style sheet is a discrete file), type a name into the File Name field, choose Style Sheet Files (*.css) from the Save As Type drop-down menu, and click Save.

7. In the CSS Styles Definition dialog box, select the attributes you'd like applied to that style.

8. Click OK.

Note: By default, the external style sheet you created will automatically be applied to the currently open document. Additionally, if you look in the CSS Styles panel, Dreamweaver lists the name of the external style sheet with a .css extension and lists all styles defined within it.

Linking to External Style Sheets

As mentioned many times, one of the grand benefits to an external style sheet is that it can be created once and then applied to any number of HTML documents. When you do this, all the redefined HTML tags, contextual selectors, and style classes will either be automatically applied (as in the case of a redefined HTML tag) or be available for application (in the case of style classes).

To link an external style sheet to a Dreamweaver document, follow these steps:

1. In the document to which you want to link the external style sheet, open the CSS Styles panel (Window > CSS Styles).

2. Click the Attach Style Sheet button .

3. When the Attach External Style Sheet dialog box appears, click the Link radio button. From there, click the Browse button to the right of the File/URL field.

4. In the Select Style Sheet File dialog box, navigate to the CSS file you wish to attach, select it, and click OK.

After the external style sheet has been attached to the document, notice that the external style sheet and all of its style classes are accessible through the CSS Styles panel.

 Note: Redefined tags and CSS selectors will automatically be applied to the document when the external style sheet is attached.

Applying Styles

Now that you've gone through all the trouble of creating a style sheet (whether embedded or external), it's time to learn how to use it in a page. Because both a redefined tag and a CSS selector are automatically applied to the document in which they're created, you can't apply them manually. However, you can (and are supposed to) manually apply style classes to selected items:

 Note: You can apply a style class to an entire page by selecting the <body> tag with the Tag Selector and then following the steps listed here.

1. Select the element(s) in your page to which you wish to apply the style class.

2. If it isn't already, open the Property Inspector.

3. Select the style you'd like to apply from the Property Inspector's Style drop-down menu.

> **Note:** All of the styles in your style sheet (whether embedded or external) are listed in the Property Inspector's Style drop-down menu.

Alternatively, you can apply a style using the CSS Styles panel. To do so, just follow these steps:

1. Select the element on your page to which you would like to apply the style.

2. If it isn't already, open the CSS Styles panel by choosing Window > CSS Styles.

3. From here, select the style class that you would like to apply.

> **Note:** important to remember that style classes are always preceded by a period (.) in the CSS Styles panel.

4. Choose Apply from the CSS Styles panel's options menu.

> **Note:** When you select a redefined tag, the Apply button is disabled

Removing Styles

You may find yourself in a situation where you want to remove a style class from an element:

1. Select the element from which you want to remove the style class.

2. If it isn't already, open the Property Inspector by choosing Window > Properties.

3. From here, select None from the Styles drop-down menu.

> **Note:** If you've applied multiple styles to a given element on your page, you'll have to repeat the process a few times until all of the styles have been removed.

Editing Styles

Style classes, redefined tags, or CSS selectors are by no means fixed in stone. One of the best features of CSS is that you can create a style, apply it to any number of elements, and then go back and change that style and have all of the elements to which it was applied change accordingly. To edit a style, just follow these steps:

1. In the document whose style sheet (embedded or external) you wish to edit, select Manage Styles from the Property Inspector's Style drop-down menu.

2. When the Edit Style Sheet dialog box appears (Figure 10.8), select either the external style sheet you want to edit (displayed as *filename*.css) or the embedded style sheet you want to edit (displayed by default as <style>).

Figure 10.8 The Edit Style Sheet dialog box

3. Click the Edit button ⬚Edit...⬚.

4. When the dialog box displaying all of the styles of the selected embedded or external style sheet appears (Figure 10.9), select the class, redefined tag, or contextual selector you would like to edit, and click the Edit button ⬚Edit...⬚.

Figure 10.9 The secondary "edit style sheets" dialog box lets you select the specific class, redefined tag, or contextual selector you'd like to edit.

5. From here, the CSS Style Definition dialog box appears, in which you can make any changes to the class, redefined tag, or contextual selector.

6. Once you've finished, click Apply to be returned to the secondary "edit style sheets" dialog box. Click Done to be returned to the main Edit Style Sheet dialog box and then Done again to be returned to the Document window.

Using Premade Style Sheets

Beyond the methods described earlier, you can also create a new document based on a library of predesigned Cascading Style Sheets. To do so, just follow these steps:

1. Choose File > New.

2. When the New Document dialog box appears, you've got a couple of choices:

- To open one of the premade *external* style sheets, select the CSS Styles option from the Category list box in the General tab. From there, choose one of the style sheets listed in the CSS Style Sheets list box (of which there are many).

- To create an HTML file that has an existing external style sheet attached to it, select Page Designs (CSS) from the Category list box. From there, select one of the options from the Page Designs (CSS) list box.

3. Click the Create button .

4. If you selected the Page Designs (CSS) option, you'll be prompted to save the HTML file. In addition, you'll be prompted to copy all of the document's dependant files (including the actual CSS file) to the location where you saved the HTML document.

Understanding Layers

As has been mentioned before, the Web is not particularly well suited as a design medium. It's pretty difficult to get things looking exactly as you would like. This was not much of a problem for most people using the Web in the early days of HTML. However, things started to change as more and more traditional print designers, who were accustomed to total control over their creations, began migrating into the world of web design. This is where Dynamic HTML (DHTML) comes into the picture. One of the most powerful features of DHTML is the ability to position elements on a page using an absolute system of coordinates. This feature alone, which makes web design much more like traditional print design than ever before, is tremendously exciting.

Dreamweaver makes the absolute positioning of elements, something that would be very time consuming and tedious if you had to hand-code the DHTML, quite effortless through the use of a great feature called layers.

Creating Layers

The process of creating layers is quite easy and, like many features in Dreamweaver, can be accomplished different ways.

Note: Because layers are made possible by Dynamic HTML, they are only supported by browsers that are version 4 and above.

First, a layer can be inserted into your Dreamweaver document using the Insert menu:

1. In the document into which you want to insert the layer, place your cursor where you'd like the layer to be initially placed.

2. Choose Insert > Layout Objects > Layer. The top-left corner of the layer (which is created with a default size) is automatically inserted where your cursor is.

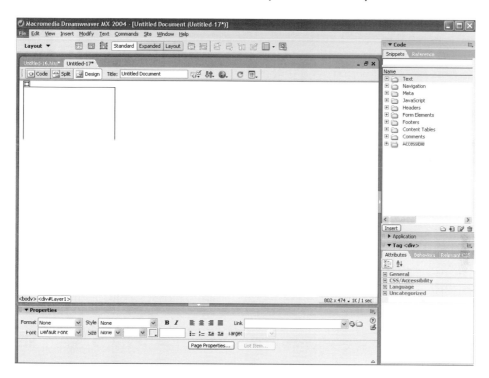

Because a layer is a specific kind of object within Dreamweaver, it can also be inserted into a document with the Insert bar. However, unlike with the Insert menu, you can also use the Insert bar to draw a layer:

1. In the document into which you want to insert the layer, open the Insert bar (Window > Insert) and make sure you are in the Layout section.

2. Click the Draw Layer button.

3. Move your cursor to the location in your page where you want to create the layer—notice that your cursor has changed to crosshairs.

4. Click and drag so that the outlines are equal to the desired size of the layer.

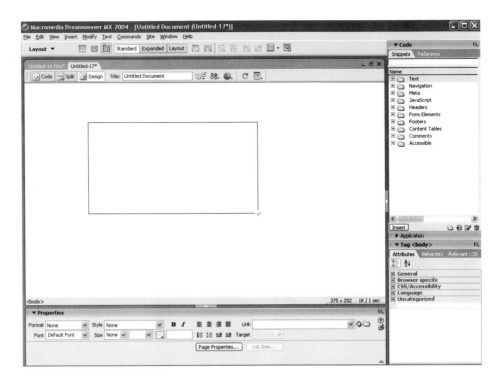

5. When the outlines are the dimensions you want the layer to be, release your mouse button.

If you have your document's invisible elements turned on, you'll notice that a small yellow icon is also inserted into the document. This represents the actual layer's corresponding HTML code tag and can be clicked to select the particular layer. As with other invisible elements, this icon appears only when you're working within Dreamweaver. It won't be visible when your page is viewed in a browser.

As you'd assume, the process of creating the layer is only the first step you need to take. While relatively simple looking, layers are fairly complicated objects, and you need to do a certain amount of massaging and manipulating to get the maximum use out of them. It behooves you to get intimately familiar with the different ways in which they can be manipulated

In the following sections, you'll get a chance to explore a bucket load of topics geared toward helping you get the most of layers.

Adding Content to Layers

One of the benefits of layers is that content can be placed exactly where you want it within your page and any content that can be added to a normal Dreamweaver document can be inserted into a layer. Thus, the first step in learning how to work with layers is to learn how to add content to them. To add content to a layer, follow these steps:

1. In the document where the layers reside, click your cursor anywhere within the layer. When you do this, it will go from being dormant to being live: its edges turn solid black and a handle appears in the top-left corner.

2. After you confirm the cursor is inside the confines of the layer, follow the same procedure you'd follow to insert content into a page under normal circumstances. Remember, you can insert anything into a layer (text, images, multimedia, and so on).

Selecting Layers

To manipulate a layer (whether it has any content or not), you must first select it. In the document that has the layer you wish to select, choose one of the following options:

*   Click the edge of a dormant layer. If the layer is active (that is, you've clicked somewhere within it) but not selected, click its handle.

*   Click the layer's icon , which represents the layer's code and appears when the layer is initially inserted.

> **Note:** If the layer's marker isn't visible, it's more than likely that that you've turned off your document's invisible elements (of which the layer marker is one). To turn them back on, choose View > Visual Aids > Invisible Elements. If It doesn't become visible, you might also have to turn the layer marker on using the Edit Preferences dialog box: choose Edit > Preferences, select Invisible Elements from the Category list, and select the Anchor Points For Layers option.

When selected, the layer's resize handles will appear (Figure 10.10).

Figure 10.10 When a layer is selected, its resize handles appear.

In addition to the options described below, you can select a layer by choosing Window > Layers and clicking its name in the Layers panel. To learn more about the Layers panel, see the section "Arranging Layers" later in this chapter.

Deleting Layers

You will probably reach the point where you'll want to delete a layer. While the process itself is pretty easy, it's extremely important to remember that if you delete a layer, all of its content goes in the garbage as well.

To delete a layer, select it using one of the methods described in the preceding section, then either press Delete/Backspace or right-click/⌘-click and choose Cut from the pop-up context menu.

Resizing Layers

When layers are created (whether with the Insert menu or the Insert bar), they have an initial width and height. Don't worry; their dimensions are hardly fixed: they can be changed on a whim using two different techniques.

 Note: A layer will automatically expand to accommodate content.

One of the most intuitive and user-friendly ways to resize a layer is by manually dragging its resize handles. Select the layer that you want to resize and choose from the following options:

- Click the handles in the middle of the layer's left or right side to resize horizontally.
- Click and drag the handles in the middle of the layer's top or bottom to resize vertically.
- Click and drag the handles on any of the layer's four corners to resize both horizontally and vertically at the same time.

When the layer has reached the desired size, release your mouse button.

Although dragging is a great way to quickly and easily resize a layer, it doesn't offer you pixel-precise control. Say, for instance, you need a layer whose dimensions are 121×54. If you resized by dragging, it would be hit or miss. With the Property Inspector, however, you can set the exact dimensions of a layer.

To resize a layer numerically, select the layer whose dimensions you want to change and open the Property Inspector (Window > Properties). Enter values for the layer's width and height (in pixels) into the W and H fields, respectively. Then press Return/Enter, or click anywhere off the Property Inspector, to apply the changes.

Note: If your layer is populated with a fixed-size object (like an image), its size cannot be changed to be smaller than the object itself.

You can also resize the layer by using the keyboard. Just select the layer and press Option/Ctrl+arrow and it will be resized incrementally in the direction of the arrow key you're pressing.

Moving Layers

Another benefit of layers is that they can be used to position content anywhere on your page. This means you have to be able to easily change their location. Once again, Dreamweaver provides you with two primary ways to move a layer: by dragging and with the Property Inspector.

To move a layer by dragging, select the layer and drag it by its handle to its new location. When it's in the desired location, release the mouse button.

You can also move your layer using absolute units (pixels) relative to the top (Y) and left (X) of the page in which it resides. To do so, select the layer and open the Property Inspector (Window > Properties). Enter values (in pixels) in the L and T fields for the distance you want to move from the left edge and top of your page, respectively. Then press Return/Enter, or click anywhere off the Property Inspector, to apply the changes.

Changing Layer Background Color or Image

A cool feature of layers (which can be used in many different creative ways) is that their background color can be changed.

To change a layer's background color, select the layer and open the Property Inspector (Window > Properties). Click the Bg Color swatch to open the Color palette. There, click the color you wish to use. Remember, to mix your own custom color, you can always open the color picker by clicking the color wheel icon in the Color palette.

You certainly aren't limited to just changing the background color of a layer; you can also add a background image.

To add a background image to a layer, select the layer and open the Property Inspector (Window > Properties). Click the Browse For File button to the right of the Bg Image field 📁. When the Select Image Source dialog box appears, navigate to the location where the image is located, select it, and click OK.

Setting Layer Overflow

A little earlier, we discussed how to resize a layer. I mentioned that, under normal circumstances, a layer will expand to accommodate content. However, there are situations when the layer's dimensions will have been set to be smaller than the content itself. In situations such as these, what happens to the extra content that is outside the confines of the layer? This is where something called *layer overflow* comes into the picture.

Essentially, the four layer overflow settings determine how the browser copes with that extra content.

Unfortunately, layer overflow has pretty spotty browser support. Currently, only Netscape 6, Internet Explorer 4, and later versions can properly cope with layer overflow. Also, keep in mind that Dreamweaver won't display a layer's overflow property; to see it, you'll need to preview the page in a browser.

To set the layer's overflow property, select the layer and open the Property Inspector (Window > Properties).

From the Overflow drop-down menu, select one of the following options:

Visible The layer's dimensions will be totally ignored and all the content will be displayed.

Hidden The content that falls outside the layer will be cut off and not displayed.

Scroll Horizontal and vertical scroll bars will appear in the layer regardless of the layer's dimensions and the size of the content.

Auto Scroll bars will appear only if the size of the content exceeds the dimensions of the layer.

Controlling Layer Visibility

Another cool feature of layers is that you can determine whether or not they are visible. On the surface, this might seem to be somewhat of a useless property over which to have control. Why create layer content only to make it invisible? However, when you think about the fact that the visibility of a layer can be controlled in Dreamweaver with behaviors (something you looked at in Chapter 9), the ability to control their visibility makes a lot more sense. For instance, you could have a layer appear when the user moves their mouse over a certain area in your web page and then have it disappear when their cursor is moved away.

To set the visibility of a layer, select the layer and open the Property Inspector (Window > Properties).

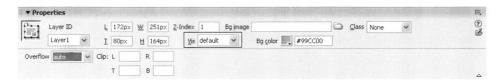

Select one of the options from the Vis drop-down menu:

Default Lets the browser determine whether or not the layer is visible. Most browsers use Inherit as their default setting for a layer's visibility.

Inherit Causes the visibility of all layers nested in one layer to be determined by the parent layer in which they are embedded.

Visible Causes the layer to be visible in the browser.

Hidden Forces the layer and all of its contents to be invisible in the browser.

You can also change the visibility of a layer with the Layers panel. To do so, open the Layers panel (Window > Layers) and click the "eyeball" column to set a layer's visibility:

- A closed eye (shown at left in Figure 10.11) indicates that the layer's visibility has been set to Hidden.

- An open eye (at right in Figure 10.11) means that the layer's visibility has been set to Visible.

- No eyeball icon means that the layer's visibility has been set to Inherit, which causes the visibility of all layers nested in one layer to be determined by the parent layer in which they are embedded.

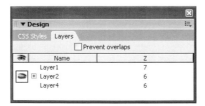 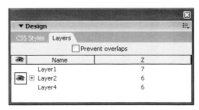

Figure 10.11 At left, Layer2 is hidden; at right: it's visible.

Setting Layer Clipping Area

The *clipping area* is an interesting but not often used layer feature. Essentially, the clipping area acts as a mask that hides (and doesn't delete) the layer's contents outside a predefined square. The square is defined by four values: top, bottom, left, and right. The L (left) and R (right) sides of the clipped area are measured from the left side of the layer. The T (top) and B (bottom) sides of the clipped area are measured from the top of the layer.

Here's how to set a layer's clipping area:

1. Select the layer whose clipping area you wish to set and open the Property Inspector (Window > Properties).

2. In the Clip section, enter a value (in pixels) for the left side of the visible area into the L field.

3. Enter a value (in pixels) for the right side of the visible area into the R field. If the value for the right side of the visible area is not larger than that of the left side, the layer's content will be totally invisible.

4. Enter a value (in pixels) for the top of the visible area into the T field.

5. Enter a value (in pixels) for the bottom of the visible area in the B field. If the value for the bottom of the visible area is larger for that of the top, the layer's content will be invisible.

6. Press Return/Enter, or click anywhere off the Property Inspector, to apply your changes.

Arranging Layers

While the vast majority of the stuff you can do to layers is carried out with the help of the Property Inspector, there is an additional tool with which you can manipulate and manage the layers in your document: the Layers panel.

Accessible by choosing Window > Layers, the Layers panel (Figure 10.12) lists all of the current layers in your document and lets you rename a layer, prevent layer overlap, set the stacking order of your layers, nest layers, and set layer visibility.

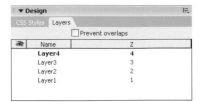

Figure 10.12 The Layers panel

Naming Layers with the Layers Panel

By default, when you create a layer (either with the Insert menu or the Insert bar), it is created with a standard default name: Layer1, Layer2, Layer3, and so on. To give the layers in your page a new name, follow these steps:

Note: If you want to use a behavior to control the way a given layer behaves, it will need a unique name.

1. From the document where the layer you wish to rename resides, open the Layers panel (Window > Layers).
2. Double-click the layer name.
3. When the Layer Name field becomes active, type in a new name.
4. Press Return/Enter, or click anywhere off the Layers panel.

Preventing Layer Overlap

Another cool feature of layers is that, because they can be positioned anywhere on a page, they can be placed on top of one another (see Figure 10.13). The relationship between layers in a stack (that is, which one is on top) is set by the Z Index, something we'll discuss shortly.

Figure 10.13 Layers can be placed on top of one another, creating an overlap.

However, you'll probably encounter a situation in which you'll want to prevent the layers from overlapping. To do this, open the page in which you wish to prevent layer overlap, open the Layers panel (Window > Layers), and check the Prevent Overlaps check box. This option affects all layers on the page.

Setting Layer Stacking Order

When two or more layers overlap, a spatial relationship determining the position of all the layers in an imaginary three-dimensional stack is instantly established. You can think about overlapping layers as a stack of papers. If one of the sheets of paper is at the bottom of the pile, its content might only be partially visible, depending on how the remaining sheets are positioned. On the other hand, the sheet on the top of the stack will have all of its content visible.

The numerical value that represents the order of each layer in the stack, called the *Z Index*, can be manipulated to your heart's content using the Layers panel:

1. From the page in which you wish to prevent layer overlap, open the Layers panel (Window > Layers).

2. Double-click the layer's Z Index (in the Z column).

3. When the Z Index field becomes editable, enter a new value (remember, a high number means a higher place in the stack).

4. To apply your changes, press Return/Enter or click anywhere off the Layers panel. The layers displayed in the Layers panel will automatically reorganize themselves in the new stacking order.
   The lower a layer's Z Index, the lower it will be in the stack.

Note: You can also change a layer's Z Index by using the Property Inspector.

Nesting Layers

When you nest layers, you place one layer within another. The layer in which the other is placed acts as a parent, partially controlling the nested layer's properties. When you move the parent layer, the nested child layer moves as well.

To nest two layers using the Layers panel, follow these steps:

1. From the document that contains the layer you wish to nest, open the Layers panel (Window > Layers).

2. In the Layers panel, ⌘/Ctrl-drag the layer you wish to nest over the layer you wish to act as the parent. Notice that the cursor will change to a document icon and the target parent layer will be highlighted with a faint blue box.

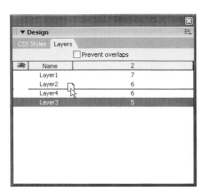

3. When your cursor is over the layer that will act as the parent, release your mouse button. Notice that an expand/collapse icon will appear to the left of the parent layer and the child layer will be represented as a subset of the parent.

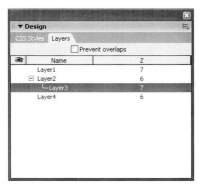

Managing and Publishing Your Site

11

Creating a website, large or small, can be a complicated process. You have to consider not only design and usability issues but also logistical ones such as asset management, site organization, and server management. On top of this, if you are working as one member of a team, such things as access and project management become an issue as well. For those who are relatively new to web design, the realization that creating a website is far more than just placing text and images can be a little daunting. Don't worry; Dreamweaver can handle it, and so can you.

Chapter Contents

Manipulating Local Sites

Back in Chapter 2, you learned how to set up a rudimentary Local Site (something that is absolutely vital if you want to take advantage of Dreamweaver's true power and potential). You also learned the absolute rudiments of the Files panel, focusing primarily on how you can create and manipulate a site map.

Note: Because the process of creating a Local Site has already been covered, it will not be covered in this chapter. If you are having trouble remembering how to set up a Local Site, it's important to refresh your memory before continuing: see the section "The Fine Art of Local Sites" in Chapter 2.

In the following sections, you will explore how to use the Files panel to manage and manipulate a Local Site. Included will be a discussion on how to open files, create new files, move files, check the integrity of your Local Site's links, repair broken links, search your Local Site, create Design Notes, and switch to another Local Site, all from within the Files panel.

Opening Files from within the Files Panel

Although you can manually open files using the File > Open command, you can also open HTML documents in your Local Site directly from within the Files panel. This is particularly handy if you are doing other things from within this panel and need to quickly open up a document.

Note: Although the Files panel offers you easy access to the files in your Local Site, you can use its built-in file explorer to access any of the files on your hard drive without having to leave the Dreamweaver MX 2004 workspace. However, remember that if you don't save the file to the Local Site, it won't be included when you upload to your remote server.

To open a document from within the Files panel, follow these steps:

1. Open the Files panel (Window > Files).
2. If you aren't already working in a defined Local Site, select a site from the Site drop-down menu (Figure 11.1).
3. Navigate to where the file is located within the Local Site and select the file.

Site drop-down menu

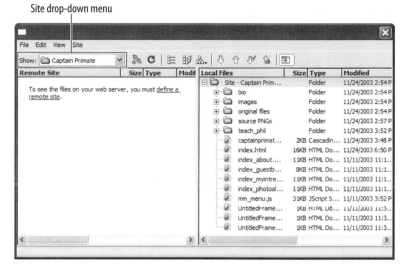

Figure 11.1 The Site drop-down menu in the Files panel lets you select the specific Local Site with which you would like to work.

Note: To drill down into a Local Site, click the expand (+) icon just to the left of a folder to open it.

4. Choose *one* of the following options to open the selected document:

- Double-click the file's icon (to the left of the actual filename).
- Right-click/Control-click the filename and choose Open.
- Choose File > Open from the Files panel menu.

Creating New Documents from within the Files Panel

Although you can create new HTML documents in Dreamweaver by using the File > New command, you might find it helpful to know that you can also easily create them directly from within the Files panel itself. This is quite helpful if you want to create *placeholder documents,* that is, HTML files that are located within your Local Site but to which no content has yet been added.

To create a new document from within the Files panel, follow these steps:

1. From within a defined Local Site, select the folder (or subfolder) where you want the new file to be created.

2. Open the context menu (right-click/Control-click) and choose New File, or choose File > New from the Files panel menu.

Note: If the Files panel's drop-down menu is not visible, click the Expand/Collapse button .

3. A new HTML file (called untitled.html or untitled.htm by default) will appear in the selected folder; notice that the name of the newly created file is an editable field (Figure 11.2).

 Note: The filename extension (either html or htm) with which the new file is created is determined by the Add Extension When Saving option, which is located in the General category of the Preferences dialog box (Edit > Preferences).

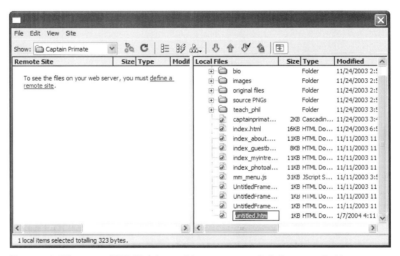

Figure 11.2 When a new HTML file is inserted, its name automatically becomes editable.

4. Without clicking anywhere, type the desired name for the newly created file.
5. When you finish typing the name you want to give to the newly created file, click anywhere off the newly created file or press Return/Enter.

 Note: You cannot create a new file that doesn't have a name. If you attempt to do so, Dreamweaver will give you an error message.

Creating New Folders in Your Site

For the sake of organization and orderliness, your Local Site should be separated into a series of folders and subfolders. When you initially define a Local Site (in an area where there aren't any existing files), you'll only have one folder in the site, your local root folder. However, as you progress in your creative endeavors, you'll want to create additional subfolders. This can easily be done from directly within the Files panel.

The way you create and organize folders and subfolders within your Local Site is often at least partially determined by your site's information architecture:

1. In a defined Local Site, select the folder (or subfolder) where you want the newly created folder to be located.

Note: If you are starting with a new Local Site in which no files are located, you'll need to select the Local Root Folder (the topmost folder in the right side of your Files window).

2. Open the context menu (right-click/Control-click) and choose New Folder, or choose File > New Folder from the Files panel menu.

Note: If the Files panel's drop-down menu is not visible, click the Expand/Collapse button .

3. A new folder (called untitled by default) will appear in the selected folder; notice that the name of the newly created folder is an editable field (Figure 11.3).

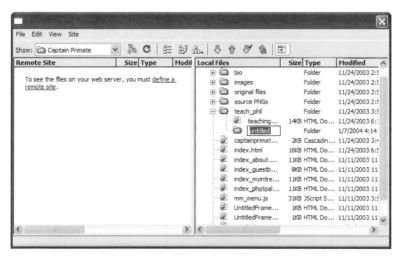

Figure 11.3 When a new folder is inserted, its name automatically becomes editable.

4. Without clicking anywhere, type the desired name for the newly created folder. Because folders aren't HTML documents, they don't need an extension, just a name.

5. When you finish typing the name, click anywhere off the newly created folder or press Enter/Return.

Note: You cannot create a new folder that doesn't have a name. If you attempt to do so, Dreamweaver will give you an error message.

Moving Files While Maintaining Links

One of the coolest features of the Files panel is that you can move a file to any location within the Local Site. This doesn't sound like much on the surface, but when you drill down a little deeper, it's quite significant. As you already know, a website is a series of files that are connected together using links. For instance, when you create a hyperlink from one document to another, a path (whether it's absolute or relative) references the document to which you are linking and provides the browser with its exact location. Without the correct path, the browser won't be able to locate the document to which you are linking and will spit out the dreaded 404 Error message.

Likewise, when you insert an image (or any other media file) into a Dreamweaver document, you create a reference to the file itself (you don't actually embed the file into the document). In order for the browser to properly display the media file (image, Flash movie, and so on) the path has to remain unchanged. If either file is moved (either the referencing HTML document or the media file itself), the path will change and the media file won't display.

This is where the power of the Files panel shines. If you move any file, folder, or subfolder, Dreamweaver automatically scans your entire Local Site, locates any file that references the moved document(s), and makes the necessary changes to all associated paths. This is a phenomenally powerful feature: it saves you the embarrassment of possibly having a broken link whenever you reorganize your site, and it saves you from having to tediously update link upon link upon link (especially if your site is particularly large).

Note: Dreamweaver will update paths only when you are working from within the Files panel. If, for instance, you move stuff around using your operating system's file management functions (Windows Explorer, for example), the paths of the files within your Local Site will *not be updated*.

CHAPTER 11: MANAGING AND PUBLISHING YOUR SITE ■

Keeping Things Neat and Tidy

As you've figured out by now, websites can get extremely complicated. In a site that is even marginally complex, you can have hundreds and hundreds of HTML files, images, and multimedia files. As a result, it's a good idea to organize each section of your website into discrete folders. Another good tactic is to have a single folder in which all your site's images reside. This way, all of your HTML files can reference that one folder and you'll always know where to find an image.

To move a file or folder around in your Local Site, follow these steps:

1. With a defined Local Site open to the Files panel, select the file or folder that you want to move.

Note: If you are moving the file to a location deep within the structure of your site, make sure you've already expanded all of the appropriate folders and subfolders so that the file can be placed exactly where it needs to go.

2. Drag it to the location where you want it and release your mouse button. Notice that your cursor changes and the location at which the cursor is located is highlighted by a blue box (Figure 11.4).

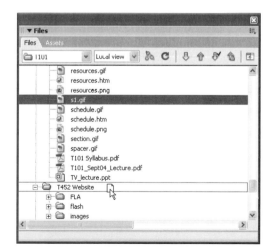

Figure 11.4 Moving files in the Files panel

To move a file or folder to a specific location, either you can click, drag, and release it over the actual target folder, or you can release it over one of the other files within the target folder (the result will be the same, whichever method you use).

3. After you move the file or folder, the Update Files dialog box (Figure 11.5) will open. Within it, you'll see a list of all the documents that include a link to the file(s) you've just moved.

Figure 11.5 The Update Files dialog box

4. To update all the associated files, click the Update button. A progress bar along the bottom will indicate the updating progress. When the process is finished, the Update Files dialog box will automatically close, returning you to the Files panel.

Using these steps, you can also move entire folders complete with all their contents. All you need to do is repeat the preceding steps. However, instead of selecting and dragging a single file, you select and drag an entire folder.

Checking Links Sitewide

During the process of creating a site of any significant size, you can end up with broken links. Maybe you accidentally mistyped the path of a Flash movie you inserted into a document, or you moved some of your Local Site's files without using the handy-dandy Files panel. You can also accumulate "orphaned" files—files that still exist in the Local Site but are no longer linked to any file. Both broken links and orphaned files can be a serious problem—broken links because they are unprofessional and serve as a major turn-off for your audience, and orphaned files because they consume disk space. However, if you were to manually sift through an entire sire looking for broken links and orphaned files, you'd potentially spend a lot of time in front of your computer. Fear not, fellow traveler in the land of web design, Dreamweaver MX 2004 provides you the ability to check for broken links and orphaned files:

1. Open the Files panel (Window > Files).

2. Choose Site > Check Links Sitewide from the Files panel's drop-down menu.

3. The Link Checker tab of the Results panel (Figure 11.6) will open, and your entire Local Site will be scanned. When the scan is finished, the tab will display the total number of files, number of broken links, number of orphaned files, and number of external links.

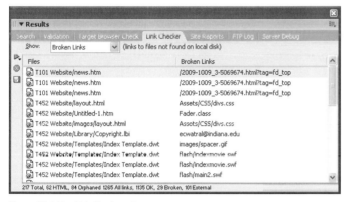

Figure 11.6 The Link Checker tab

Note: The Link Checker tab reports on the number of external links in your site. It doesn't, however, have the ability to determine whether the external file to which you are linking is still in the same location as when you originally created the link.

4. To view a list of the broken links, orphaned files, or external links, choose the appropriate option from the Show drop-down menu (in the top-left corner of the Link Checker tab).

Note: If you want to rerun the search, click the Check Links button, which acts as a drop-down menu from which you can decide whether you want to check the links for the entire site or just for the currently open document.

From here, you can fix the broken links that Dreamweaver found, a process that is covered in the next section.

Fixing Broken Links

Now that you've learned how to locate all the broken links within your Local Site, it would be wise to learn how to fix them. Remember, a broken link can refer to any file whose position or name has changed, whether that's a text file, HTML file, or image. Here's how to repair your broken links:

1. Follow steps 1 through 4 as described the previous section.

2. Choose Broken Links from the Show drop-down menu. The Link Checker tab's Files column is a list of all the files in which broken links were found. In the Broken Links column, you'll see the specific broken link (path) within each document.

3. Select the broken link you want to fix. Notice that the path becomes an editable field and a browse button appears just to the right of the link (Figure 11.7).

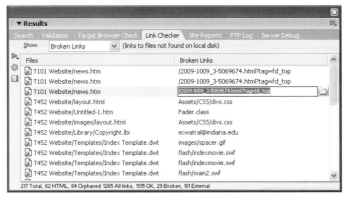

Figure 11.7 When you click the path of one of the broken links, it becomes editable and a browse button appears to its right.

4. Click the browse icon 📁 to open the Select File dialog box.

5. Navigate to the image or file referenced in the broken link, and click the OK button. The link will update in the Broken Links column.

6. Press Enter/Return or click anywhere off the editable Broken Links field.

7. If there are other broken links to this file, Dreamweaver will ask you whether you want to fix all references. Click Yes, and you'll save yourself a lot of time. If you click No, only the single link will be fixed and all the remaining broken links to that particular file will need to be fixed separately. Once you've updated the link, Dreamweaver will remove it from the Link Checker tab of the Results panel.

8. Repeat steps 3 through 7 until you've fixed all the broken links in your Local Site.

Using the Find and Replace Function

The Find and Replace function is easily one of the most underutilized and incredibly useful tools in all of Dreamweaver MX 2004. With it, you can search for either text elements within your document or specific tags within your HTML source code and easily replace them with any other string of text or tag that you desire.

> **Note:** One of the drawbacks of the Find and Replace tool is that it doesn't include any text-based Library Items when it's searching in the currently open document. However, when the scope is set to search the entire Local Site, it will include Library Items. For more information on the Library and Library Items, see Chapter 7.

This can save you hours of time spent manually searching for (and changing) content within individual pages or an entire Local Site. To use Dreamweaver's Find and Replace tool, follow these steps:

1. Choose Edit > Find and Replace to open the Find and Replace dialog box (Figure 11.8).

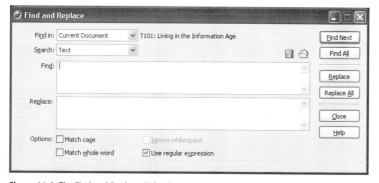

Figure 11.8 The Find and Replace dialog box

2. Choose the scope of your search by selecting one of the options from the Find In drop-down menu:

   Selected Text Confines the search to any text that you currently have selected.

   Current Document Confines the scope of the search to the document that you are currently working within.

   Open Documents Confines the scope of the search to all the current documents that you have open in Dreamweaver.

   Entire Local Site Expands the search scope so that the currently open Local Site is included.

Selected Files in Site Limits the search solely to those files and folders that are currently selected in the Files window.

Folder Lets you specify the folder in which you want the search to be confined. To specify the folder, click the Browse button that appears after you choose the Folder option. When the Choose Search Folder dialog box appears, navigate to the desired folder and click Select.

3. Select the specific search you'd like to perform from the Search drop-down menu. Based on your choice, the Find and Replace dialog box will change to display the options for your specific search type.

From here, you can explore the specifics of each type of search, described in the following sections.

 Note: To learn how to search your code, see Chapter 12.

Searching for Text

If you chose Text from the Search drop-down menu, the Find and Replace dialog box will change to reflect a set of options specific to a text search (Figure 11.9).

Follow these steps to set the options for a text search:

1. Type the text for which you want to look into the Find field.

2. To replace the searched-for text with some other text, enter it into the Replace field.

3. If you want to limit the search to text whose case exactly matches that of the text you entered into the Find field, select the Match Case option.

4. If you want the search to search for complete words that match exactly with the text you entered in the Find field, select the Match Whole Word option.

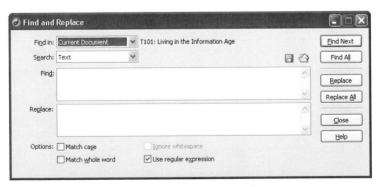

Figure 11.9 Text search options in the Find and Replace dialog box

5. If you want the search to ignore any differences in the number of spaces within the text that the search finds and the text upon which the search was based, select the Ignore Whitespace option. For example, if you were searching for the words "my dog has fleas" and your document contained the words "my dog has fleas" (two spaces between each of the words instead of one), the search would ignore the extra spaces and locate the string of text regardless.

6. If you want certain characters and short strings of characters to be converted into expression operators, select the Use Regular Expression option.

Note: Expression operators are characters (or short strings of characters) used as a sort of shorthand to describe character combinations in text. To find out more about expression operators, refer to Dreamweaver's help files (Help > Using Dreamweaver) and search for "regular expressions."

7. When you finish setting your search criteria, click one of the following buttons to initiate the search:

    Find Next Locates the next occurrence of the text, opens the appropriate file (if you've selected Entire Local Site or Folder as the search's scope), and selects it.

    Find All Generates a report (in the form of a list) of all the locations where it located the text.

    Replace Locates the first occurrence of the text and replaces it with the text you entered into the Replace With field. If your search scope goes beyond the currently open document, Dreamweaver will open the file in which it finds the text (in a new window) and replace it.

    Replace All Generates a report (in the form of a list) showing files in which it carried out the replacement.

8. The results of your search will display in the Search tab of the Results panel (Figure 11.10). You can display the found text by double-clicking any of the occurrences in the Search tab to open the file in which the text was located.

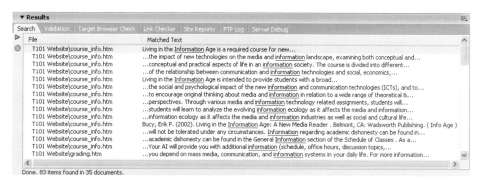

Figure 11.10 The Search tab displays the results of your search.

Note: The process of searching for text in the HTML source code is almost identical to that of searching for text. The only difference, as its name suggests, is that a search for text in the source code will locate all occurrences of the text regardless of whether it appears in an image name, a hyperlink, or textual content defined by HTML tags.

Saving and Loading Searches

One of the great features of the Find and Replace function is that you can save searches for future use. This is particularly handy if you've got a large site with a lot of text that needs regular minute updating. All you have to do is create a search, save it, and then load it whenever you want.

To save a search, just follow these steps:

1. Using the Find and Replace dialog box (Edit > Find and Replace), compose a search using the techniques described previously.
2. Click the Save Query button 🖫.
3. When the Save Query dialog box appears, enter a name for the saved query into the File Name field, navigate to the location where you would like the query saved, and click Save.

Note: Queries are saved as discrete files with a .dwr extension.

To load a saved query, just follow these steps:

1. Open the Find and Replace dialog box (Edit > Find and Replace).
2. Click the Load Query button ✉.
3. When the Load Query dialog box appears, navigate to the location of the saved query, select it, and click Open.
4. From there, the search will be loaded into the Find and Replace dialog box.

Manipulating Remote Sites

Remember that managing and manipulating your Local Site is really only half of what the Files panel is used for. You can also use it to manage and manipulate your remote site, which is the online counterpart of your Local Site that sits on a web server somewhere and can be accessed by anyone with a web browser and an Internet connection.

One of the neatest things about Dreamweaver is that the line between a Local Site and a remote site is very transparent. With many other visual web authoring tools, you can create your website, but you must then employ an FTP client to upload it to your intended web server. With Dreamweaver, however, the FTP client is seamlessly built right into the Files panel. As a result, some very tricky, time-consuming, or seemingly impossible procedures can be pulled off effortlessly.

In the following sections, you'll learn how to use the Files panel to create, manage, and manipulate a remote site. You'll start off by learning how to configure a remote site and go on to explore how to connect to the remote site, upload and download files, use the Check In/Check Out feature, synchronize your local and remote sites, and refresh your remote site.

Note: An FTP (File Transfer Protocol) client is a program with which you move files from your computer to another computer somewhere else on the Internet.

Setting Up a Remote Site

Before you get too much ahead of yourself thinking of all the groovy things you can do with the Files panel, you need to configure your remote site. The process itself is actually part of setting up a Local Site; Macromedia assumes that when you configure a Local Site, you will also configure its complementary remote site. As a result, it's just a matter of setting some additional properties for your remote site:

1. Open the Edit Sites dialog box (Site > Manage Sites).
2. Select the Local Site whose remote component you want to configure and click Edit.
3. If it isn't already visible, click the Advanced tab.

Note: The Basic tab of the Site Definition dialog box provides you with a step-by-step wizard for setting up your site—included in which are steps for setting up your remote site.

4. Choose Remote Info from the Category list. This section is pretty bare: just a single drop-down menu. Don't worry; this is as it should be.

From here, you'll need to use the Access drop-down menu to determine how you access your remote site. For a description of the two most common methods (FTP and LAN), as well as their associated properties, continue on to the next sections.

Note: The Testing Server category comes into play when you use Dreamweaver MX 2004 to create a dynamic database-driven site—a topic that's introduced in Bonus Chapter 1 on the CD.

Connecting to Your Remote Server Using FTP

As mentioned previously, FTP is how you connect and transfer files to a computer somewhere else on the Internet to which you do not have direct access. Chances are, unless you find yourself in the fortunate position of having access to a web server over a LAN (local area network), you'll use FTP to access your remote server. To set up your remote site so that it's accessed by FTP, follow these steps:

1. Follow steps 1 through 3 as described in the previous section.

2. Select FTP from the Access drop-down (Figure 11.11).

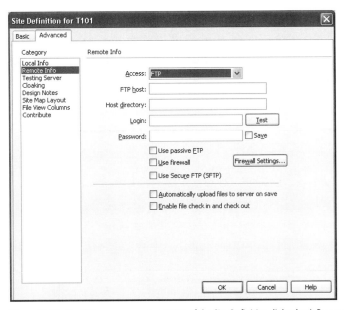

Figure 11.11 The FTP access property section of the Site Definition dialog box's Remote Info category

3. Now you have access to all the properties specific to FTP access. In the FTP Host field, enter the name of the FTP host (i.e., ftp.*yourhostname*.com).

Note: If, for some reason, you aren't sure of the exact hostname of your web server (or any of the other associated necessary info), contact the company that is providing you with server space; the folks there will be able to tell you exactly what you need to know.

4. In the Host Directory field, type the exact path (for example, usr/www/htdocs) of the location where publicly accessed documents reside on your web server.

5. Enter your login into the Login field.

6. Enter your password into the Password field.

> **Note:** Because a web server is a secure computing environment, a unique login and password is required each time you wish to upload files to or download files from your remote site. If you want to avoid having to retype your login and password each time you connect to your remote site, check the Save option. However, this can cause some security problems: anyone who has access to your computer will automatically have access to your server.

7. If your remote site resides on a server that uses a firewall, make sure you've got the Use Passive FTP option selected. If you don't, you might not be able to connect to your remote site.

8. If you are working from behind a firewall (software that increases security on a computer network), make sure you have the Use Firewall option selected. You'll need to enter the information for a proxy server in Preferences dialog box (Edit > Preferences).

> **Note:** For help with firewall-related issues, contact the system administrator for your Internet service provider.

9. Choose any desired options:

- If you want files to be automatically uploaded when they're saved, select the Automatically Upload Files to Server on Save option. Remember, in order for this option to function, you need to be connected to the Internet whenever you save.

- To enable the Check In/Check Out feature, select the Enable File Check In and Check Out option. Don't worry too much about what this does right now—you'll get a chance to explore it in depth later in the chapter.

10. Click the Test button. Dreamweaver will attempt to connect to your remote site based on the information you provided. If the test is successful, Dreamweaver will tell you.

> **Note:** In order for Dreamweaver to test an FTP connection, you must be connected to the Internet.

11. When you're finished, click OK.

Connecting to Your Remote Server Using a LAN

If you are lucky enough to work somewhere that owns and maintains its own web server (to which you have direct access), you don't need to use FTP. Instead, you'll use the Local/Network option. The Local/Network option is extremely easy to configure because it assumes that you'll have direct access (through a LAN) to the computer that is acting as your web server.

To set up the connection to your Local Site using Local/Network:

1. Follow steps 1 through 3 described previously in "Setting Up a Remote Site."

2. Choose Local/Network from the Access drop-down menu (Figure 11.12).

3. Click the browse button to the right of the Remote Folder field.

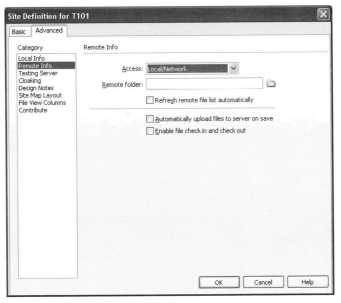

Figure 11.12 The Local/Network access property section of the Site Definition dialog box's Remote Info category

4. When the Choose Remote Folder dialog box opens, navigate to the folder in which the publicly accessible documents reside on the web server, open it, and click Select.

5. Choose any desired options:

   • If you want the list of files on the remote site to automatically update whenever Dreamweaver (or any other program) adds a new file, select the Refresh Remote File List Automatically option.

   • To enable the Check In/Check Out feature, select the Enable File Check In and Check Out option (we'll explore in depth what Check In/Check Out does later in the chapter).

- If you want files to be automatically uploaded when they're saved, select the Automatically Upload Files to Server on Save option. Remember, for this option to function, you need to be connected to the Internet whenever you save.

6. When you're finished inputting the settings for the Local/Network access option, click OK.

Connecting to a Remote Site

Now that you've properly configured your remote site, it's time to learn how to connect to it using Dreamweaver MX 2004's built-in FTP client.

> **Note:** Because the vast majority of Dreamweaver users don't have direct access to a web server, this section of the chapter will focus exclusively on using FTP to connect to your remote site (as opposed to Local/Network).

To connect to your remote site using the FTP client, follow these steps:

1. From within the Files panel (Window > Files) of the Local Site to whose remote server you wish to connect, click the Connect button .

> **Note:** In order to successfully connect to the web server (remote site) by FTP, you must be hooked up to the Internet and must have properly configured the remote site via the Site Definition dialog box, as discussed earlier in "Setting Up a Remote Site."

2. Dreamweaver opens a session (that's a fancy term for a connection) with the web server on which your remote site is sitting. If you didn't select the Save Password and Login option when you configured the remote site, you'll be prompted to input your login and password.

3. If everything has been configured properly (and your web server isn't experiencing any problems), a dialog box will appear relating the progress of the connection, and then the remote site will appear in the left side of the Files panel (Figure 11.13).

> **Note:** If you don't see your remote site in the left side of the Files panel, click the Expand/Collapse button.

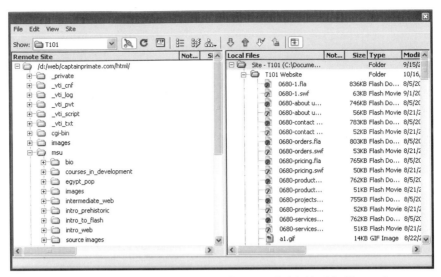

Figure 11.13 Once you connect to your remote site, it will appear in the left side of the Files panel.

4. If you would like, as soon as you connect to your remote site, you can disconnect by clicking the Disconnect button [icon] (which replaces the Connect button).

Uploading to a Remote Site

The whole point of having a built-in FTP client in Dreamweaver MX 2004 is to upload files to your web server (remote site) so that the entire Web world can experience your glorious site. Because of this, you might assume that the Files panel makes it easy to upload files, and you'd be right! Macromedia has made a sometimes difficult process into something quite effortless:

1. Make sure you're connected to the remote site to which you wish to upload (remember to click the Expand/Collapse button if it isn't visible in the Files panel).

2. From the Local Site section of your Files panel, select the file you want to upload to your remote site. You can upload any number of files all at once; simply select all the files you want to upload at this step.

3. Do one of the following:
   - Click and drag the file from the Local Files section of the Files panel to the Remote Site section.

Note: If, in the directory to which you're uploading your file, there is a file with the same name as the one you're uploading, the one one on the remote site will be overwritten.

- Click the Put Files button 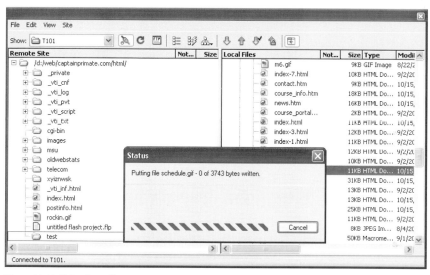.
- Choose Site > Put.

4. If the document you are uploading has any associated files (inserted Flash movies or images, for example), Dreamweaver will prompt you with the Dependent File dialog box. To upload all documents' associated files, click Yes. If you don't want to upload all the associated files, click No.

5. A window will appear showing the progress of your upload (Figure 11.14). When the upload is complete, the file will appear in the Remote Site section of the Files panel.

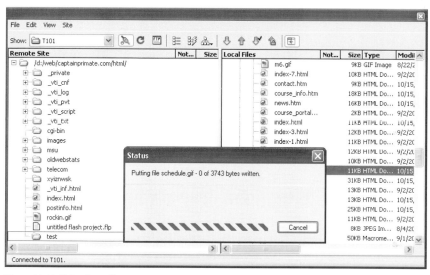

Figure 11.14 Uploading a file to your remote site

Downloading from a Remote Site

Downloading a file or files from a remote site is just as easy as uploading:

1. Make sure you're connected to the remote site to which you wish to download (remember to click the Expand/Collapse button to display both the Local Site and Remote Site in the Files panel).

2. From the Remote Site section of your Files panel, select the file you want to download. You can also select multiple files.

3. Do one of the following:
    - Click and drag the file from the Remote Site section of the Files panel to the Local Files section.

- Click the Get Files button .
- Choose Site > Get.

4. If the document you are downloading has any associated files (inserted Flash movies or images, for example), Dreamweaver will prompt you with the Dependent File dialog box. To download all documents' associated files, click Yes. If you don't want to download all the associated files, click No.

5. A window will appear showing the progress of your upload. When the upload is complete, the file will appear in the Remote Site section of the Files panel.

Checking Files In and Out of a Remote Site

Back when you were learning how to configure your remote site, one of the steps was to choose whether you wanted to enable the Check In/Check Out feature. In this section, you'll learn more about that feature as well as how to put it to good use.

Here is a horrible scenario for you to consider. Say you are one member of a distributed web design team working on a project. Say you download from the remote server a file that requires the addition of some content, a task for which you are responsible. Remember, when you download a file from a server, you aren't really taking the file, per se; you're only making a copy of the file. The file itself still hangs out on the server, while the copy is stuck on your hard drive. In our scenario, unbeknownst to you, a short time after you download the file, the graphic designer of the project downloads the same file to make some changes to the layout. When you're finished adding the necessary content to the file, you upload it to the server. Unfortunately, when the graphic designer finishes her changes, she uploads the file and replaces the one on the server, which has all the changes you've made, with her version of the file. The humanity! Hours of work down the tube!

As simplistic as this scenario is, this kind of tragedy happens quite often. How can it be avoided? This is where Dreamweaver MX 2004's Check In/Check Out feature comes into the picture: when you enable the Check In/Check Out feature, you can check files out from the remote site. When they're checked out, the file on the server becomes locked, prohibiting anyone else from downloading it and making changes to it. When you're finished editing the file, you check it back into the server and it then becomes accessible again to other individuals.

Note: The Check In/Check Out feature only works for those who are accessing the remote site with Dreamweaver. If one of your team members is accessing the web server with another FTP client, they can upload and download files with no restrictions.

When a file has been checked out, a small check mark appears next to it in the Remote Site section of the Files panel, indicating that it is locked to all other users (Figure 11.15).

Another cool thing about the Check In/Check Out feature is that it can be configured to display the name (as well as the e-mail address) of the individual who checked out a particular file (Figure 11.16).

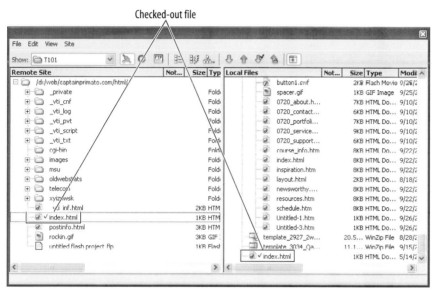

Figure 11.15 A file that's been checked out has a small green check mark next to its name.

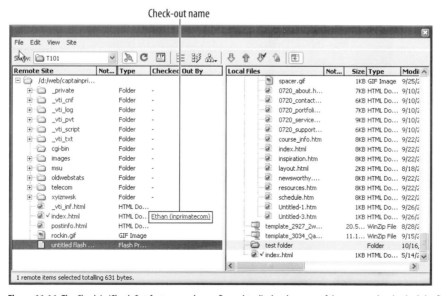

Figure 11.16 The Check In/Check Out feature can be configured to display the name of the person who checked the file out.

To configure a remote site's Check In/Check Out feature, follow these steps:

1. Choose Site > Manage Sites.

2. When the Manage Sites dialog box appears, select the Local Site whose Check In/Check Out feature you want to configure, and click Edit.

3. Choose Remote Info from the Category list.

4. If it isn't already selected, select the Enable File Check In and Check Out option. Once this is done, a series of additional options will appear (Figure 11.17)

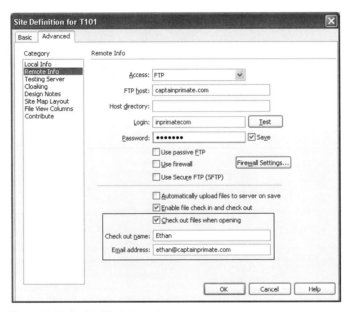

Figure 11.17 Check In/Check Out options

5. Choose the desired options:

- If you want the file to be automatically checked out when the user downloads it, select the Check Out Files When Opening option.

- To display your name next to the checked-out file, enter a name into the Check Out Name field.

- To display your e-mail address next the checked-out file, enter it into the Email Address field.

Note: Users accessing the same remote site through Dreamweaver can click the address of the individual who checked out a given file to launch their e-mail program.

6. When you're finished configuring the Check In/Check Out features, click OK.

Now that you've configured Check In/Check Out, you can take advantage of its features:

To check out a file, within the Local Site from which you want check out a file, select the file in the Remote Site section of your Files panel. Then either click the Check Out Files button or choose Site > Check Out.

To check a file back into the remote site, in the Local Site section of the Files panel, select the file that needs to be checked back into the remote site. Then click the Check Files In button or choose Site > Check In.

> **Note:** When you check a file back into a server, the copy in your Local Site becomes read-only (represented by a small padlock icon to the right of the filename in the Files panel). To turn this feature off, select the file, right-click/Control-click to open the context menu, and select Turn Off Read Only.

Synchronizing Files between a Local and Remote Site

Sometimes you get into a situation where you aren't exactly sure whether the files on your remote site or your Local Site are the most up-to-date. It would be a painful process to go through all of your directories to check which files have the most recent time/date stamp. Fortunately, Dreamweaver MX 2004 provides a one-step way to ensure that both Local and Remote Sites have all the most up-to-date versions of the files: Synchronize.

> **Note:** When you synchronize a Local Site and Remote Site, you can also automatically delete the files on one site that do not appear on the other.

To synchronize a Local Site and Remote Site, follow these steps:

1. Make sure you are connected to your remote site (and both are showing in the Files panel).

2. In the Files panel (Window > Files), choose Site > Synchronize.

3. When the Synchronize Files dialog box appears (Figure 11.18), choose the scope of the synchronization from the Synchronize drop-down menu:

- If you want to sync the entire site, choose Entire *Site Name*.
- If you want to sync only selected files or folders, choose Selected Local Files Only.

Figure 11.18 The Synchronize Files dialog box

4. From the Direction drop-down menu, choose the direction in which the synchronization process will flow:

   Put Newer Files to Remote Dreamweaver determines the newest versions of files in the Local Site and uploads them to the remote site.

   Get Newer Files from Remote Dreamweaver finds the newest versions of files on your remote site and downloads them to your Local Site.

   Get and Put Newer Files The newest versions of files will flow from your local server to your remote server and vice versa.

5. If you want to delete from the remote site files that aren't located in the Local Site, select the Delete Remote Files Not on Local Drive option.

6. When you're finished setting all the options in the Synchronize Files dialog box, click the Preview button. Dreamweaver will open a dialog box displaying all the files that are slated to be included in the synchronization.

7. Deselect any file you don't want included in the synchronization by clicking the check box directly to its left, and then click OK.

8. When the process is finished, you'll be prompted to keep a record of the changes. If you want to, click the Save Log button. Dreamweaver will provide a dialog box to set the location where you want the log saved. If you don't want to save a log, click the Close button.

Refreshing a Remote Site

When you refresh a site (either local or remote), Dreamweaver will reread the contents of any selected directory to see if the contents have changed. If they have, it will automatically update the view. This is particularly helpful if files have been added or removed by other users during the course of your FTP session.

Note: If you enabled the Refresh Local Files Automatically option in the Site Definition dialog box, you'll only have to refresh a remote site because your Local Site will automatically refresh when any changes are made.

CHAPTER **11**: MANAGING AND PUBLISHING YOUR SITE

To refresh a site, have a Local Site and a remote site open in the Files panel and select the topmost folder of the site (local or remote) you wish to refresh. Then just click the Refresh button 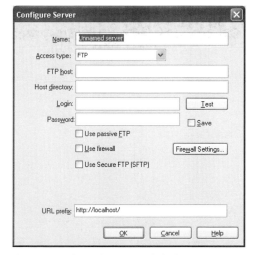.

Creating a Site-less Connection to a Remote Site

Up until this point, any connection you made to a remote site could only be done after you had first set up a Local Site. This can sometimes be frustrating—especially when you are working on files that belong to a remote site that resides on someone else's computer. This is where a site-less connection comes into the picture—it allows you to connect to a remote FTP server from within Dreamweaver without having to actually create a Local Site. There are, however, some caveats. If you make a site-less connection to a remote server using Dreamweaver, you cannot perform sitewide operations such as link checking.

To set up a site-less connection to a remote server, just follow these steps:

1. Choose Site > Manage Sites.
2. When the Manage Sites dialog box appears, click the New button and select the FTP and RDS server option from the drop-down menu.
3. When the Configure Server dialog box appears (Figure 11.19), enter a name for the connection into the Name field.
4. Choose FTP from the Access Type drop-down menu.
5. Now you have access to all the properties specific to FTP access. In the FTP Host field, enter the name of the FTP host.

Figure 11.19 The Configure Server dialog box

Note: If, for some reason, you aren't sure of the exact hostname of your web server (or any of the other associated necessary info), contact the company that is providing you with server space; the folks there will be able to tell you exactly what you need to know.

6. In the Host Directory field, type the exact path (for example, usr/www/htdocs) of the location where publicly accessed documents reside on your web server.

7. Enter your login into the Login field.

8. Enter your password into the Password field.

Note: Because a web server is a secure computing environment, a unique login and password is required each time you wish to upload files to or download files from your remote site. If you want to avoid having to retype your login and password each time you connect to your remote site, check the Save option. However, this can cause some security problems: anyone who has access to that PC will automatically have access to your server.

9. If your remote site resides on a server that uses a firewall, make sure you've got the Use Passive FTP option selected. If you don't, you might not be able to connect to your remote site.

Note: For help with firewall-related issues, contact the system administrator for your Internet service provider.

10. If you are working from behind a firewall (software that increases security on a computer network), make sure you have the Use Firewall option selected. You'll need to enter the information for a proxy server in Preferences dialog box (Edit > Preferences).

Note: Passive FTP enables your local software to set up the FTP connection rather than requesting that the remote server set it up. If you're not sure whether you use passive FTP, check with your system administrator.

11. When you're finished, click OK. The Files panel will display the contents of the remote server you specified. From there, you'll be able to upload and download files using the techniques described earlier in this chapter.

Communicating with Design Notes

Design Notes are one of the coolest features in Dreamweaver. In a situation where more than one person is working on a given site, there has to be some behind-the-scenes communication about any number of topics; Design Notes provide that.

> **Note:** Even though they are geared toward working in a group, Design Notes are also useful for leaving yourself helpful reminders in a situation where you are the sole designer on a project.

Essentially, Design Notes are tiny little files that work like digital sticky notes, attaching themselves to any file in a Local Site. When the file is moved (or uploaded to a remote site), the Design Note moves with it, remaining permanently attached until it is deleted.

> **Note:** Design Notes are saved with a MNO extension in a subfolder (called _notes) that is automatically created in the root folder of your site.

For example, say you're working on a file in which the primary content has yet to be added by your content manager (let's call him Ed). You can attach a Design Note to the file in question that says something like, "Hey Ed, I've finished off all the layout and design of this file. It needs the content. Remember, when you add everything, to make sure that all the dates read 2004 as opposed to 2003." When Ed opens the file in question, the Design Note automatically opens.

Whether in a Remote Site or Local Site, Design Notes are displayed in the same way, as a little yellow bubble to the right of a file (Figure 11.20).

> **Note:** The Design Note icon will be displayed *only* after you click the Files panel's Expand/Collapse button.

In the following sections, you are going to explore how to set up and configure Design Notes, as well as how to create, attach, and view them.

Design Note

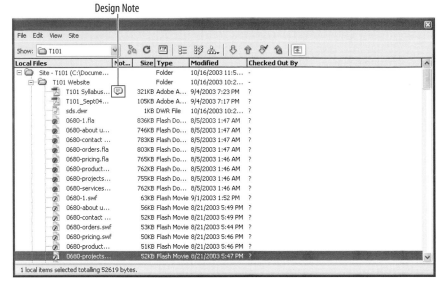

Figure 11.20 Design Notes are represented by a little yellow bubble to the right of the file to which they are attached.

Configuring Design Notes

Before you can take advantage of Design Notes, your Local Site (or Remote Site) needs to be configured to deal with them:

1. Open the Manage Sites dialog box (Site > Manage Sites).

2. Select the site for which you want to enable Design Notes, and click Edit.

3. The Site Definition dialog box will open. If it isn't already, make sure you open the advanced section by selecting the Advanced tab. From there, click the Design Notes option in the Category list box.

 Note: If you're already using Design Notes, you can click the Clean Up button to delete any Design Notes that aren't associated with a file.

4. If it isn't already selected, click the Maintain Design Notes check box.

5. If you want your Design Notes uploaded to the Remote Site, click the Upload Design Notes for Sharing option (if it isn't already selected).

6. Click OK.

Creating Design Notes

Once you've configured your site to deal with Design Notes, the process of attaching them to a file is easy:

> **Note:** Design notes can not only be attached to HTML files, but also any other files you have in your site. In addition, you can attach design notes to folders.

1. With the Files panel open, select the file to which you want to attach a Design Note.
2. From the File menu or from the context menu, choose Design Notes. This will bring up the Design Notes dialog box (Figure 11.21).

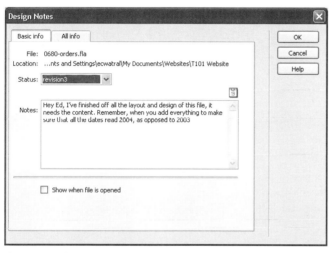

Figure 11.21 The Design Notes dialog box

3. If you want to include the status of the file, select one of the options from the Status drop-down menu.
4. If you want to add the current date to the Design Note (in mm/dd/yy format), click the Insert Date button 🗓.
5. In the Notes field, type in the text for the Design Note.
6. If you want the note to automatically open when the file to which it is attached opens (as opposed to having to be opened manually), select the Show When File Is Opened check box.
7. Click OK.

> **Note:** To make more detailed custom Design Notes, use the All Info section of the Design Notes dialog box.

Viewing Design Notes

There are several ways to open a Design Note. The first way happens automatically if you've enabled the Show When File Is Opened option described in the previous section. The second way involves manually opening the note:

1. With the Files panel open, select the file with the attached Design Note you want to open.

2. Choose from the following options:
   - Double-click the Design Note icon.
   - Choose File > Design Notes.
   - Open the file's context menu and choose Design Notes.

3. Any of these options will automatically bring up the Design Notes dialog box, and the Design Note in question will be displayed.

Cloaking Files

A great feature in Dreamweaver MX 2004 is the ability to *cloak* specific file types or complete folders—and we're not talking about Romulans and Klingons. Cloaking lets you exclude folders or specific file types from sitewide operations such as put/get, synchronization, inclusion in the Assets panel, and sitewide link checking. It's a pretty handy feature if you are working on a large site and are trying to work on one specific area of the site without affecting other areas.

Enabling Cloaking

Before you can cloak folders in your site, you must first enable the cloaking feature for your Local Site. To do so, follow these steps:

1. Choose Site > Manage Sites to open the Manage Sites dialog box. Select the site for which you want to enable cloaking, and click Edit.

2. Select the Cloaking option in the Category list box (Figure 11.22).

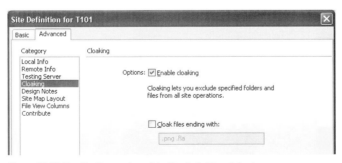

Figure 11.22 The Cloaking section of the Site Definition dialog box

3. If it isn't already selected, select the Enable Cloaking check box.

4. If you want to cloak specific file types, click the Cloak Files Ending With check box, and then enter the specific extensions associated with the files you want to cloak into the text field.

5. When you're finished, click OK.

Cloaking Site Folders

Now that you've enabled cloaking for your site, you can go ahead and cloak any folder or subfolder (and by extensions, all of its contents). Follow these steps to cloak a site folder:

1. Open the Files panel (Files > Site).

2. Select the specific folder you want to cloak.

3. In the Files panel, choose Site > Cloaking > Cloak.
   Dreamweaver will automatically cloak the selected folder (see Figure 11.23).

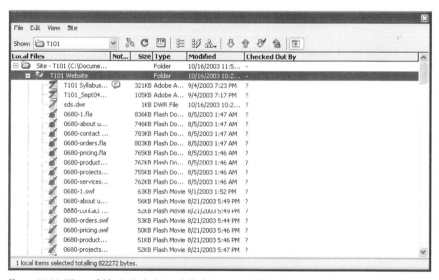

Figure 11.23 When a folder is cloaked, it and all of its associated files are crossed out with a red hatch mark.

Note: To uncloak a folder, select it in the Files panel and choose Site > Cloaking > Uncloak. You can also uncloak all cloaked folders in your Local Site by choosing Site > Cloaking > Uncloak All.

Handcrafting Code in Dreamweaver

Traditionally, Dreamweaver has been known as a tool for visual web development: what you see is what you get (WYSIWIG), drag and drop, that kind of stuff. However, this is only half of the story. Even in its earliest version, Macromedia incorporated tools for hand coding HTML into Dreamweaver. As new versions of the program came out, more and more hand-coding tools were incorporated. The most recent version of the program features a bevy of extremely powerful tools that not only allow dyed-in-the-wool, hard-core hand coders to do their thing, but also allow those who aren't necessarily completely familiar with HTML to fiddle with the code in a relatively safe and accessible way.

12

Chapter Contents
Viewing and Navigating Code
Creating and Editing Code
Checking Your Code
Working with XHTML

Viewing and Navigating Code

Before you can even start whipping your code into shape, you've got to know how to get at it and how to move around it. In this section, you are going to explore how to view code, how to select specific tags when you are working in Design View, how to color code your HTML so that it's more accessible, and how to navigate your code.

Viewing Code

Obviously, one of the most important prerequisites to working with HTML in Dreamweaver is to be able to get at the code. For those who normally work in Dreamweaver's visual authoring environment, this might not necessarily be as obvious as it is to those who are used to working directly on the code in Dreamweaver.

In order to access your code, you have a few options:

To enter Code View (Figure 12.1), either choose View > Code or click the Show Code View button located in the Document Toolbar.

To enter Split Code and Design view, also simply called "Split view" (Figure 12.2), either choose View > Code and Design or click the Split ⬚ Split button located in the Document toolbar.

> **Note:** To adjust the size of the panes in Split view, simply drag the bar that separates the two.

To open the Code Inspector (Figure 12.3), choose Window > Code Inspector.

Figure 12.1 Code View

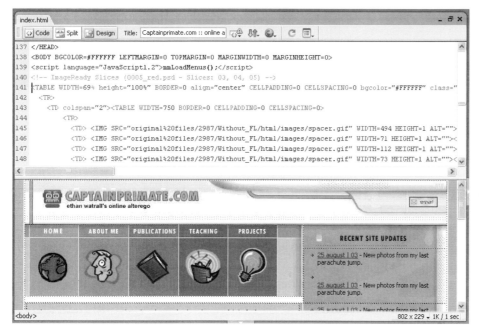

Figure 12.2 Split Code and Design view

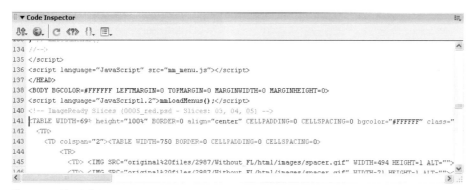

Figure 12.3 The Code Inspector

> **Note:** The Code Inspector is an artifact from earlier versions of Dreamweaver in which you couldn't directly display your HTML in the Document window.

Selecting HTML Tags with the Tag Selector

There are many instances in which you need to select specific tags while working in Design view. For example, what if you wanted a behavior to execute when the page loaded? To do this, you would need to first select the <body> section of the document and then insert the behavior. Or, what if you wanted to edit the properties of a specific element but you found that it was difficult (or impossible) to select in Dreamweaver's visual authoring environment? This is where the Tag Selector comes in.

Located at the bottom of the Document window (Figure 12.4), the Tag Selector displays a list of all the tags associated with a currently selected element or the current position of the cursor.

The tags display in a hierarchical manner, allowing you not only to view the current tag, but also the "tree" of tags in which the current tag exists—all the way up to the <body> tag.

To select the specific element associated with a specific tag, all you need to do is click the tag in the Tag Selector. So, for example, as illustrated in Figure 12.5, if you were to place your cursor in a block of text and then click the <p> tag, the entire paragraph would be selected.

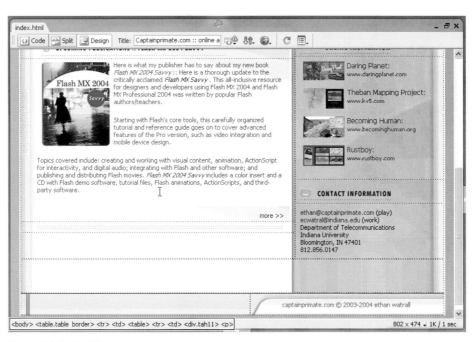

Figure 12.4 The Tag Selector

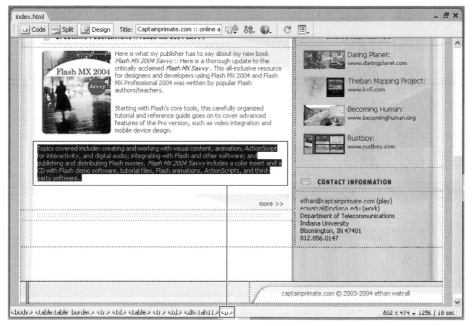

Figure 12.5 Selecting a specific tag in the Tag Selector—in this case, the <p> tag—results in the associated element being selected in the Document window.

Color Coding Your HTML

As the size and complexity of your page increases, so will the amount of HTML you'll need to cope with. As many hand coders will attest, the larger an HTML document gets, the higher the chance will be that code tends to run together, making it harder and harder to find the specific portion of the document you want to edit. This is where color coding your HTML comes to the rescue.

Note: By default, your code is always colored in Dreamweaver

You can specify colors for general categories of tags and code elements, such as form-related tags or JavaScript identifiers. The end result is that while there is still the same amount of code, it's easier to zero in on specific kinds of code.

To color code your HTML, just follow these steps:

1. Choose Edit > Preferences.

2. When the Preferences dialog box appears, select Code Coloring from the Category list box (Figure 12.6).

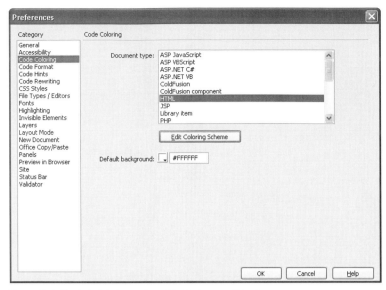

Figure 12.6 The Code Coloring section of the Preferences dialog box

3. Select the specific type of document whose color coding scheme you'd like to manipulate from the Document Type list box.

Note: If you want to set the background color of Code View (or the Code Inspector) for a specific document type, click the Default Background color swatch and choose a color from the color picker.

4. Click the Edit Coloring Scheme button [Edit Coloring Scheme].

5. When the Edit Coloring Scheme dialog box appears (Figure 12.7), select the specific element whose color you want to edit from the Styles For list box.

6. Change the color of the code element (both for the code's text and its background) by clicking the appropriate color swatch and choosing a color from the color picker.

7. To style the code element, click the Bold **B**, Italic *I*, or Underline U button.

    Notice that, as you edit the color/style of the specific code elements, you'll get a generic preview of your code's overall color scheme in the Preview section of the Edit Coloring Scheme dialog box.

8. When you are finished, click OK to exit the Edit Coloring Scheme dialog box.

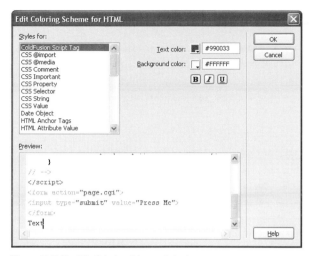

Figure 12.7 The Edit Coloring Scheme dialog box

9. Repeat the process for any other document types, and then click OK to exit the Preferences dialog box.

Determining How Code is Displayed

In the previous section, you explored how to color code your HTML syntax in order to make it more accessible. In this section, you'll see the Code View options, which make your code more user-friendly and approachable.

To access the Code View options, either choose View > Code View Options or click the View Options button in the Document toolbar.

Select one or more of the options to toggle it on or off:

Word Wrap When turned on, this option forces all of the lines of your code to wrap so they can be displayed within the Document window without a horizontal scroll bar.

Line Numbers As its name suggests, this option numbers each of the lines of your code (Figure 12.8). This is particularly useful if you are discussing your code with one of your colleagues and you need to refer to a specific section in the document. All you need to do us say, "Hey Bob, check out line 234. Isn't that some wicked syntax?"

Highlight Invalid HTML When turned on, this option highlights any of your HTML code that is invalid or incorrect (Figure 12.9).

Syntax Coloring This option turns your HTML's color coding on and off.

Auto Indent When turned on, this option automatically indents each new line of code at the same level as the previous line of code.

```
86   mm_menu_1111155006_0.addMenuItem("Curriculum Vitae");
87   mm_menu_1111155006_0.addMenuItem("Teaching Philosophy");
88   mm_menu_1111155006_0.hideOnMouseOut=true;
89   mm_menu_1111155006_0.bgColor='#000000';
90   mm_menu_1111155006_0.menuBorder=1;
91   mm_menu_1111155006_0.menuLiteBgColor='#000000';
92   mm_menu_1111155006_0.menuBorderBgColor='#333333';
93   window.mm_menu_1111155459_0 = new Menu("root",240,16,"Tahoma",10,"#FFFFFF","#000000","#FE31BA","#CCCCCC","left","middle",3,0
     true,true,true,0,false,true);
```

Figure 12.8 Line numbers can be displayed along the left side of the Document window in Code View.

```
151   <TR>
152       <TD COLSPAN=2 ROWSPAN=3>  <IMG SRC="images/logo.jpg" WIDTH=565 HEIGHT=77 ALT=""></TD>
153       <TD COLSPAN=2><IMG SRC="original%20files/2987/Without_FL/html/images/top1.jpg" WIDTH=185 HEIGHT=19 ALT=""></TD>
154   </TR>
155   <TR>
156       <TD> <IMG SRC="images/serch.jpg" ALT="" WIDTH=112 HEIGHT=37 border="0"></TD>
157       <TD> <a href="#"><IMG SRC="images/email.jpg" ALT="" WIDTH=73 HEIGHT=37 border="0" usemap="#Map"></a></TD>
158   </TR>
159   <TR>
160      |TD COLSPAN=2> <IMG SRC="original%20files/2987/Without_FL/html/images/top2.jpg" WIDTH=185 HEIGHT=21 ALT=""></TD>
161   </TR>
162   <TR>
163       <TD WIDTH=494 HEIGHT=127 ROWSPAN=2><TABLE WIDTH=494 BORDER=0 CELLPADDING=0 CELLSPACING=0 bgcolor="#CCCCCC">
```

Figure 12.9 The Highlight Invalid HTML option forces Dreamweaver to highlight any funky code.

Searching Code with Find and Replace

Back in Chapter 11, you learned how to use the Find and Replace function to search for specific text. In this section, you are going to explore how to use the Find and Replace function to search for and, if you wish, replace a specific tag in your document or your entire site. By using Find and Replace, you can save yourself lots of time spent manually searching for (and changing) content within individual pages or an entire Local Site. To use Dreamweaver MX 2004's Find and Replace tool to search your code, just follow these steps:

1. Choose Edit > Find and Replace to open the Find and Replace dialog box.

2. Choose the scope of your search by selecting one of the options from the Find In drop-down menu:

   Selected Text Confines the search to any text that you currently have selected.

   Current Document Confines the scope of the search to the document that you are currently working within.

Open Documents Confines the scope of the search to all the current documents that you have open in Dreamweaver.

Folder Lets you specify the folder in which you want the search to be confined. To specify the folder, click the Browse button that appears after you choose the Folder option. When the Choose Search Folder dialog box appears, navigate into the desired folder and click Select.

Selected Files in Site Limits the search solely to those files and folders that are currently selected in the Site window.

Entire Current Local Site Expands the search scope so that the currently open Local Site is included.

3. Select Specific Tag from the Search drop-down menu.

4. Select the specific tag for which you want to search from the Tag drop-down menu. The Find and Replace dialog box will change to display the tag options (Figure 12.10).

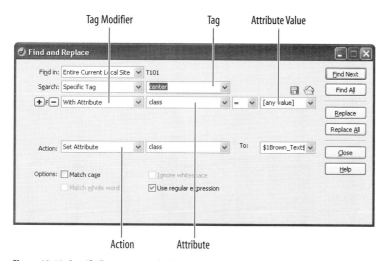

Figure 12.10 Specific Tag options in the Find and Replace Dialog box

5. If you want to search for *all* occurrences of a tag, click the minus button ⊟ and skip to step 7.

6. To limit the search further by specifying the attributes of the tag upon which you are basing the search, choose one of the following options from the Tag Modifier drop-down menu:

With Attribute Sets an attribute that must be present in the tag for it to be located by the search. You can select the specific attribute from the Attribute drop-down menu.

Without Attribute Lets you search for any tag devoid of a specific attribute, which you can select from the Attribute drop-down menu.

Containing Lets you search for a tag that contains either some specific text or an additional tag nested within the previously selected tag.

Not Containing Enables you to modify the search so that it searches for any tag that doesn't contain some specific text or a specific nested tag.

Inside Tag Lets you set a tag, chosen from the drop-down menu (located to the right of the Tag Modifier drop-down menu), that must be nested.

Not Inside Tag Lets you define a tag in which the tag you are searching for cannot be nested for the search to locate it.

 Note: To add additional search criteria, click the plus button ⊞ and redo step 6.

7. Set an action that Dreamweaver MX 2004 will take when the tag is located. Choose one of the following options from the Action drop-down menu:

Replace Tag and Contents Lets you enter something (usually a combination of both a tag and associated content) into the With field that will replace the searched-for tag.

Replace Contents Only Lets you enter something into the With field that will replace the content contained within the searched-for tag.

Remove Tag and Contents Removes the tag and its associated contents from the HTML source code.

Strip Tag Removes the searched-for tag, but the tag's associated content will remain unchanged.

Change Tag Lets you change the searched-for tag to another tag (which is chosen from the Tag drop-down menu).

Set Attribute Lets you change the tag's attribute. Select a new attribute from the drop-down menu (located to the right of the Action drop-down menu) and set the attributed value in the second drop-down menu (located to the right).

Remove Attribute Removes a specified attribute from the searched-for tag.

Add Before Start Tag Lets you specify something (text or tag) that you want to be added before the searched-for tag's opening element.

Add After End Tag Lets you specify something (text or tag) that you want to be added after the searched-for tag's closing element.

Add After Start Tag Lets you specify something (text or tag) that you want added after the searched-for tag's opening element.

Add Before End Tag Lets you specify something (text or tag) that you want added before the searched-for tag's closing element.

8. You can narrow your search with one or both of the following check boxes:

   - To limit the search to text whose case exactly matches that of the text you entered into the Search field, select the Match Case option.

   - To find only complete words that match exactly with the Search text, select the Match Whole Word option.

9. If you want the search to ignore any differences in the number of spaces within the text that the search finds and the text upon which the search was based, select the Ignore Whitespace option. For example, if you were searching for the words "my dog has fleas" and your document contained the words "my dog has fleas" (two spaces between each of the words instead of one), the search would ignore the extra spaces and locate the string of text regardless.

10. If you want certain characters and short strings of characters to be converted into expression operators, select the Use Regular Expression option.

> **Note:** Expression operators are characters (or short strings of characters) used as a sort of shorthand to describe character combinations in text. To find out more about expression operators, refer to Dreamweaver MX 2004's help files (Help > Using Dreamweaver) and search for "regular expressions."

11. When you finish, click one of the buttons along the right side of the Find and Replace dialog box to initiate the search.

12. The results of your search will display in the Search tab of the Results panel (Figure 12.11). You can display the found tag(s) by double-clicking any of the occurrences in the Search tab to open the file in which the tag is located.

Figure 12.11 The search dialog box displays the results of your tag search.

Creating and Editing Code

Now that you've got a good idea how to view and navigate your code, it's time for you to start exploring how you actually go about creating and editing code. In the following sections, you'll explore a wide variety of techniques and tools available that allow you to take full control of your code regardless of whether you live, breath, and dream HTML or are an HTML novice.

Inserting and Editing Code in Design View

Although the vast majority of the work that you'll do with your code will happen in Code View, you aren't totally cut off from your HTML in Design view. In this section, you are going to explore how to insert and edit HTML when working in Design view.

Inserting HTML in Design View

There are definitely situations in which you might want to add HTML into your document without having to enter into Code View. Honestly, the process is rather easy. All you have to do is follow these steps:

1. In Design view, place your cursor in the location where you want to insert the HTML.

2. Right-click/Control-click and select Insert HTML from the context menu.

3. When the Insert HTML "windoid" appears (Figure 12.12), simply type the HTML that you would like to insert.

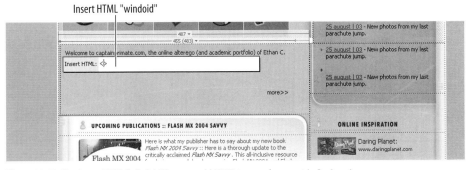

Figure 12.12 The Insert HTML "windoid" lets you add HTML to your document in Design view.

4. When you are finished inserting the HTML, simply click anywhere off the "windoid" and the code will be inserted into the Document.

Editing HTML in Design View

Earlier in the chapter, we discussed using the Tag Selector to select specific tags when you are working in Design view. Well, the Tag Selector also has built-in functionality that lets you edit a specific tag and its attributes directly from within Design view.

Let's take a look at how:

1. In the Tag Selector, right-click/Control-click the tag that you want to edit, and select Edit Tag from the context menu.

2. When the Edit Tag "windoid" appears (Figure 12.13), make any changes to the tag that you'd like.

3. When you are finished editing the tag, click anywhere off the Edit Tag "windoid," and the HTML will be updated.

Figure 12.13 The Edit Tag "windoid" lets you edit HTML tags in Design view.

Using Code Hints

So, you're happily pounding away at your keyboard, entering HTML in Code View, when your brain takes a complete vacation and you can't remember the syntax of a tag that you want to use. Never fear, this is where Code Hints come into the picture.

Before you can actually take advantage of Code Hints, you must turn the feature on and set its options. Let's take a look at how:

1. Choose Edit > Preferences, and select Code Hints from the Category list (Figure 12.14).

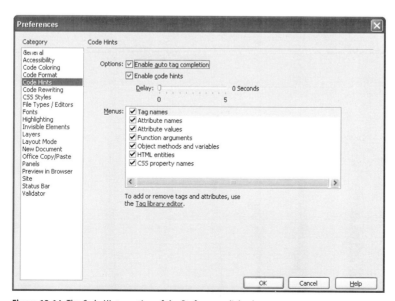

Figure 12.14 The Code Hints section of the Preferences dialog box

2. To turn Code Hints on, click the Enable Code Hints check box.

3. If you want Dreamweaver to automatically add a closing tag after you've typed an opening tag, click the Enable Auto Tag Completion check box.

4. To set the time that it takes for the Code Hints menu to appear, adjust the Delay slider.

5. To set the specific type of code hints you want to display while you are typing, simply choose any of the options from the Menus list box.

6. When you are finished, click OK.

Essentially, when you enable Code Hints, a handy little menu containing a huge list of tags (Figure 12.15) pops up whenever you type an opening (that is, left angle) bracket, <.

```
268    <TD colspan="2" height="100%" ><TABLE WIDTH=750 BORDER=0 CELLPADDING=0 CELLSPACING=0 height="100%">
269        <TR>
270            <TD COLSPAN=2 background="original%20files/2987/Without_FL/html/images/tiling_main.jpg" WIDTH=750 HEIGHT=100% > <IMG SRC=
       "original%20files/2987/Without_FL/html/images/spacer.gif" WIDTH=750 HEIGHT=1 ALT=""></TD>
271        </TR>
272        <TR>
273            <TD background="original_files/2987/Without_FL/html/images/bot1.jpg" WIDTH=406 HEIGHT=40 ALT>
274        <> a        ding-top:14; color:505050; font-style: italic;" class="tahl1" align="center"></div></TD>
275        <> abbr
276        <> acronym    "original%20files/2987/Without_FL/html/images/bot2.jpg" WIDTH=344 HEIGHT=40 >
           <> address   adding-top:14;color:505050" class="tahl1" align="center"> captainprimate.com @ 2003-2004 ethan watrall</div></TD>
           <> applet
       >   <> area
277        </T  <> b
278    </TABLE  <> base
279    </TR>    <> basefont
280 </TABLE>    <> bdo
281 <!-- End ImageReady Slices -->
282 <map name="Map">
283    <area shape="rect" coords="5,9,56,27" href="mailto:ethan@captainprimate.com">
```

Figure 12.15 The Code Hints menu displays a list of tags from which you can choose.

You can manually scroll through the menu to find the tag you want. Alternatively, if you keep on typing the tag in Code View, Dreamweaver will jump to the tag in the Code Hint menu that it thinks you are entering.

 Note: To close the Code Hint menu at any time, just press the Esc key.

When you've found the specific tag that you would like to insert, all you have to do is double-click it, or select it and press Enter/Return.

Now, the great thing about Code Hints is that they aren't designed just for tags; they also work on tag attributes. Once you've inserted the opening tag, start typing the beginning of an attribute and Dreamweaver will open up another Code Hint menu. This time, however, the menu will contain all of the attributes associated with that specific tag. The joy doesn't stop there! After you've selected a specific attribute, Dreamweaver will automatically open another Code Hint menu that contains all of the possible *values* of that specific attribute.

Editing Attributes with the Tag Inspector

The Tag Inspector, which is accessible by choosing Window > Tag Inspector, is a handy tool that lets you select a given tag (either in Code View or Design view) and then edit all of its attributes in an accessible and user-friendly manner. The great thing about the Tag Inspector is that you don't have to be intimately familiar with each and every attribute of a given tag.

To edit a tag's attribute with the Tag Inspector, just follow these steps:

1. If you are working in Code View, click anywhere within the tag whose attributes you want to edit. If you are working in Design view, click the element related to the tag.

Note: Alternatively, if you are working in Code View, you can select the tag itself from the Tag Selector.

2. Open the Tag Inspector by choosing Window > Tag Inspector.
3. When the Tag Inspector appears (Figure 12.16), make sure the Attributes tab is selected.

Figure 12.16 The Tag Inspector

4. To customize the way in which the specific selected tag's attributes are displayed in the Tag Inspector (Figure 12.17), do one of the following:

   To group attributes by category (General, Browser Specific, CSS/Accessibility, Language, and Uncategorized), click the Show Category View button ▦ .

   To group attributes alphabetically, click the Show List View button ⥯ .

5. Click the attribute whose value you want to set.

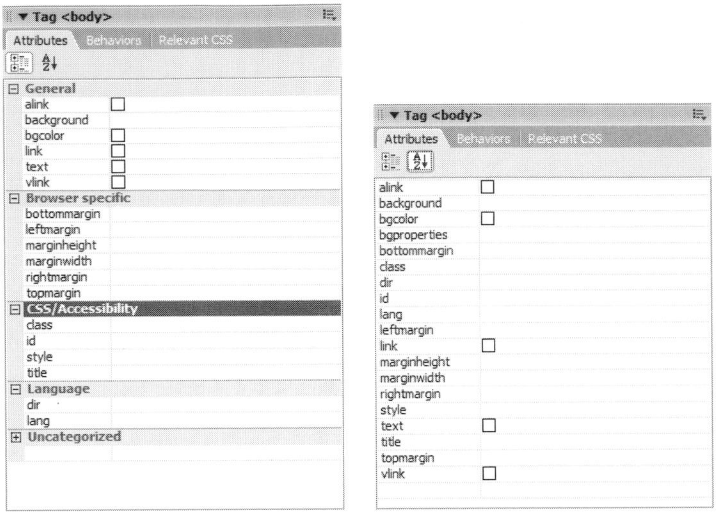

Figure 12.17 You can organize the selected tag's attributes (left) into several broad categories or (right) in an alphabetical list.

6. When the attribute's value (which is listed in the column on the right) becomes editable, make any changes you want. Changes are automatically applied.

The way in which you make the change depends on the type of attribute. In the case of attributes that take a color value, such as the bgcolor attribute, you can either directly input the hex color code or click the Color swatch and choose a color from the color picker (Figure 12.18).

In the case of an attribute with a finite set of values, such as the lang attribute, a drop-down menu will display all of the possible options (Figure 12.19).

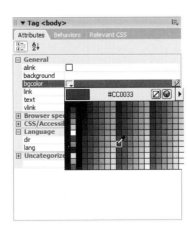

Figure 12.18 To set a value for bgcolor, you can click the swatch and select a color from the color picker.

When it comes to an attribute that takes any text or numeric value, such as the leftmargin attribute, for example, all you have to do is enter a value directly into the field (Figure 12.20).

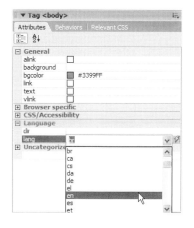

Figure 12.19 To set the value for lang, select one of the options from the drop-down menu.

Figure 12.20 In the case of leftmargin, as with many attributes, you manually enter a value into the field.

Adding Content to the <*head*> Section of Your Document

The <head> section of your HTML document can contain important parts of your page, such as keywords, a description, or an automatic refresh. For those who are intimately familiar with HTML, the <head> content (which is just a series of additional tags) can just be hand coded. However, once again, what about people who might not necessarily be so comfortable with the ins and outs of HTML?

Well, the good folks at Macromedia have included a quick and easy way to manipulate the <head> section of your document without ever having to touch the HTML. Let's take a look at how:

1. Make sure you have the Insert bar open (Window > Insert) and are working in the HTML section.

2. Click the Head button, and select an option from the subsequent drop-down menu.

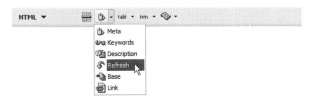

3. A dialog box will appear, specific to the tag type you chose. Refer to the following sections for a full description of each.

There is some overlap among the Head options: Meta, Keywords, Description, and Refresh are all, essentially, versions of the <meta> tag with different attributes and values, while Base and Link represent completely different tags. But in each case, Dreamweaver will insert the correct code in the <head> section of your document, changing the content of the tags as necessary behind the scenes so that you don't need to know the syntax.

Setting Meta Properties of the Page

The <meta> tag is a <head> element that contains information about the page such as its name, copyright status, author, character encoding, and PICS rating.

To set the properties of the <meta> tag, just follow these steps:

1. In the HTML section of the Insert bar, click the Head button and select Meta.

 Note: The information contained within the <meta> tag is really just a generic type of information called metadata—which can used by any number of other software programs or applications.

2. When the Meta dialog box appears (Figure 12.21), select one of the options from the Attribute drop-down menu. The Name attribute signals that the tag to be inserted contains descriptive information about the page; the HTTP-Equivalent attribute signals that the tag contains HTTP header information about the page.

Figure 12.21 The Meta dialog box

Platform for Internet Content Selection (PICS)

The PICS specification enables labels to be associated with Internet content. It was originally designed to help parents and teachers control what children access on the Internet, but it also facilitates other uses for labels, including code signing and privacy. The PICS platform is one on which other rating services and filtering software have been built. For more information on PICS, check out www.w3.org/PICS/.

3. Enter the value of the tag into the Value field. A <meta> tag's value can be absolutely anything you want. Some values are well defined. However, if you would like, you can specify your own value also—such as humorlevel, difficulty, or copyright.

4. Finally, enter the value's content into the Content field. Content is pretty much the equivalent of a tag's attribute value. For example, if you were setting the content of a humorlevel value, you could enter not so funny, mildly funny, or incredibly hilarious into the Content field.

Note: Because the scope of the <meta> tag is pretty wide open (barring widely used ones like description and keywords) and up to you, you can come up with any kind of content you want for a given value.

5. When you are finished, click OK.

Setting the Page's Keywords

Many search engine bots read the contents of the Keywords portion of your code and use the information to index your page in their databases.

Note: A search engine bot is just a small, relatively self-contained program that automatically browses the Web gathering information for search engines to index.

To set your page's keywords, open the HTML section of the Insert bar, click the Head button, and select Keywords. When the Keywords dialog box appears (Figure 12.22), all you need to do is enter all of the keywords you want associated with your site. When you are finished entering the keywords, click OK.

Figure 12.22 The Keywords dialog box

Note: The vast majority of search engine bots only glean the first 255 characters of your keywords. As a result, it's far wiser to go for substance over volume and use several choice keywords instead of a whole list.

Setting the Page's Description

Much as they do with the Keyword element, many search engine bots use the content of the Description portion of your page to index the page in their databases. In addition, many search engines display this information on their results page.

Note: As with the Keyword element, only 255 characters are gleaned from your page's description. As a result, keep it short, sweet, and to the point.

In the HTML section of the Insert bar, click the Head button and select Description. When the Description dialog box appears (Figure 12.23), all you need to do is enter a description for your page. When you are finished entering the page's description, click OK.

Figure 12.23 The Description dialog box

Setting the Page's Refresh Properties

The Refresh portion of your code lets you set a specific amount of time (in seconds) after which the page refreshes—by reloading the current page or loading a new one entirely. This is a useful trick in many kinds of situations. For example, you can create a splash page that automatically switches to the home page of your site after a few seconds. Or you can use Refresh to redirect your users to a page's new URL if it has changed.

To set the refresh properties, just follow these steps:

1. In the HTML section of the Insert bar, click the Head button and select Refresh.

2. When the Refresh dialog box appears (Figure 12.24), enter a value (in seconds) into the Delay field to determine the amount of time that must pass before the page refreshes.

Figure 12.24 The Refresh dialog box

3. Choose one of the following:

   • If you want the browser to load a different page after the time has elapsed, click the Go to URL radio button and then enter the document to which you would like your users redirected into the text field. If the document that you want loaded is in your Local Site, click the Browse button. When the Select File dialog box appears, navigate to the location of the file, select it, and click OK.

   • If you want the browser to reload the current page after the time has elapsed, click the Refresh This Document radio button.

4. When you are finished configuring the Refresh code, click OK.

Setting the Page's Base Properties

The Base element allows you to set a document (or URL) for all the document-relative paths in the page. To set the page's Base, just follow these steps:

1. In the HTML section of the Insert bar, click the Head button and select Base.

2. When the Base dialog box appears (Figure 12.25), click the Browse button.

Figure 12.25 The Base dialog box

3. When the Select File dialog box appears, navigate to the Local Site's file in to which all document-relative paths in your page will be considered relative, select it, and click OK.

4. Select one of the options from the Target drop-down menu. The choice you make determines the specific window in which linked documents will open by default.

 Note: The Target options are explained in Chapter 6.

5. When you are finished, click OK.

Setting the Page's Link Properties

The Link element allows you to define a relationship between the current document and another document.

 Note: The Link element is *not* the same thing as a normal hyperlink. In the case of the Link element, the name is used to refer to a relationship, not a hyperlink.

To set the properties of a Link element, just follow these steps:

1. In the HTML section of the Insert bar, click the Head button and select Link.

2. When the Link dialog box appears (Figure 12.26), you need to start off by setting the document to which you are creating a relationship. To do this, click the Browse button.

Figure 12.26 The Link dialog box

3. When the Select File dialog box appears, navigate to the place in your Local Site where the file is located, select it, and click OK.

4. Enter a unique identifier for the link into the ID field.

5. Enter a name for the relationship into the Title field.

6. Enter the type of relationship between the current document and the one you defined earlier into the Rel field. This value is completely up to you and could include anything—such as next, previous, help, appendix, glossary, home, and so on.

7. Enter the *reverse* relationship between the current document and the linked document into the Rev field. This value could include anything you want—just like the Rel value.

8. When you are finished, click OK.

Inserting HTML Tags with the Tag Chooser

The Tag Chooser, which is only accessible when you are working in Code View or in the code side of Split view, allows you to insert and customize hundreds of kinds of tags from an extensive Library.

Note: The cool thing about the Tag Chooser is it not only allows you to insert HTML tags but tags from other languages as well, including ASP, CFML, PHP, WML, ASP.NET, JSP, and JRun.

To insert a tag with the Tag Chooser, follow these steps:

1. Place your cursor at the location in the HTML where you would like to insert the tag.

2. Choose Insert > Tag.

Note: If you are not in Code View when you choose Insert > Tag, Dreamweaver will automatically shift you into the code section of Split view.

3. When the Tag Chooser appears (Figure 12.27), you have a couple of options as to how to locate the specific tag you'd like to insert:

• Select the category of the tag you want (HTML, ASP, PHP, etc.), and then select the specific tag from the list box on the right side.

• Expand the tag's category by clicking its plus sign; you'll see a series of subcategories. Expand subcategories until you see the tag you want to insert, and then select the tag from the list box on the right.

Note: When you select a tag from the Tag Chooser's right list box, a description will appear in the bottom of the window. If the description isn't visible, click the Tag Info button.

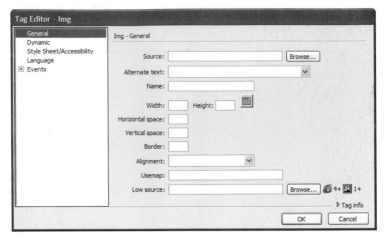

Figure 12.27 The Tag Chooser

4. Once you've selected the specific tag you'd like to insert, click the Insert button [Insert].

5. When the Tag Editor appears, enter the tag's attributes, and then click OK. The Tag Editor will display different attributes for different tags, organized into as many as six categories (depending on the exact tag)—General, Browser Specific, Style Sheet/Accessibility, Language, Content, and Events. Figure 12.28 displays the Tag Editor as it appears if you were inserting an <img> tag.

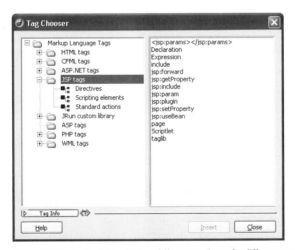

Figure 12.28 The Tag Editor displays different attributes for different tags— here, the ones for the <img> tag.

Working with Snippets

Although the Tag Chooser allows you to insert and customize any number of different tags in a quick and user-friendly manner, you are still just inserting a *single* tag. What if you wanted to insert a block of HTML that consisted of multiple tags? This is where the Snippets panel comes into the picture. Accessible by choosing Window > Snippets, the Snippets panel (Figure 12.29) is a library of predefined blocks of code that are more than just the sum of their tags.

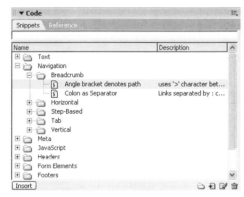

Figure 12.29 The Snippets panel

The cool thing about the Snippets panel is that it isn't just about the blocks of code (Snippets) that ship with the program. You can also convert a block of code that you've created into a Snippet and save it for future use—thereby allowing you to avoid having to rewrite it every time it's needed. So, for instance, say you created a particularly cool-looking table whose attributes would take you a while to re-create. With the help of the Snippets panel, you could take the code for that table, convert it into a Snippet, and then insert it into any document you wanted.

Note: Another cool thing about Snippets is that they can be inserted in either Code View or Design view.

The following sections explore how to insert Snippets into your document, how to create your own Snippets, and how to manage your library of Snippets.

Inserting Snippets into a Document

The process by which you insert a Snippet into your page is quite easy:

1. In either Code View or Design view, place your cursor in the location where you'd like to insert the Snippet.

Note: In some cases, certain Snippets, such as those that contain <head> elements, can be inserted only in Code View.

2. If it isn't already, open the Snippets panel by choosing Window > Snippets.
3. Expand one of the categories by clicking its plus sign.

Note: Notice that a description of the particular Snippet appears in the Description column of the panel.

4. Select the specific Snippet that you would like to insert, and click the Insert button ⌊ Insert ⌋.

Note: You can also double-click the Snippet to insert it into your document.

Creating and Deleting Snippets

As mentioned earlier, you can produce your own Snippets out of code you've created:

1. If it isn't already, open the Snippets panel by choosing Window > Snippets.
2. Select the block of code that you want to turn into a Snippet. This can be done in either Code View or Design view. If you are working in Design view, all you need to do is select the element or elements that are associated with the code that you want to turn into a Snippet.
3. Click the New Snippet button 🗗 .
4. When the Snippet dialog box appears (Figure 12.30), enter a name for the Snippet into the Name field and a description in the Description field. This information will appear in the Snippets panel.
5. You have a couple of choices as to how the Snippet will be inserted into a document:
    - Select the Wrap Selection radio button if you want your Snippet to be composed of two blocks of code—one that gets inserted before the selection and one that gets inserted after the selection.
    - If you want your Snippet to be inserted exactly in the same location as the selection (or the location of the cursor), select the Insert Block radio button.

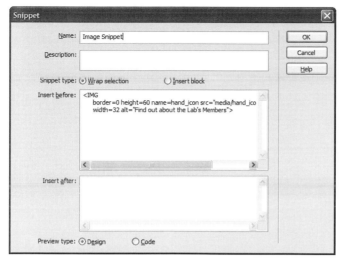

Figure 12.30 The Snippet dialog box

6. Type in your code. If you selected the Wrap Selection radio button, enter the code that you would like inserted before and after the selection into the Insert Before and Insert After fields, respectively. If you selected the Insert Block option in step 5, enter your Snippet's code into the Insert Code field.

> **Note:** You'll notice that the code you selected in step 2 appears "pre-entered" in the Insert Before or Insert Code field. You can leave it as is, delete it and replace it with some other code, or edit it to suit your needs.

7. Select the appropriate preview type: Design or Code. If you select Design, Dreamweaver renders the code and shows it to you in the Preview pane of the Snippets panel as it would appear in a browser. If you select Code, then Dreamweaver shows the actual code in the Preview pane.

8. When you are finished, click OK and your Snippet will be inserted into the Snippets panel.

You might get to the point in which you've accumulated far too many Snippets in the Snippets panel for you to cope with. In situations such as these, you might find yourself wanting to delete some. Doing so is simple: just select a Snippet in the Snippets panel and click the Remove button 🗑 . When the prompt appears, select Yes to delete the Snippet or No to leave it where it is.

Editing Snippets

Once you create a Snippet, you aren't stuck with its initial properties. You can easily go back and edit it. Likewise, you can edit any of the pre-made Snippets that ship with Dreamweaver. Let's take a look at how:

1. If it isn't open already, open the Snippets panel by choosing Window > Snippets.

2. Select the specific Snippet that you would like to edit.

3. Click the Edit Snippet button .

4. When the Snippet dialog box appears, make any edits you want.

5. When you are finished, click OK.

Note: Snippets are not like Library Items in that whenever you change the "parent," all of the "children" change. When you edit a Snippet, any instances that had been previously inserted won't change at all.

Checking Your Code

After you've spent time crafting your web page, it's time for the final step—checking your code. In Dreamweaver MX 2004, there are a couple of different ways for you to make sure that your HTML is as lean, mean, and functional as humanly possible. This section shows how to clean up your HTML, validate your HTML, and, as a last resort, get help with your HTML syntax.

Cleaning Up Your HTML

In the grand scheme of things, HTML is a very forgiving medium. You can easily insert empty tags or redundant tags and the browser will display the page regardless. However, releasing sloppy HTML onto the world is not a habit that you want to get into. As a result, Dreamweaver has a built-in feature that lets you clean up your HTML.

To improve your code, choose Commands > Clean Up HTML. When the Clean up HTML/XHTML dialog box appears (Figure 12.31), select any or all of the following options. Once you are finished choosing options, click OK.

- To remove any pairs of tags that don't have any content between them, select the Empty Container Tags check box.

- To remove all redundant tags, select the Redundant Nested Tags check box. What exactly is a redundant tag? Well, in the following line of HTML, the <i> tags around the word *Spain* are redundant and would therefore be removed.

```
<i>the rain in <i>Spain</i> falls mainly on the plain </i>
```

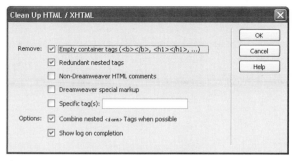

Figure 12.31 The Clean Up HTML/XHTML dialog box

- To delete any comment that wasn't inserted by Dreamweaver, select the Non-Dreamweaver HTML Contents check box.
- To delete any Dreamweaver-specific comments, select the Dreamweaver Special Markup check box.

Note: When you are working with Library Items or Templates, Dreamweaver inserts special comments that allow it to refer to the parent Template or Library Item. If you remove any special Dreamweaver markup when the document is cleaned up, these comments will be removed and the document will be detached from the Template or Library Item.

- To delete particular tags, select the Specific Tag(s) check box and then enter the tag(s) you want removed into the adjacent text box.

Note: To remove more than one tag, list them all and separate each with a comma.

- If your document has any nested <font> tags that you want combined, select the Combine Nested <font> Tags check box.
- To display a log of all the actions take during the cleanup, click the Show Log On Completion check box in the Options section.

Note: If you are working with some HTML that was initially generated by Microsoft Word (which is notorious for bloating HTML with all sorts of weird, unnecessary junk), you can deal with that specifically by choosing Commands > Clean Up Word HTML

Validating HTML

Beyond cleaning up your HTML, you can do a far more detailed check of its syntax. The process, which is called validation, also checks your code for less serious problems and gives you some helpful suggestions about formatting your code so that it conforms to certain standards.

 Note: When you are validating an HTML document, as opposed to an XHTML document, HTML 4.0 is used as the code version against which your document is checked.

For example, if, when you validate your document, Dreamweaver finds that the <body> tag's topmargin attribute is missing, it will tell you. All in all, validating your HTML is a great way to catch any problems or sloppy code, and it generally allows you to make your HTML more streamlined and well written.

To validate your HTML, choose File > Check Page > Validate Markup. Dreamweaver will validate your document and display the results in the Validation tab of the Results panel (Figure 12.32). An explanation of each error is displayed in the Description column.

 Note: The same information that is listed in the Description column can be gotten by selecting a specific result and then clicking the Info button.

Figure 12.32 The results of the validation are displayed in the Validation section of the Results panel.

From here, you have a few options:

- To open up Code View to the specific place in the document where an error exists, double-click a result.

- To output the report as an HTML document, which can then be printed or saved for future reference, click the Browse Report button 🌐.

- To save the results of the report as an XML file, click the Save Report button 🖫. When the Save As dialog box appears, enter a name for the saved report into the File Name field, navigate to the location where you want the file saved, and click the Save button.

Getting Help with HTML Syntax

OK, let's face it. Even with all of the help that Dreamweaver MX 2004 offers for those who might not necessarily live, breath, and sleep code, HTML can sometimes be confusing and daunting.

This is where the Reference panel comes into the picture. Accessible by choosing Window > Reference, the Reference panel (Figure 12.33) provides you with a comprehensive resource for a wide variety of commonly used web languages, such as HTML, ASP, CFML, PHP, SQL, CSS markup, and JavaScript.

Many of the "listings" on each tag or element are taken from the works of respected tech publisher O'Reilly and contain complete descriptions of the tag, its syntax, and an example of how it could be used.

Figure 12.33 The Reference panel

Working with XHTML

Since its inception in the early 1990s, HTML has gone through several versions, the culmination of which is HTML 4.01. Unfortunately, there isn't going to be an HTML 5.0. Why? Well, you first need to bear in mind that HTML was originally designed for a very different environment than today's very demanding hi-tech Internet—namely, exchange of data and documents between scientists associated with CERN, the birthplace of the Web. Since then the language has been hacked and stretched into an unwieldy monster, and the prevalence of sloppy markup practices makes it hard or impossible for some user agents (e.g., browsers, spiders, etc.) to make sense of the Web. After a decade of use and ad hoc evolution, there is a strong need for a more flexible and more portable language. This is where XML enters the picture.

XML, which stands for Extensible Markup Language, is a structured set of rules for how one might define any kind of data to be shared on the Web. It's called "extensible" because anyone can invent a tag for a particular purpose, and as long as everyone uses the tag (both the author and an application itself), it can be adapted and used for many purposes—including, as it happens, describing the appearance of a Web page.

The problem with XML is that, quite honestly, the web world at large really isn't ready for it. Structurally speaking, it's fairly different from HTML. As a result, most browsers aren't equipped to deal with it in the same way that they are equipped to deal with HTML. Also, legions of web designers and developers are steeped in the traditions of HTML and would find it difficult to completely shift gears and start working with a totally different language with which to create their grand designs. This is where XHTML comes into the picture.

XHTML is the bridge between HTML and XML. Think of XHTML (Extensible Hypertext Markup Language) as the next incarnation of HTML. XHTML 1.0 is the first step toward a modular and extensible Web based on XML. It provides the bridge for web designers to enter the Web of the future while still being able to maintain compatibility with today's HTML 4–based browsers. With a few notable exceptions, XHTML syntax looks very much like HTML 4. So, if you're familiar with HTML 4, XHTML will be easy to learn and use.

The cool thing about Dreamweaver is that, while all web pages are, by default, created using HTML 4.01, XHTML 1.0 (which is the current XHTML standard) is supported. In the following sections, you can explore how to create XHTML documents, convert documents from HTML 4.0 into XHTML, and validate XHTML documents.

Creating XHTML Documents

Creating an XHTML page from scratch is really quite easy. All you need to do is follow these steps:

1. Choose File > New.

2. When the New Document dialog box appears, select any of the available document types.

3. Click the Make Document XHTML Compliant check box in the bottom-right corner of the dialog box.

4. Click the Create button. Note that, as illustrated in Figure 12.34, your new document's XHTML compliance will be displayed in the title bar.

Figure 12.34 "XHTML" will be displayed in Dreamweaver's title bar for any XHTML-compliant document.

Note: All documents types, not just HTML, can be made XHTML compliant in Dreamweaver MX 2004.

Converting HTML Documents to XHTML

If you've created an entire page, or even an entire site, using HTML 4, never fear! You can easily convert any HTML 4 document into XHTML with a minimum of muss and fuss: just choose File > Convert > XHTML.

In some cases, you might get a dialog, like one in Figure 12.35, indicating that several elements of your HTML document couldn't be fixed during the conversion. Just click OK and the document will be converted into XHTML.

Figure 12.35 Dreamweaver will alert you to parts of your HTML code that don't produce valid XHTML code.

Note: If the page you are trying to convert is based on a Template, Dreamweaver will tell you that it is unable to convert it to XHTML and will prompt you to convert the actual Template file or manually detach the document from its parent Template.

Validating XHTML Documents

Just as in the case of an HTML document, you can validate an XHTML document to make sure that the syntax is correct and the code doesn't contain any irregularities.

To validate an XHTML document, choose File > Check Page > Validate As XML. Dreamweaver will validate your document and display the results in the Validation section of the Results panel (Figure 12.36). An explanation of each error is displayed in the Description column.

Figure 12.36 The results of the XHTML validation are displayed in the Validation section of the Results panel.

From here, you have a few options as to what you can do:

- To open up Code View to the specific place in the document where an error exists, simply double-click a result.

- To output the report as an HTML document, which can then be printed or saved for future reference, click the Browse Report button.

- To save the results of the report as an XML file, click the Save Report button. When the Save As dialog box appears, enter a name for the saved report into the File Name field, navigate to the location where you want the file saved, and click the Save button.

Extending Dreamweaver

Easily one of the most exciting things about Dreamweaver MX 2004 is the fact that it is specifically designed to be not only highly customizable, but also extensible. You can mold the program so that it is best suited for your needs, and you can also extend it in ways that weren't originally built into the version of the program that you purchased. Ultimately, whether you customize or extend Dreamweaver, the point is to make the program be the most it can be for your needs—thereby allowing you to unshackle your creativity and produce the best interactive experience for your audience.

Chapter Contents
Automating Tasks with Commands
Extending Dreamweaver with Extensions
Changing the Dreamweaver Interface

You've already experienced this to a certain extent with some of the topics that were covered back in Chapter 2. However, in this chapter, you are going to take the next step and explore some more complex topics.

Automating Tasks with Commands

During the process of creating a website, however big or small, you'll be doing a lot of tasks over and over again. What if you could record tasks that have many steps and then replay them whenever you wanted? In Dreamweaver MX 2004, this isn't just a pipe dream, it's a reality. With the help of the new History panel, you can choose any of the steps that you've carried out since you started a new document and compile them into a command that can be saved and run anytime you please. The commands themselves, which are something like macros, are retained permanently (regardless of whether or not you're working in the document they were created in) and become accessible through the program's Commands menu. To actually run a command, all you need to do is select it from Dreamweaver's Commands menu.

Note: The History panel displays a list of the steps you've performed in the currently active document since you opened it. The History panel does not show steps you've performed in other documents. The slider in the panel initially points to the last step that you performed. Beyond creating commands, you can use the History panel to undo or redo individual steps or multiple steps at once. You can apply steps from this panel to the same object or to a different object in the document. However, you cannot rearrange the order of steps in the History panel.

In the following sections, you'll explore how to create and manage commands.

Creating Commands

The process by which you create a command is quite easy; all you need to do is follow these steps:

1. Manually carry out a series of steps that you would like to turn into a command.
2. Open the History panel by choosing Window > History. You'll notice that the steps you've taken in the currently active document are listed in the panel. The earliest steps are listed at the top of the panel, while the most recent are listed at the bottom (Figure 13.1).
3. Select the steps that you would like included in the command. To select multiple steps, hold down the Shift key.

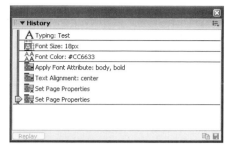

Figure 13.1 The History panel. Note the list of steps carried out.

Note: You might have noticed that some of the steps' associated icons have a small red *x* in their lower-right corner or are separated from one another by a line. This means that because of its specific nature, that specific step can't be made into a command. If you try to include one of these kinds of steps in a command, the command won't be saved.

4. Click the Save Selected Steps As Command button located in the lower-right corner of the History panel.

5. When the Save As Command dialog box appears (see Figure 13.2), enter a name for the command in the Command Name field.

Figure 13.2 The Save As Command dialog box

Note: It's a really good idea to give your command a descriptive name. By doing this, you'll be able to distinguish the purpose of each specific command when you view the Commands menu.

6. When you're finished, click OK.

Note: After you've converted a series of steps into a command, it appears in the Commands menu.

Renaming or Deleting Commands

Although you give a command a name when you initially create it, you might find yourself wanting to change its name during the course of your work. And as you work more and more with Dreamweaver, you'll begin to accumulate more and more commands, which will inevitably clog up the Commands menu. So it's a good idea to remove commands that you no longer use.

To rename or delete a command, first choose Commands > Edit Command List. The Edit Command List dialog box appears (Figure 13.3):

To rename a command, double-click its name. When the command name becomes editable, simply type a new name. When you are finished, click the Close button ⌐ Close ⌐.

To delete a command, select it and click the Delete button ⌐ Delete ⌐. When the pop-up alert appears, asking you whether you want to delete the command, click Yes.

Figure 13.3 The Edit Command List dialog box

Extending Dreamweaver with Extensions

Back in Chapter 9, you were first introduced to behaviors as great tools to add interactivity to your website and extend the power of Dreamweaver MX 2004. The wonderful thing is that, much as with plug-ins for other programs, an entire community of behavior developers has sprung up. The definite added bonus is that, unlike the plug-in industry, the majority of developers distribute their behaviors free for anyone to download. And it isn't just behaviors that are being created; developers are creating commands and objects as well—many of which are free to anyone who wants to download them.

The most complete resource for downloadable extensions is the Macromedia Exchange (www.macromedia.com/exchange), where you'll not only be able to download behaviors for Dreamweaver MX 2004, but also free components, extensions, and add-ons for a host of other Macromedia programs, including Flash MX 2004, Cold-Fusion MX, Fireworks MX 2004, JRun, and HomeSite (Figure 13.4).

All you need to take advantage of this virtual wealth of free downloadable behaviors is an Internet connection and a small (free) program called Macromedia Extension Manager. Designed to let you install and manage downloaded components over multiple Macromedia programs, Extension Manager is vital if you want to take advantage of free downloadable components.

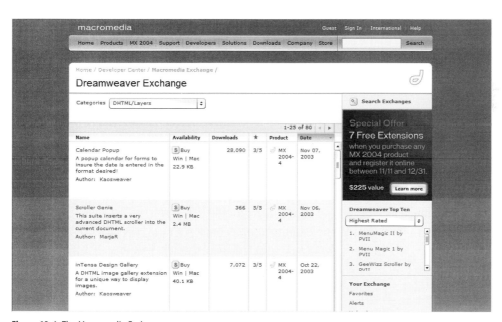

Figure 13.4 The Macromedia Exchange

Behaviors, Commands, and Objects—Oh My!

Many people can become confused as to the difference between behaviors, objects, and commands. You already know that behaviors are simply pre-packaged little JavaScript programs that you can insert into your HTML using the Behaviors panel. What about objects and commands?

Commands are simply a prepackaged series of instructions for Dreamweaver that, once downloaded, get stored in the Commands menu. Like behaviors, commands might insert JavaScript into your HTML. On the other hand, they might instruct Dreamweaver to format your document in a certain way—such as clean up the HTML. Besides any custom commands that you create using the History panel, Dreamweaver MX 2004 actually comes with a few pre-made commands—such as Set Color Scheme and Create Web Photo Album—all of which are accessible though the Commands menu.

Objects, on the other hand, are slightly different from commands and behaviors. As you've already seen, objects are basically things that can be inserted into your HTML document—form elements, images, SWF files, and so on. Most commonly, objects are inserted with the Insert bar. When you download new objects, you essentially add additional buttons to your Insert bar and thereby increase the number of elements that can be inserted into your HTML document. Each installed object, when used, provides its own unique dialog box, allowing the user to set the particular properties of that specific inserted element.

To use Extension Manager to add new behaviors to Dreamweaver, follow these steps:

1. With the Extension Manager open (Figure 13.5), choose File > Install Extension. Alternatively, you can click the Install New Extension button .

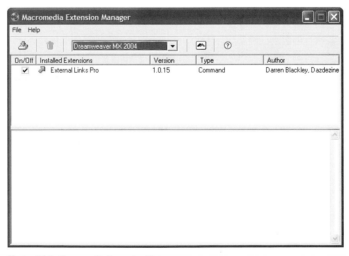

Figure 13.5 Macromedia Extension Manager

2. When the Select Extension to Install dialog box appears, navigate to where you downloaded the extension (which has a .mxp extension), select it, and click Install.

3. After the extension is installed, it will be visible in Extension Manager's list (and available for use in the program for which it was designed). If the extension is a behavior, it will be accessible through the Behaviors panel. If it is a command, it will be accessible through the Commands menu. If it is an Object, it will be accessible with the Insert bar.

Changing the Dreamweaver Interface

Back in Chapter 2, you learned how to modify Dreamweaver's interface to better suit the characteristics of your own workflow. This is all fine and good, but what if you want to do things to extend and manipulate the interface in ways that Macromedia never really intended for the average user? Unlike other programs out there whose interface is locked up in compiled executable programs, Dreamweaver (as well as many other Macromedia products) draws the configuration of its interface from a series of files that are open and editable by anyone who has the gumption to do so. So, the main program menu, the Insert bar, and even various dialog boxes can be fiddled with to suit your needs.

In the following sections of the chapter, you are going to dive into learning how to customize the interface in more drastic ways.

Manipulating the Main Program Menu

Unquestionably one of the coolest things about customizing Dreamweaver is the fact that you can easily change and manipulate the program's main menu. So, for instance, you could add another menu entirely, add menu items to current menus, or reorganize the current menu items in one of the menus.

All menus in Dreamweaver are controlled by a single XML file that is located in Dreamweaver's Configurations/Menus folder. The file, which is called menu.xml, can be opened using a wide variety of editors (such as Windows Notepad or BBEdit) and then edited to your heart's content.

> **Note:** The syntax of the code in the menu.xml file is based on JavaScript. As a result, those who have some experience with JavaScript will be far better equipped to exert total control over the properties of the menu information contained in the file.

You might ask why you couldn't just use Dreamweaver to edit the file. While Dreamweaver can be used to edit XML, there are some problems with editing the menu.xml file within Dreamweaver. Basically, when you run Dreamweaver, the file is in use. Saving any changes to the file on the fly while it's in use can have some pretty serious results. So, here is what you can do—create a copy of the menu.xml file and call it something different. This way, you can make any changes you want to it using Dreamweaver without actually fiddling with the file that is currently being used by the program.

Whether or not you are using Dreamweaver to edit the menu.xml file, it is *always* important that you create a backup. This way, if the changes you make cause problems (which can range from a menu not functioning to Dreamweaver not being able to properly launch), you can always replace the edited file with the backup of the original, thereby restoring the original configuration.

To add your own custom menu or menu item to Dreamweaver's main program menu, first you need to understand the anatomy of the menu.xml file. First off, given the fact that the file controls all menus in Dreamweaver, it is quite large. If you want to edit the main program menu, you'll need to scroll down quite a way until you see this gray comment line:

<!-- This is the Main menu bar -->

After this line, everything pertains to the main program menu.

From here, as illustrated in Figure 13.6, you can see that the code for each individual menu is contained within two elements (that look something like an HTML tag): <menu> and </menu>.

 Note: All submenus are contained within the <menu> tag as well.

The other thing you need to realize is that the <menu> element has attributes that control the way in which the menu itself behaves:

name The name attribute, which is required, sets the name of the menu as it appears in the program. For example, if you want your menu to be titled Websites, you'd enter name="Websites".

id The id attribute, which is required, is a unique identifier for that menu.

```
2563    <menu name="_Help" id="DWMenu_Help">
2564        <menuitem name="Getting Started and T_utorials" enabled="true" arguments="'DWTutorial'" file="Menus/MM/CSHelp.htm"    id="DWMenu
2565    <separator />
2566        <menuitem name="Using Dreamwea_ver" key="F1" enabled="true" arguments="'DWUsing'" file="Menus/MM/CSHelp.htm" id="DWMenu_Help_UD
2567        <menuitem name="Using _ColdFusion" key="Cmd+F1" arguments="'CFUsing'" file="Menus/MM/CSHelp.htm" id="DWMenu_Help_CFUsing" />
2568        <menuitem name="Re_ference" key="Shift+F1" enabled="true" command="dw.toggleFloater('reference')"    checked="dw.getFloaterVisib
2569        <menu name="_Extensions" id="DWMenu_Help_Extending">
2570            <menuitem name="_Extending Dreamweaver" arguments="'Extending'" file="Menus/MM/CSHelp.htm" id="DWMenu_Help_DWExtending" />
2571            <menuitem name="_API Reference" arguments="'API'" file="Menus/MM/CSHelp.htm" id="DWMenu_Help_DWAPI" />
2572            <menuitem name="Creating and Su_bmitting" file="Commands/Extension Help.htm" id="DWMenu_Help_Extensions" />
2573    </menu>
```

Figure 13.6 This piece of the code refers to the Help menu—note the <menu> and </menu> elements that designate the beginning and the end of the menu.

platform The platform attribute, which isn't required, determines whether the menu is available in the Macintosh or Windows version of Dreamweaver. If you want the menu to be visible just on a Mac, enter the code platform="mac". However, if you want the menu to be visible on a Windows machine, enter platform="win". If you want the menu to be visible on both platforms, simply don't include the platform attribute.

As illustrated in Figure 13.7, a good example of the use of the platform attribute can be seen at the very top of the main menu bar section of the menu.xml file. You'll note that there is a menu named Apple. For those who are used to working on a Mac, you'll recognize this as the Apple menu (designated by a little apple icon in the Mac OS)—which doesn't appear in the Windows OS.

So, now that you know the structure and the attributes of a menu in the main menu bar, you can easily add your own custom menu. In Figure 13.8, you'll note that a new menu, called Websites, has been added after Dreamweaver's Help menu.

```
1723   <menu name="Apple" id="DWMenu_Apple" platform="mac">
1724       <menuitem name="About Macromedia Dreamweaver MX 2004" command="dw.showAboutBox()" enabled="true" id="DWMenu_Apple_About" />
1725       <menuitem name="Ke_yboard Shortcuts..." platform="mac" enabled="true" file="Commands/Keyboard Shortcuts.html" id="DWMenu_Edit_F
1726   </menu>
```

Figure 13.7 The platform attribute associated with the Apple menu designates it as a Mac-only menu.

```
2588   <menu name="Websites" id="DWMenu_websites">
2589   </menu>
```

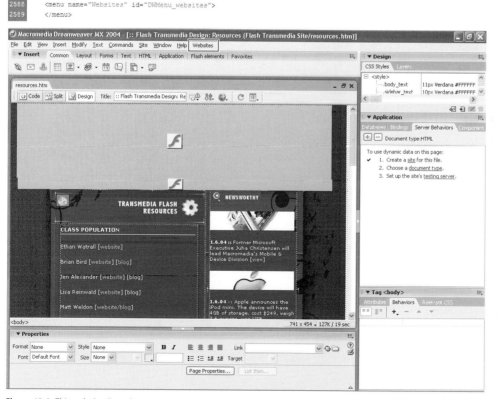

Figure 13.8 This code (top) results in a new menu called Websites to be inserted after Dreamweaver's Help menu (bottom).

The thing about this code is that it only defines the shell of the menu itself—basically just a new entry in the main menu bar. The menu doesn't actually have anything in it until you add some menu items.

Adding New Menu Items to Menus

Once you have created a new menu, you can start adding menu items to it. It's important to realize that menu items work in much the same way that menus do. Also, you can add menu items not only to your own custom menus, but even to the program's default menus.

Instead of being defined by the <menu> element, options and commands on a menu are defined by the <menuitem> element. And, like the <menu> element, the <menuitem> element has several attributes.

Note: To take full advantage of creating custom menu items, it's a good idea to have at least a passing understanding of JavaScript—because there are far more attributes associated with the <menuitem> element than the <menu> element and the syntax of each attribute's values is based on JavaScript syntax.

name The name attribute, which is required, sets the name of the menu item as it appears in the menu. For example, if you were creating a menu item that opened up Macromedia's website, you'd enter something like name="Visit Macromedia's Website".

id The id attribute, which is required, is a unique identifier for that menu item.

platform The platform attribute, which isn't required, determines whether the menu is available in the Macintosh or Windows version of Dreamweaver; it takes a value of "mac" or "win", as explained in the preceding section.

file The file attribute specifies the file used to configure a menu item that is set by the dynamic attribute. These files, which are HTML documents, are most commonly located in the Configure/Menus/MM folder and use JavaScript to dynamically manipulate the Dreamweaver interface.

dynamic The dynamic attribute specifies a menu item that is configured by the file specified by the file attribute.

arguments The arguments attribute lets you specify a comma-separated list of arguments that are passed to the file specified by the file attribute. Each argument must be separated by a single quote (') inside the attribute's double quote (").

checked The checked attribute specifies a JavaScript function that returns a value of true if the menu item is supposed to have a check mark next to it when it has been activated.

command The command attribute, which is arguably one of the most important of the <menuitem> element's attributes, specifies the JavaScript function that executes when the menu item is selected.

domrequired The domrequired Boolean attribute determines whether or not Dreamweaver's Design and Code View need to be synchronized before the code specified by the <menuitem> attributes is executed. A value of true requires that Design and Code View be synchronized, while a value of false doesn't.

key The key attribute sets a keyboard shortcut that can be used to activate the menu item. If you are using the key attribute, make sure that the plus (+) sign is used to separate multiple keys in the combination—for instance, Ctrl+L. In addition, be sure to use the proper key abbreviation: Alt, Opt, Ctrl, Cmd, Shift, and so on.

Now that you've got a basic understanding of the syntax and attributes of the <menuitem> element, you can go ahead and start adding items to your menu. As an example, Figure 13.9 illustrates the code required to create a menu, each item of which would launch a specific website.

> **Note:** Although this section discussed adding a custom menu item to a custom menu, you can use the same steps to add a custom menu item to one of Dreamweaver's existing menus.

```
2588  <menu name="Websites" id="DWMenu_websites">
2589      <menuitem name="Macromedia.com" command="dw.browseDocument('http://www.macromedia.com/')" id="DWMenu_web_macromedia" />
2590      <menuitem name="Captainprimate.com" command="dw.browseDocument('http://www.captainprimate.com/')" id="DWMenu_web_capprimate" />
2591      <menuitem name="Amazon.com" command="dw.browseDocument('http://www.amazon.com/')" id="DWMenu_web_amazon" />
2592      <menuitem name="Adobe.com" command="dw.browseDocument('http://www.adobe.com/')" id="DWMenu_web_adobe" />
2593  </menu>
```

Figure 13.9 The code required to create a menu in which there are several items, each of which launches a specific website

Reorganizing Objects in the Insert Bar

You may have noticed that it's completely impossible to reorganize the order of the tabs in the Insert bar in the same way that you would if you were working with any other panels. Unfortunately, this is just a fact of life. Even though it may appear similar to other panels, the Insert bar is not really a panel and therefore isn't governed by the same rules of customization.

However, in much the same way that you can create a custom menu in the main menu bar (using the techniques outlined in the previous sections), you can reorganize the tabs in the Insert bar to better suite your personal workflow.

As with Dreamweaver's menus, the configuration (and to a certain degree, the appearance) of the Insert bar is controlled by the Insertbar.xml file (Figure 13.10), which is located in the Configuration/Objects folder.

```
142    <button id="DW_Chars_Registered" image="Characters\Registered.gif" MMString:name="insertbar/registered" file="Characters\Reg
143    <button id="DW_Chars_Trademark" image="Characters\Trademark.gif" MMString:name="insertbar/trademark" file="Characters\Tradema
144    <separator />
145    <button id="DW_Chars_Other" image="Characters\Other.gif" MMString:name="insertbar/other" file="Characters\Other.htm" />
146  </menubutton>
147  </category>
148  <category id="DW_Insertbar_HTML" MMString:name="insertbar/category/html" folder="HTML">
149    <button id="DW_HR" image="Common\HR.gif" MMString:name="insertbar/hr" file="Common\HR.htm" />
150    <menubutton id="DW_Insertbar_Head" MMString:name="insertbar/head" image="Head\Meta.gif" folder="Head">
151      <button id="DW_Head_Meta" image="Head\Meta.gif" MMString:name="insertbar/headMeta" file="Head\Meta.htm" />
152      <button id="DW_Head_Keywords" image="Head\Keywords.gif" MMString:name="insertbar/headKeywords" file="Head\Keywords.htm" />
153      <button id="DW_Head_Description" image="Head\Description.gif" MMString:name="insertbar/headDescription" file="Head\Descriptio
154      <button id="DW_Head_Refresh" image="Head\Refresh.gif" MMString:name="insertbar/headRefresh" file="Head\Refresh.htm" />
155      <button id="DW_Head_Base" image="Head\Base.gif" MMString:name="insertbar/headBase" file="Head\Base.htm" />
156      <button id="DW_Head_Link" image="Head\Link.gif" MMString:name="insertbar/headLink" file="Head\Link.htm" />
157    </menubutton>
158    <menubutton id="DW_Insertbar_TableTags" MMString:name="insertbar/tabletags" image="Tables\TableTag.gif" folder="Tables">
159      <button id="DW_Tables_TableTag" image="Tables\TableTag.gif" enabled="_VIEW_CODE" MMString:name="insertbar/tableTag" file="Tab
160      <button id="DW_Tables_Tr" image="Tables\Tr.gif" enabled="_VIEW_CODE" MMString:name="insertbar/tableTR" file="Tables\Tr.htm" (
161      <button id="DW_Tables_Th" image="Tables\Th.gif" enabled="_VIEW_CODE" MMString:name="insertbar/tableTH" file="Tables\Th.htm" (
162      <button id="DW_Tables_Td" image="Tables\Td.gif" enabled="_VIEW_CODE" MMString:name="insertbar/tableTD" file="Tables\Td.htm" (
163      <button id="DW_Tables_Caption" image="Tables\Caption.gif" enabled="_VIEW_CODE" MMString:name="insertbar/caption" file="Table:
164    </menubutton>
165    <menubutton id="DW_Insertbar_FramesTags" MMString:name="insertbar/frames" image="Frames\Frame.gif" showif="!_FILE_TEMPLATE" fold
166      <button id="DW_Frames_Frameset" image="Frames\Frameset.gif" enabled="_VIEW_CODE" MMString:name="insertbar/frameset" file="Fra
167      <button id="DW_Frames_Frame" image="Frames\Frame.gif" enabled="_VIEW_CODE" MMString:name="insertbar/frame" file="Frames\Frame
```

Figure 13.10 Although the Insertbar.xml file is large, this section of code gives you an idea of how it is structured.

 Note: Be *absolutely* sure you back up the Insertbar.xml file before you start fiddling with it. Also, if you are using Dreamweaver to edit the code, make sure you are working on a version of the file that isn't currently being used by the program.

When you look at the file's code, you'll notice that it contains both <category> and <button> elements (which have attributes much as the <menu> and <menuitem> elements discussed in the preceding sections have). The <category> element refers to the individual tabs, while the <button> elements refer to the objects within a specific tab.

To reorganize the tabs in the Insert bar, all you need to do is move any <category> element to a different location (before or after other <category> elements). If you want to reorganize an object within a specific tab, all you have to do is move its corresponding <button> element within its associated <category> element.

Adding an Object to the Insert Bar That Runs a Command

Earlier in this chapter, you learned how to create commands using the History panel. You'll remember that any command you create is stored in the Commands menu. This is all fine and good if you are a fan of using the main menu bar to access Dreamweaver's features. However, some people aren't. Some would rather use a more visual, "in-interface" approach (buttons, icons, etc.) to access the program's features. Given this, you are probably asking yourself whether you can create a button in the Insert bar to run a command that you've created. The answer is yes (granted, this would be a pretty lame section if the answer was no).

To add a custom object that runs a command to the Insert bar, just follow these steps:

1. Open the Insertbar.xml file (located in the Configuration/Objects folder).

> **Note:** Be *absolutely* sure you back up the Insertbar.xml file before you start fiddling with it. Also, if you are using Dreamweaver to edit the code, make sure you are working on a version of the file that isn't currently being used by the program.

2. Locate the specific tab into which you would like to add the object that runs your command.

> **Note:** Remember, each tab in the Insert bar is defined by the contents of a specific <category> element in the Insertbar.xml file.

3. From here, add the following code (with the appropriate attribute values for your command):

```
<button command="dw.runCommand ('my Command's HTML file here.htm', null);
" enabled="" id="aUniqueValueName" image="theTabName\ MyIconImageName.gif"
name="Enter a Tooltip for the Command's Icon here" />
```

Let's break the code down a little in order to get a better understanding of how it works:

- The command attribute is simply saying that when you click on that button, it will run the specific command. What you might not realize is that, whenever you create a command, it's stored as an HTML file (complete with an associated JavaScript file) in the Configurations/Commands folder. In the command attribute, you are simply telling Dreamweaver the name of this HTML file.

- The id attribute, much as in the case of the <menu> element we discussed earlier, is simply a unique identifier of your choosing.

- The image attribute is the icon that will appear in the Insert bar. There are a few things regarding this image about which you should be aware. First, it must be 18 pixels by 18 pixels in size. Second, you need to stick it in a folder that corresponds to the specific tab in which you want the object to appear—which you specified in the preceding code. The folders are located in the Configuration/Object folder.

- The `name` attribute simply acts as a tool tip that pops up when the user moves their mouse over the command's icon in the Insert bar.

4. When you are finished, save the file and restart/start Dreamweaver.

Changing Dreamweaver Dialog Boxes

As mentioned at the beginning of this section, Dreamweaver draws the configuration of its interface from a series of files that are open and editable by anyone who has the gumption to do so. We've already seen that this is the case with the program's main menu bar as well as the Insert bar. This is also the case with all of the program's dialog boxes, whose appearances are based on simple HTML documents—the majority of which are located in the Configuration/Commands folder. To change the appearance of a specific dialog box, all you have to do is locate its HTML file, open it, make any changes you want, and then save it.

Take, for example, the Insert Flash Text dialog box. Figure 13.11 illustrates the default appearance of the dialog box.

If you were to locate and open the Flash Text.htm file, which controls the appearance of the dialog box (located in the Configuration/Commands folder), you would be faced with a simple form (as illustrated in Figure 13.12).

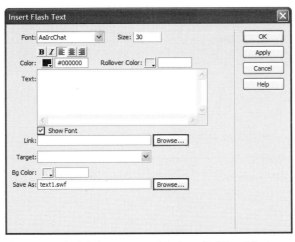

Figure 13.11 The default appearance of the Insert Flash Text dialog box.

To manipulate the appearance of the dialog box (Figure 13.13), all you would have to do is change the HTML form, save it, and then restart Dreamweaver.

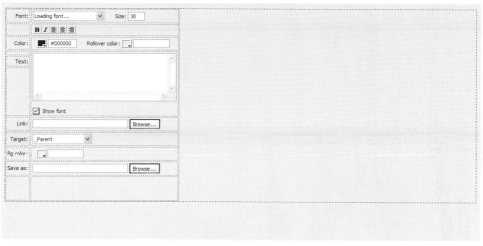

Figure 13.12 The appearance of the Insert Flash Text dialog box is controlled with a simple HTML form.

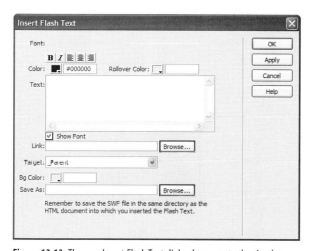

Figure 13.13 The new Insert Flash Text dialog box—note the simple text that has been added near the bottom

Collecting User Information with Forms

As much as it is used to deliver information, the Web has become a tool for gathering information too. Whether it's an e-commerce site that gathers orders, payment information, and customer data or a forum site that requires a username and password, data flows both ways on the Web.

Sending data from a web page to a server involves two parts. The first is the web page itself, where fields, buttons, menus, and more are used to collect information from the user. The second part is a program on the server that receives and uses that data.

14

Chapter Contents
Inserting Forms and <form> Tags
Setting Form Properties
Adding Objects to Your Form

This chapter focuses on the first component: the front-end interface elements, commonly called forms, that collect the data from the users. In Dreamweaver MX 2004, you can not only create the front-end form elements, you can also create the back-end server-side component—topics covered in Bonus Chapters 1 and 2 on the CD.

Inserting Forms and *<form>* Tags

A form on the Web, interestingly enough, is quite like its real-world paper counterpart. It's a structured method of communication that solicits very specific information from the user, whether they are sitting in front of their computer buying books or sitting in the bank applying for a car loan.

The process by which you create the elements that make up a form is relatively easy. The real challenge comes in understanding the nuts and bolts of a form and making sure that you've designed your form beforehand so that you'll be able to quickly and efficiently choose those elements that allow you to best serve your data collection needs (for example, using a drop-down menu to collect a user's name is definitely a bad decision—not to mention impossible—when a simple text field will do the trick just fine).

Before you can start inserting the form objects (text fields, radio button, and so on), you have to insert the actual <form></form> tags in which the form objects reside. You can actually have form objects that exist outside the <form></form> tags. However, without the tags, they can't interact with the back-end component and are therefore pretty useless. Because the form itself, which is inserted just as any other object in Dreamweaver is inserted, is an invisible element, it's represented in the Document window by a dashed red line; this will become a very important visual cue.

Note: If you do not insert the form first, any form objects that you subsequently add will be totally useless. They must reside within the red dashed lines of the form.

To insert a form into your document, follow these steps:

1. Place your cursor in the location where you want to insert the form.
2. Open the Insert bar (Window > Insert).
3. Make sure you are working in the Forms section of the Insert bar.

4. Click the Form button ▢. Alternatively, you can choose Insert > Form > Form to insert the form into your Document window.

If you have the document's invisible elements turned on, you'll notice the red dashed box (which is often referred to as the form delimiter; see Figure 14.1)—this is the form itself. Anything within it falls within the <form></form> tags.

Setting Form Properties

Like many elements in Dreamweaver, a form has a series of properties that you'll need to set in order for it to work properly. To do so, just follow these steps:

1. Open the Property Inspector (Window > Properties).

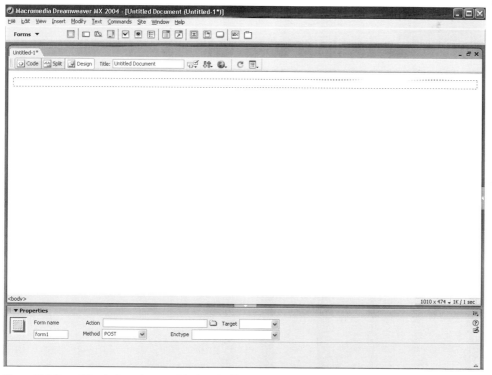

Figure 14.1 The red lines indicate the area of the form itself.

2. With your cursor inside the form delimiter, select the form by clicking the <form> tab in the Tag Selector. This gives you access to the form's properties (Figure 14.2).

Note: Remember, the Tag Selector is located in the bottom-left corner of the Document window.

Figure 14.2 Form properties in the Property Inspector

Note: The form properties are also referred to as a form handler.

3. First, you need to set the form's method, which is how the form sends the data that it collects to the server. You have two options:
   - If you use the GET method, the data is sent to the server in the form of a URL. The GET method is rarely used, for two reasons. First, when you pass data in the form of a URL to the server, you are limited in the amount of data that can be moved. Second, because the data is actually visible, sending data in the form of a URL is relatively insecure and therefore not particularly desirable.
   - If you use the POST method (the default selection), data is encrypted and sent to the server.

4. In the Action field, enter the location (relative or absolute URL) of the script, page, or program that will process the information gathered by the form.

Note: For more information on processing and using form-submitted data, see Bonus Chapters 1 and 2 on the CD for an introduction on using Dreamweaver MX 2004 to create dynamic database-driven sites.

5. When you finish setting the form properties, press Return/Enter or click anywhere off the Property Inspector.

Adding Objects to Your Form

In order for your user to submit data via a form, there must exist a method by which they can actually input their data. This is where form objects come into the picture. Form objects are the graphical portion of a form—such as buttons, check boxes, and text fields—into which the user inputs their data. In the following sections, you are going to explore how to add all manner of form objects to your form. Before this, however, let's take the time to explore a very important issue when it comes to form objects: names and values.

Understanding Names and Values

The form objects in the upcoming sections are called *input items*. Each input item, whether it's a radio button, a text box, or a drop-down menu, is represented, both in the HTML source as well as the information that is sent to the server, as two different components: a *name* and a *value*.

In Dreamweaver, the name of an input device is set with the Property Inspector (a process that you'll be carrying out each time you insert a new form object into your form). The value of an input device, on the other hand, is generated by the user. For example, say you have a text box named DogName into which the user has to type the name of their dog. If I were to come along and type my dog's name into the text box, the output to the server would look something like this:

```
DogName=Oscar
```

What the server does with the output from a form, which is delivered in this name=value structure, depends on the server-side technology being used. But to work properly, it is absolutely necessary that each form object have a name. Although Dreamweaver will automatically generate generic names for all of your form objects, it's in your best interest to create your own distinct name so that data delivered to your server won't become confusing.

Adding Text Fields

The text field is the most basic of form objects. Text fields are used to collect data that you don't know in advance, such as name, address, and favorite cheesy '70s science fiction TV series. Text fields come in several different flavors: single line, multiline, and password. In the following section, you'll learn how to create each kind of text field, as well as how to set their various properties.

You insert all three types of text fields by following the same basic steps:

1. Place your cursor in the location within the form delimiter where you wish to insert the text field.

2. Open the Insert bar (Window > Insert) and make sure you are working in the Forms section.

3. Click the Insert Text Field button 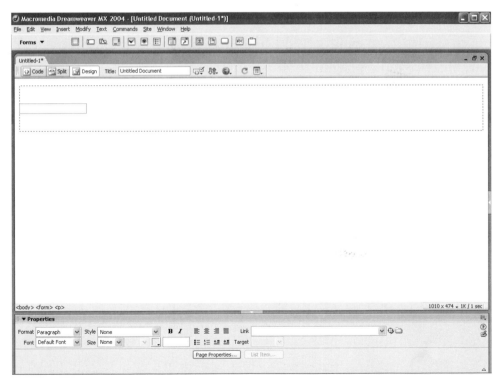. Alternatively, you can choose Insert > Form > Text Field to insert a text field (Figure 14.3).

Once the text field itself has been inserted into the document (within the form delimiter), you can set its properties with the Property Inspector. The following three sections describe how to set properties for the three types of text fields.

Creating Single-Line Text Boxes

A single-line text field is designed to accept—you guessed it—a single line of text. Although it's limited to a single line, the length of the line is quite up to you. Once you've inserted a text field, you can configure it as a single-line text box by doing this:

1. Select the text field. When selected, the text field will be highlighted with a black dashed line.

2. Open the Property Inspector (Window > Properties). Alternatively, you can double-click the text box to open the Property Inspector (Figure 14.4).

Figure 14.3 A text field

Field name

Figure 14.4 The text field properties in the Property Inspector

3. If it isn't already selected, make sure Single Line is selected as the type.

4. In the Name field, enter a unique name for the single-line text field.

> **Note:** For this and the other exercises in this chapter, keep in mind how the name/value combination factors into the overall form equation. If you are having trouble remembering how names and values work, see the section "Understanding Names and Values" earlier in this chapter.

5. Enter a numerical value into the Char Width field. As represented in Figure 14.5, the number represents the horizontal size of the text field, not the number of characters that it can accept (that is set by the Max Chars value).

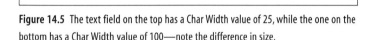

Figure 14.5 The text field on the top has a Char Width value of 25, while the one on the bottom has a Char Width value of 100—note the difference in size.

6. Enter a numerical value into the Max Chars field. This number represents the maximum number of characters (including spaces) that the user will be able to type into the text field.

7. If you want the text field to already have some text in it when the user loads the page, type it into the Init Val field. Any text in the Init Val field, which shows up when the page is initially loaded, can be deleted by the user.

8. When you finish setting the text field's properties, press Return/Enter or click anywhere off the Property Inspector and the changes will take effect.

Creating Multiline Text Fields

A multiline text field can be used for accepting any kind of text that doesn't fit well on a single line—such as the user's favorite Shakespearean soliloquy or their mother's incredible recipe for butter tarts. Note that the multiline text field starts out as a single-line text field.

Once you've inserted a text field, you can configure it as a multiline text box by selecting the text field and clicking the Multiline radio button in the Property Inspector. This will also give you access to the multiline text field properties, which you set just as you would for a single-line text field. However, there are some minute differences (Figure 14.6).

Num Lines You must enter a numerical value into the Num Lines field. As shown in Figure 14.7, the Num Lines value controls the vertical size of the multiline text field.

Wrap If you want the text that the user types into the multiline text field to wrap, choose one of the options from the Wrap drop-down menu (which is accessible in the expanded portion of the Property Inspector):

Default The user's browser decides (based on its own rules) whether the text entered into a multiline text field wraps.

Off The text won't wrap (that is, unless the user presses Return/Enter, it will be entered on a single line).

Virtual The text will wrap when it's viewed in the user's browser but won't include any line breaks when it's sent to the server for processing.

Physical The text will include line breaks both on the screen and when it's sent to the server for processing.

Figure 14.6 Multiline properties in the Property Inspector

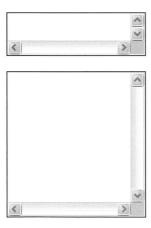

Figure 14.7 The multiline text field on the top has a Num Lines value of 2, while the one on the bottom has a Num Lines value of 10—note the difference in size.

Creating Password Fields

A password field is almost the same as the single-line text field; the only difference is that any text typed in by the user is hidden with a generic symbol such as an asterisk (*) or bullet (•) (Figure 14.8). The password field has no other function than to disguise the text from a casual passerby.

Figure 14.8 Password field

Once you've inserted a text field, you can configure it as a password field by selecting the text field and then clicking the Password radio button in the Property Inspector. The password text field properties are exactly the same as in the case of a single or multiline text field.

> **Note:** All text entered into the password text field, including Init Val text, is represented in those snazzy secret symbols.

Inserting Check Boxes or Radio Buttons

Both check boxes and radio buttons (Figure 14.9) let users choose from a series of discrete items.

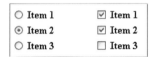

Figure 14.9 Radio buttons (left) and check boxes (right) have only two states: on (filled in) or off (left blank).

The difference between radio buttons and check boxes is that check boxes let the user pick as many options as they wish. Radio buttons, on the other hand, let the user choose only one option from a group of options.

However, the process by which you add and manipulate both check boxes and radio buttons is virtually identical. Here's how to insert either check boxes or radio buttons into your form:

1. Place your cursor in the location (within the form delimiter) where you wish to insert the radio button or check box.

2. Open the Insert bar (Window > Insert) and make sure you are working in the Forms section.

3. Click either Insert Check Box ☑ or Insert Radio Button ⊙. Alternatively, you can choose Insert > Form > Radio Button or Insert > Form > Check Box.

From here, you can set the properties of either the check box or radio button with the Property Inspector:

1. Select the object whose properties you wish to set.

2. Open the Property Inspector (Window > Properties) and enter a unique name into the Name field (Figure 14.10).

Name

Figure 14.10 Radio button/check box options in the Property Inspector

3. Enter a unique name into the Checked Value field. This name will be sent to the server if the user has selected that particular check box or radio button.

4. To determine whether the radio button or check box will be checked or unchecked when the page is initially loaded, choose one of the Initial State options. By default, check boxes and radio buttons are unchecked when a page initially loads.

5. When you finish setting the properties for a check box or a radio button, press Return/Enter or click anywhere off the Property Inspector.

Inserting Radio Groups

The Radio Group form object gives you the ability to create a radio group, which is just a group of radio buttons that you insert into your document in one fell swoop through a single dialog box. Beyond that, there are really no differences between a radio group and a regular radio button.

To insert a radio group, follow these steps:

1. Place your cursor in the location (within the form delimiter) where you wish to insert the Radio Group form object.

2. Open the Insert bar (Window > Insert) and make sure you are working in the Forms section.

3. Click the Insert Radio Group button ▤. Alternatively, you can choose Insert > Form > Radio Group.

4. When the Radio Group dialog box opens (Figure 14.11), enter a unique name into the Name field.

> **Note:** By default, when you create a radio group, it has two radio buttons. You can easily change the number by using the process described here.

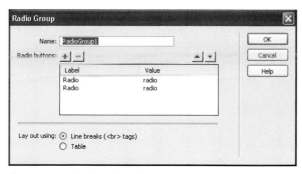

Figure 14.11 Radio Group dialog box

5. Click the first item in the Label column. When the field becomes editable, enter a new name for the radio button. This is not the name of the form object but is the text that will appear next to it.

6. Click the corresponding item in the Value column. When the field becomes editable, enter a corresponding value for that radio button.

7. Repeat steps 5 and 6 for the remaining radio buttons.

8. To add additional radio buttons to the radio group, just click the plus button ➕ and repeat steps 5 and 6 for each newly added radio button.

9. To remove a radio button from the radio group, select any of the items in the Label column and click the minus button ➖.

10. To change the order of the radio buttons in the radio group, select any of the items in the Label field and click the up button ▲ to move it upward in the stack or click the down button ▼ to move it downward in the stack.

11. Select one of the Lay Out Using options. If you choose Line Breaks, the radio buttons in the radio group will be stacked one on top of the other as if you had pressed Return/Enter after inserting the radio button. However, if you choose Table, Dreamweaver will create a table in which to place the radio buttons in the radio group.

12. When you finish setting the radio button's properties, click OK.

Creating Drop-Down Menus and Scrolling Lists

A drop-down menu (Figure 14.12) is another way to let the user choose from a number of different options. Unlike with radio buttons or check boxes, however, the options are all contained in one menu, thereby saving a fair amount of space.

Figure 14.12 The drop-down menu is designed to let you provide users with a series of options without taking up a great deal of space.

A drop-down menu, like a radio button, is a "one choice" form object, allowing users to make a single selection (as opposed to several).

The scrolling list is to the drop-down menu what the check box is to the radio button. From a scrolling list, the user can choose more than one item by ⌘/Ctrl-clicking. Also, unlike the drop-down menu, the scrolling list lets you display more than one menu item at a given time (Figure 14.13). In fact, you can control the number of items that are displayed.

Figure 14.13 The scrolling list lets you control the number of menu items that are displayed at any given time.

The scrolling list starts out as a drop-down menu, so the process to insert one is the same. You transform the drop-down menu into the scrolling list with the Property Inspector.

Follow these steps to create a drop-down menu object or a scrolling list:

1. Place your cursor in the location (within the form delimiter) where you wish to insert the menu or list.

2. Open the Insert bar (Window > Insert) and make sure you are working within the Forms section.

3. Click the Insert List/Menu button 📋. Alternatively, you can choose Insert > Form > List/Menu.

Notice that when the menu is originally inserted, it looks rather small. This is because it's not yet populated with any content. From here, you can populate the object as well as set its other properties:

1. Select the menu or list whose properties you wish to set.

2. Open the Property Inspector (Window > Properties) and choose the Menu radio button (for a single-selection drop-down menu) or the List radio button (for a

multiple-selection scrolling list). Figure 14.14 shows the properties of a list; these are just the same for a menu, except that the Height and Selections: Allow Multiple options are grayed out for a menu.

Figure 14.14 List/menu properties in the Property Inspector

3. Enter a unique name into the List/Menu Name field.

4. Click the List Values button to open the List Values dialog box (Figure 14.15). This is where you'll populate the drop-down menu.

Figure 14.15 The List Values dialog box

5. Click just below the Item Label column header and an editable field will open.

6. Type the text you want to appear in the drop-down menu's first slot.

7. Press Tab to move to the Value column, where an editable field will open.

8. Type in the value you want associated with the menu item.

9. To add additional menu items (after you typed in the value for the first item), press Tab to return to the Item Label column. Alternatively, you can click the plus (+) button in the top-left corner of the List Values dialog box. Repeat steps 6 through 10 until you've added all the items that you want to the drop-down menu.

10. When you finish populating the drop-down menu, click OK.

11. With the drop-down menu or scrolling list still selected and the Property Inspector still open, select one of the menu items in the Initially Selected list. This sets the item that will be initially selected when the page is loaded.

Note: To edit an item in a drop-down menu or scrolling list, open the Property Inspector, click the List Values button to open the List Values dialog box, and make any changes that you want.

12. If you're configuring a drop-down menu, you're done and you can skip to step 13. If you're configuring a scrolling list, though, set these additional options:

- Enter a value into the Height field. This sets the number of menu items that will be visible at any given time in the scrolling list. As illustrated in Figure 14.16, if you enter a value that is lower than the amount of items in the list, a scroll bar will appear, letting the user scroll to the items not currently displayed in the list.

- If you want the user to be able to select more than one menu item, select the Allow Multiple Selections option.

13. When you finish setting properties, press Return/Enter or click anywhere off the Property Inspector.

Figure 14.16 The scrolling list on the left has a height value equal to its number of menu items, so there is no scroll bar. The scrolling list on the right has a height value less than the number of its menu items, so there is a scroll bar.

Adding Buttons

Buttons are arguably the most important part of a form. While they don't actually collect any information from the user, they act as a bridge between the front-end form and the back-end server. Without a Submit button (the most common type of button), users could diligently fill out your form, but they wouldn't be able to send the data anywhere once they were finished.

Dreamweaver offers you three distinct kinds of buttons that you can add to your form:

Submit Carries out the action (as well as the method) that you set when you defined the properties of the form itself.

Reset Clears the form of any entered data and returns it to its initial state.

None Doesn't do a thing. The user can click it to their heart's content, but nothing will happen.

To add a button to your form, follow these steps:

1. Place your cursor in the location (within the form delimiter) where you wish to insert the button.

2. Open the Insert bar (Window > Insert) and make sure you are working in the Forms section.

3. Click the Button button ⬜. Alternatively, you can choose Insert > Form > Button.

From here, you can set the properties of the button:

1. Select the button.

2. Open the Property Inspector (Window > Properties) to access the button's properties (Figure 14.17).

Figure 14.17 Button properties in the Property Inspector

3. Set the purpose that you want the button to fulfill by selecting one of the Action options (Submit, Reset, or None).

4. To give your button a custom label, type a name into the Label field. Be wild, be crazy—break out of the mold and give your button a little flare by entering a custom label (as in Figure 14.18).

Figure 14.18 Give the button a custom label—anything you want—
by entering some text into the Label field.

> **Note:** Even if you type in a new label, the button's action won't change. A Submit button will always be a Submit button, no matter what its text label is.

5. When you finish setting the button's properties, press Return/Enter or click anywhere off the Property Inspector.

Working with File Fields

Compared to the other form objects that have been covered thus far, the file field object (sometimes also referred to as the file input field) isn't as commonly used. Essentially, a file field (Figure 14.19) lets the user browse their computer for a file that is then attached to the form and sent to the server with any other data. Say, for instance, you have created a site at which employers could advertise the positions they need filled. You could create a file field that lets the job seeker upload their résumé from their hard drive.

Figure 14.19 The file field, which lets the user browse for and then attach a document
to the form and send it to the server, is composed of a text field and a Browse button.

Here's how to insert a file field into your form:

1. Place your cursor in the location (within the form delimiter) where you wish to insert the file field.

2. Open the Insert bar (Window > Insert) and make sure you are working in the Forms section.

3. Click the Insert File Field button 🗋 . Alternatively, you can choose Insert > Form > File Field.

From here, you can set the (limited) properties of the file field object:

1. Select the button.

2. Open the Property Inspector (Window > Properties) to access its properties (Figure 14.20).

3. Enter a numerical value into the Char Width field. Remember, the number represents the horizontal size of the file field's associated text field—not the amount of characters that it can accept (that is set by the Max Chars value).

4. Enter a numerical value into the Max Chars field—this number represents the maximum number of characters that the user will be able to type into the text field.

5. When you've finished setting the file field's properties, press Return/Enter or click anywhere off the Property Inspector.

Figure 14.20 File field properties in the Property Inspector

Appendix:
Web Resources

This appendix provides a list of useful resources, including links to the official Macromedia Dreamweaver site, to other wonderful Macromedia tools, to some other great online Dreamweaver resources, and to a host of excellent general web-design and Web-development resources.

Chapter Contents

Macromedia Tools

Dreamweaver Resources

Web-Design and Web-Development
  Resources

Macromedia Tools

This list of useful tools includes the official Dreamweaver MX 2004 site, as well as links to some of Macromedia's other cool tools:

Dreamweaver MX 2004 (www.macromedia.com/software/dreamweaver) The official Dreamweaver MX 2004 website contains a 30-day limited downloadable demo. Also included are hints and tips, links to the Dreamweaver community, and purchasing and product information.

Fireworks MX 2004 (www.macromedia.com/software/fireworks) The official Fireworks MX 2004 website contains a 30-day limited downloadable demo. Also included are links to the Fireworks community, downloadable templates, and product and purchasing information.

Flash MX 2004 and Flash MX Professional 2004 (www.macromedia.com/software/flash) Interested in finding out more about Flash MX 2004 and Flash MX Professional 2004? The official Macromedia Flash web page is a great place to start. Learn about the program by taking the extensive feature tour. Get your hands dirty by downloading the 30-day limited demo.

ColdFusion MX 6.1 (www.macromedia.com/software/coldfusion) Interested in finding out more about ColdFusion MX? The official Macromedia ColdFusion web page is probably the best place to start. Learn about the program by taking the extensive feature tour, get started with introductory tutorials, and get your hands dirty by downloading the 30-day limited demo.

Dreamweaver Resources

Check out these great Dreamweaver resources:

Macromedia Developer Center (www.macromedia.com/devnet) The Macromedia Developer Center is a phenomenal resource for articles, tutorials, tips, hints, tricks, and just about everything under the sun when it comes to all of Macromedia's extensive line of products—Dreamweaver MX 2004 included.

TrainingTools (www.trainingtools.com) This site includes extensive tutorials on beginner, intermediate, and advanced Dreamweaver topics. Despite the fact that they were designed for older versions of Dreamweaver, you'll still get lots out of the tutorials.

Project VII (www.projectseven.com) This site includes all sorts of interesting intermediate and advanced tutorials, as well as a host of other tips and tricks. Project VII is also a great place for purchasing some of the neatest Dreamweaver behaviors out there.

Dreamweaver Fever (www.dreamweaverfever.com) The Dreamweaver Fever site is a great resource for Dreamweaver tutorials, news, objects, and behaviors.

Macromedia Exchange (www.macromedia.com/exchange) The Dreamweaver Exchange is the central location for downloadable Dreamweaver MX 2004 behaviors, objects, commands, and other groovy extensions. You'll also find extensions for other Macromedia products, such as Flash, ColdFusion, and Fireworks.

DW Team (www.dwteam.com) The DW Team site brings together some of the top Dreamweaver experts in the world. The site has great tutorials, tips, and free downloadable extensions.

The Dreamweaver Depot (www.andrewwooldridge.com/dreamweaver/) The Dreamweaver Depot features Dreamweaver news, tutorials, and a whole host of downloadable resources—including behaviors, commands, objects, inspectors, templates, and themes.

Yaromat (www.yaromat.com) Featuring some of the coolest downloadable extensions under the sun, the Yaromat is a definite resource for discerning Dreamweaver developers.

Massimo's Corner (www.massimocorner.com) Arguably one of the oldest Dreamweaver resources around, Massimo's Corner features tons of downloadable resources for a host of Macromedia products.

DreamweaverFAQ (www.dreamweaverfaq.com) Dedicated to serving the Dreamweaver community, DreamweaverFAQ.com offers a variety of tutorials and answers to frequently asked questions.

Dreamweaver and Fireworks Extensions by David G. Miles (www.z3roadster.net/dreamweaver) A bare essentials kind of site that offers a host of downloadable objects, commands, and behaviors for Dreamweaver.

UltraDev Cookbook (www.hiran.desilva.com/ultradev) Created by Hiran DeSilva, the UltraDev Cookbook site features a host of great tutorials that, while originally designed for creating dynamic database-driven applications with UltraDev, are perfectly usable for Dreamweaver MX 2004. (Note: At time of printing, the demos were temporarily down.)

MX Extensions (www.mxextensions.com) The MX Extensions site features a ton of resources, downloadable extensions, tutorials (both text and video), and news geared to support all of your Macromedia MX needs (especially dynamic database-driven applications).

Dreamweaversites (www.dreamweaversites.com) The Dreamweaversites site features downloadable Dreamweaver templates (both for purchase and for free), a list of extensive resources, as well as some cool interactive Viewlet-based tutorials.

Web-Design and Web-Development Resources

These are some good general web-design and -development resources:

Builder.com (www.builder.com) Run by CNET, Builder.com has everything under the sun for the web developer, including discussion boards and lots of great articles and free scripts.

Webmonkey (www.webmonkey.com) This site has great articles on all manner of topics from beginner to advanced. A definite must!

Webdeveloper.com (www.webdeveloper.com) This site includes resources, tech info, daily news, and analytical features essential for the web-development community.

Computer Arts (www.computerarts.co.uk) The Computer Arts site, which is the digital component of the print magazine of the same name, features news, product reviews, and extensive tutorials that cover all sorts of digital design programs (including Flash).

Index

names for, **155–156**, *155–156*
nesting, **153**
non-resizable, **159**, *159*
from preset layouts, **150–153**
saving, **165–166**
scrollable, **159–161**, *160*
size of, **153–154**, *154*
sources of, **156–157**, *157*
splitting for, **147–150**, *148–150*
Frames panel, **155**, *155*
frameset files, 147
framesets, **161–162**, *161*
    borders for, **162–163**, *162*
        color of, **163–164**
        thickness for, 163, *163*
FTP for remote server connections, **304–305**, *304*, 307

G

geekspeak, 20
General tab, 41, *41*
Get and Put Newer Files option, 314
Get Current HTML option, 241
GET method, 376
Get More Styles option, 121
Get Newer Files from Remote option, 314
GIF (Graphics Interchange Format) images, 82
Go To Alt URL option, 230
Go To URL dialog box, 235–236, *236*
Go To URL option, 230, 343
Graphics Interchange Format (GIF) images, 82
Green project, 209
Grid Settings dialog box, 34–35, *35*
grids, 34–35, *35*
grouping attributes, 337, *338*
groups, panel
    collapsing and expanding, **28**, *28*
    creating, **30–31**, *31*
    docking, **28–30**, *28–29*

H

handles
    for cropping, 93, *93*
    for Flash movies, 203, *203*

for images, 90, *90*
for layers, 280
for tables, 132, *132*
Head Content area, 172
<head> section
    content in, **339–340**
    for style sheets, 255
<head> tag, 222
headers in tables, 126
headlines, 10–11, *10*
height
    of boxes, **262**
    of pop-up menu cells, 250
Height attribute, **262**
help for HTML syntax, **353**, *353*
Hidden option, 283–284
Hide Underline on Rollover option, 60
High option, 205
highlight color
    for Library Items, **196**
    for pop-up menus, 251
    in Templates, **184**, *185*
Highlight Invalid HTML option, 330
highlighting, 12
hints, code, **335–336**, *335–336*
History panel, 358–359, *359*
Horizontal Position attribute, 259–260
horizontal rules, **70–71**, *70–71*
horizontal scrolling, 160
hotspots, **114–116**, *115–116*
HTML and HTML tags, 268
    changing, **268–269**, *269*
    cleaning up, **350–351**, *351*
    color coding, **327–329**, *328–329*
    converting to XHTML, **355**, *355*
    CSSs for, 254
    editing, **334–335**, *335*
    help for, **353**, *353*
    inserting, **334**, *334*, **345–346**, *346*
    selecting, **326**, *326–327*
    validating, **352–353**, *352*
.html extension, 292
HTTP-Equivalent attribute, 340
Hyperlink dialog box, 104, *104*
hyperlinks, **101–102**
    checking, **296–297**
    color of, 56, *56*, 59–60, 66
    e-mail, **112–114**, *113*

fixing, **298**, *298*
Flash Buttons for, **119–121**, *120*
image, **105–106**, *106*
image maps for, **114–116**, *115–116*
Jump Menus for, **117–119**, *117*, *119*
to moved files, **294–296**, *295–296*
named anchors for, **108–111**, *108–111*
Point to File icon for, **107**, *107*
properties for, **59–60**, *59*, **269–270**, *270*, **344–345**, *344*
text, **102–105**, *103–104*

I

IA diagrams (information architecture diagrams), **3–4**, *3*
Icon Labels option, 51
icons
    for invisible elements, 109
    in navigation, 20
id attribute
    for Insert bar commands, 369
    for <menu>, 364
    for <menuitem>, 366
ID field for Link properties, 344
Ignore Whitespace option, 301, 333
<ilayer> tag, 283
image attribute, 369–370
image links
    borders for, **106**, *106*
    creating, **105–106**, *106*
image maps, **114–115**
    hotspots for, **115–116**, *115–116*
    links in, **116**
Image Placeholder dialog box, 84, *84*
images, **81**
    aligning, **85–88**, *85–88*
    alt tag for, **90–91**, *91*
    as assets, 171
    background
        in pages, 57–58
        in styles, 259
        in tables, **145**
    borders for, **92**, *92*

for editing sites, 53
for site-less connections, 315
for Site Map layouts, 48, 50
Margin attributes, **262**
Massimo's Center site, 391
Match Case option, 300, 333
Match Whole Word option, 300, 333
measurement units
for layers, 281
for rulers, 34
Menu Commands list, 32
Menu Position option, 251
<menu> tag, 364
menu.xml file, 363–364
<menuitem> element, 366 367
menus
adding items to, **366–367**, *367*
on forms, **384–386**, *384–386*
Jump Menus, **117–119**, *117, 119*
modifying, **363–366**, *364–365*
pop-up, **247–251**, *247–251*
Merge Selected Cells Using Spans option, 130
merging table cells, **130**, *130*
Meta dialog box, 340, *340*
meta properties, **340–341**, *340*
<meta> tag, 340–341
Middle option, 87, *87*
minimizing response time, **7–9**
Modify Page Properties dialog box, 52
Move Content To New Region menu, 190
Move Event Value Down option, 227
Move Event Value Up option, 227
movies, Flash. *See* Flash movies
moving
files, **294–296**, *295–296*
layers, **281**, *281*
layout cells, **135–136**, *135–136*
panels between groups, 30, *30*
multiline text fields, **379–380**, *380*
multimedia, **199**
ActiveX Controls for, **214–219**, *215–219*
Flash movies. *See* Flash movies
Java applets, **209–211**
Netscape plug-ins, **211–214**, *213*
Shockwave files, **207–209**

multiple documents, styles across, 254
multiple navigation roads, **21**
multiple table rows and columns, 129
multiple URLs, opening, **235–236**, *236*
MX Extensions site, 391

N

name attribute
for Insert bar commands, 370
for <menu>, 364
for <menuitem>, 366
for meta properties, 340
Named Anchor dialog box, 108, *108*, 110
named anchors, **108–111**, *108–111*
names
commands, **360**
domain, 46
on forms, **377**
frames, **155–156**, *155–156*
Jump Menu items, 118
layers, 286
Library Items, **194**
local sites, 45
panel groups, 31
placeholders, 84
styles, 267
navigation, **13–14**
branding in, **17**, *18*
breadcrumb trails in, **19**, *19*
color in, **17**
consistency in, **14–16**, *15*
labels in, **20**
multiple roads in, **21**
between open documents, 35
simplicity in, **16**
visual vocabulary in, **20–21**
nesting
<font> tags, 351
frames, **153**
layers, **287–288**
Netscape and Netscape plug-ins, **211–212**
ActiveX Controls accessible by, **218**, *218*
borders for, **213**, *213*
previewing, **213–214**
URLs for, **213**, *213*

Never Underline option, 60
New CSS Style dialog box, 267–268, *267*, 271
New Document dialog box
for creating documents, 41, *41*
for style sheets, 275
for Templates, 188
for XHTML documents, 355
New Editable Region dialog box, 179–180, *179*
New Favorites Folder, 173
New Folder option, 293
New From Template dialog box, 188, *189*
New Library Item option, 192, 194
New Optional Region dialog box, 181, *181*
New Panel Group option, 31
New Repeating Region dialog box, 182, *182*
New Snippet option, 348
New Style option, 75
New Template option, 177
No Border option, 206
No Resize option, 159
NoFrames content, 167
Non-Dreamweaver HTML Contents option, 351
non-resizable frames, **159**, *159*
None buttons, 386
Normal option for whitespace, 261
Not Containing option, 332
Not Inside Tag option, 332
notes. *See* Design Notes
Nowrap option, 261
Num Lines field, 380
Number of Columns option, 50
numbered lists, **72**, *72*

O

Oak project, 209
<object> tag, 218
objects vs. behaviors and commands, **362**
Open Browser Window behavior, 226, 236–237, *236*
Open dialog box, 146
open documents, navigating between, 35
Open Documents option, 299, 331

Split Frame Down option, 149, *149*
Split Frame Left option, 148, *148*
Split Frame Right option, 148, *148*
Split Frame Up option, 149, *149*
splitting
        cells, **131**, *131*
        for frames, **147–150**, *148–150*
stacking order of layers, **287**
Standard view, **124–126**, *124–125*, 128, 132
Start Count option, 75
status bar
        for browser text, **239–240**, *239–240*
        settings for, 36–38, *37*
Stay On This Page option, 230
storyboards, 5–6
Strip Tag option, 332
Style attributes, 263
Style Definition dialog box, 267, 269–270
Style menu, 65, 68–69, *69*, 257
Style option, 75
<style> section, *255*
styles, 253–254
        applying, **272–273**
        attributes for, **256–265**
        for borders, 263
        classes for, 254, **266–268**, *267–268*
        for code elements, 328
        creating, **266**, *266*
        deleting, 273
        editing, **274–275**, *274*
        external style sheets for, 270–272
        for lists, 75
        for pop-up menus, 249
        premade style sheets for, **275–276**
        for redefining hyperlink properties, **269–270**, *270*
        selecting, **68–69**, *69*
        for tags, **268–269**, *269*
        for text, **64**
        working with, **254–256**, *255–256*
Subject line, 113–114
Submit buttons, 386
Swap Image dialog box, 245–246, *246*

Swap Image Restore behavior, 246
SWF files, 121, 201
symbols, inserting, **75–76**, *76*
synchronizing files, **313–314**, *314*
syntax, help for, **353**, *353*
Syntax Coloring option, 330

T

Tab Index field, 105
Table dialog box, 124, *124*
Table Width setting, 125
tables, 123
        aligning, **126**, **133**, *133*
        background color in, **144**, *144*
        background images in, **145**
        border color in, **143**, *143*
        border thickness in, **142–143**, *143*
        cells in. *See* cells
        content in, **140–142**, *141*
        in Expanded view, 125
        importing data for, **145–146**, *146*
        layout. *See* layout tables
        in Layout view, **127–128**, *128*
        rows and columns for, 125, **128–130**, *129*, **136–139**, *137*, *139*, **183–184**, *183*
        shape of, **128**
        size of, 125–126, **128**, **131–133**, *131–132*
        in Standard view, **124–126**, *124–125*
        in Templates, **181–183**, *182*
Tag Chooser, **345–346**, *346*
Tag Editor, 346, *346*
Tag Inspector, **337–339**, *337–339*
Tag menu, 268
Tag Selector
        for editing HTML, **334–335**
        for selecting HTML, **326**, *326–327*
target browsers, **39–41**, *39–40*
Target field, menus, 248
targets, frame linking with, **164–165**, *165*
Template Editor, 178–182
Templates, 62, 172, **175–176**
        applying, **188–190**, *189–190*
        copying, **187**

creating, **176–178**, *176–178*, **188**, *189*
        deleting, **187**
        detaching pages from, **190**
        editable regions in, **179–180**, *179*
        editing, **185**
        highlight colors in, **184**, *185*
        optional regions in, **180–181**, *181*
        renaming, **186–187**
        repeating regions or tables in, **181–183**, *182*
        saving, **185–186**
        tag attributes in, **183–184**, *183*
terminology for labels, 20
text, **63**
        aligning and indenting paragraphs, **69–70**
        aligning to
                Flash movies, **206**
                images, **85–86**, *85–86*
        breaking up, **70–71**, *70–71*
        in browser status bar, **239–240**, *239–240*
        color of, **65–66**, *65*
                Flash Text, 80
                legible, **12–13**, *13*
                in styles, 258
        in CSSs, **68–69**, *69*
        dates, **76–77**, *77*
        Flash Text, **78–80**, *79*
        fonts for, **66–68**, *67*
        for Java applets, **211**
        legible, **12–13**, *12–13*
        lists, **72–75**, *72–74*
        local, formatting, 68
        for pop-up menus, 249
        properties for, **58**
        scannable, **10–12**, *10–12*
        searching for, **300–302**, *300–301*
        size of, **64–65**, *64*
        special characters, **75–76**, *76*
        spell checking, **78**, *78*
        styling, **64**
        in text fields, **242–243**, *242*
Text Align attribute, 261
text blocks, 11, *11*
Text Color field, 58
Text Color swatch, 65

keyboard shortcuts in, **31–33**, *32*

panels in, **27–32**, *28–31*

rulers in, **33–34**, *33–34*

Workspace Setup dialog box, 26, *26*

Wrap Selection option, 348–349

Wrap setting for multiline text fields, 380

writing for web, **9–10**

X

XHTML (Extensible Hypertext Markup Language)
documents, **354**
converting HTML to, **355**, *355*
creating, **355**, *355*
validating, **356**, *356*

XML (Extensible Markup Language), 354

Y

Yaromat site, 391

Z

Z Index for layers, 234–235, 286–287

Soluti👁ns™ FROM SYBEX®

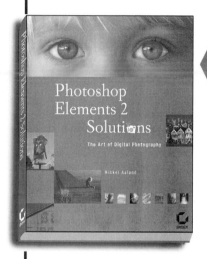

Photoshop® Elements 2 Solutions™
by Mikkel Aaland
ISBN: 0-7821-4140-4
US $40.00 💿 full color throughout

iMovie™ 3 Solutions™: Tips, Tricks, and Special Effects
by Erica Sadun
ISBN: 0-7821-4247-8
US $40.00 💿 full color throughout

DVD Studio Pro® 2 Solutions
by Erica Sadun
ISBN 0-7821-4234-6
US $39.99 💿 📀

Acrobat® 6 and PDF Solutions
by Taz Tally
ISBN 0-7821-4273-7
US $34.99 💿

SYBEX®
www.sybex.com